The Singing Winger

COLIN GRAINGER

WITH **HYDER JAWÁD**

deCoubertin
B O O K S

First published as a hardback by deCoubertin Books Ltd in 2019.

First Edition

deCoubertin Books, 46B Jamaica Street, Baltic Triangle, Liverpool, L1 0AF.
www.decoubertin.co.uk

ISBN: 978-1-909245-95-2

A CIP catalogue record for this book is available from the British Library.

Cover design and typeset by Leslie Priestley.

Printed and bound by Replika Press Pvt. Ltd.

To

Duncan Edwards

1 October 1936 – 21 February 1958

&

Jim Iley

15 December 1935 – 17 November 2018

Acknowledgements

ALL BOOKS HAVE AT LEAST ONE AUTHOR. THIS ONE HAS TWO – SORT OF. But the reality is that books are almost always collaborations, even though the name or names on the cover rarely say so. Consequently, the authors wish to thank the following for their input into this project and for their support:

Lesley Constable; Colin Grainger junior; Doreen Grainger; the late Jim Iley; Jean Kitchen; Andy Mills; Christian Radley; Kim Radley; Wayne Tomlinson; Tony Topping; and Chris Worrall. The deCoubertin Book team of Jack Gordon Brown, James Corbett, Simon Hughes, Megan Pollard, and Leslie Priestley deserve special thanks for not only supporting the project when it was just a rough manuscript but also for bringing their expertise to the table.

The Singing Winger is the product of nearly a hundred hours of interviews with Colin Grainger, in addition to research provided by contemporary sources such as *Charles Buchan's Football Monthly*, official programmes for the matches in which he played, and his own personal scrapbook.

Contents

CHAPTER ZERO

Exordium

Heroes and martyrs

You would have loved them

Dynasty [noun]: *A succession of people from the same family who play a prominent role in business, politics, or another field.*

I HAVE NEVER BEEN A FAN OF *DYNASTY* AS A WORD. IT CONTAINS ALL sorts of negative connotations, not least the implied suggestion that you acquired something – fame, a career, a wife, a name – through the family rituals and institutions of which you are a part. *Dynasty* suggests entitlement. *Dynasty* diminishes the blood and sweat you expended to achieve your goals. *Dynasty* alienates outsiders. But how hollow my words seem when juxtaposed alongside the reality that sporting prowess dominated the Grainger-Holliday genealogy for half a century. I learnt from a young age that being part of that genealogy afforded me both ready-made role models and inherent pressures. Everywhere I turned there was a football player.

Even before I was born, my cousin, Jack Grainger (born 1912), was forging a career for himself as a full-back with Barnsley and Southport. World War Two took what should have been the best part of his career but he did play as a guest for Liverpool. His younger brother, Dennis Grainger (born 1920), enjoyed a moderately successful post-war career with Leeds United and Wrexham. My oldest brother, Jack Grainger (born 1924), was already turning himself into a Rotherham United legend while I was still at school. By the time I signed my first professional contract in 1949, as a super-skinny but super-fast seventeen-year-old with Wrexham, newspapers could never write about me without making reference to my brother. By 1956, when I was a full England international left winger, my cousin, Edwin Holliday (born 1939), signed for Middlesbrough. My younger sister, Lilly, helped to grow our football family when she married Jim Iley, then a left-half with Sheffield United, and later of Tottenham Hotspur and Newcastle United, in 1958.

You dream of being the best football player in the world but even when you have played at Wembley, and scored twice on your England debut against Brazil, you have stop and ask yourself if you are even the best player in your household.

There are a lot of Football League appearances among that list of names. But none of those fine people are the heroes of my life. And nor am I. My heroes are always martyrs. My heroes are my parents. My mam. My dad. I wish you could have met them. You would have loved them. But they are long gone and there are not many of us around who still remember them. For me, now, in good times and bad, they enter my thoughts and they blossom like the calla lily in May. It was because of them that I spent most of my working life performing to audiences as both a football player and a singer. Life was so good that I sometimes felt guilty taking money for doing what I would have done for nothing.

I still perform today, but only in my mind's eye. And there is only ever an audience of two: My mam. My dad. And theirs is the applause that matters most of all. They were the ones who toiled so I did not have to. They were the ones who fashioned my future with a simple command: Son, no way you're ever going down a pit.

Over the course of my story, you will hear these nine words a lot, and I offer no apologies for the repetition. If something is precious, you desire to share it in perpetuity – even if, in this case, it is only a simple sentence. Even if the sentence means more to me than it could ever mean to you.

CHAPTER I

Havercroft Memories
1933-53: Kinship, childhood, national service, Wrexham

The heart of an angel

IN THE LATE-VICTORIAN ERA, THE ENGLISH CLASS SYSTEM DEFINED itself with such assurance that people had their futures mapped out for them even before they were born. And so it was with my dad. By the time he began working in 1910, he did what his had father had done and what his father's father had done: underground coal mining, a job that seemed design to create bad hygiene and hasten death. In West Riding, not a lot changed over many decades – academics call it social determinism – and yet, paradoxically, every day felt different, fresh and new, as if our tiny colliery village of Havercroft spun on its own axis.

Before I was born, the Depression had become the defining feature of life for mining communities. From a young age, I heard the passed-down tales of what genuine hardship meant and how adversely it manifested itself. Like the occasion my dad came home from work. It was evening time, early 30s, I would guess, and

3

he displayed what one family member described as a haunting emptiness in his eyes. He took off his coat, put it on a hook, and said softly to my mam: 'So sorry, Lily, no money today.'

A pregnant pause but no complaint. My mam never complained. She knew, as everybody knew, that my dad always grafted, eight hours a day, five days a week, often through the night. The problem was productivity. He could spend the entire day lying on his back, striving with the coal cutters, or with a pick and shovel. He could sweat so much that his eyes stung. But if production was low at the end of his shift, even through no fault of his own – tough luck. He would go home with no wages.

Such was the scourge of the Depression; that centrifugal force whose tentacles spread indiscriminately to every corner of the globe, destroying livelihoods and communities, turning places like Havercroft into paradigms of social anxiety.

How forlorn my dad must have felt, standing there, his face stained with soot, his overalls blackened like charcoal, presenting himself as a metaphor for the economic volatility of our times. Most days were not like that, of course. Most days he would return with a brown envelope full of money to give to my mam. Then his eyes would sparkle, and she would smile, and we all knew there would be a beef joint on Sunday.

The worst of times were rare, the best of times common. And I look back on my past now with the same wide-eyed enthusiasm that I possessed when those days were my present, when the future lay before me all bright, all beautiful, all ready to enlighten.

So many memories. They enter my mind like flashes of lightning, never in any particular order. But only one memory is constant because it defined my childhood. It was when I heard for the first time my dad's command:

Son, no way you're ever going down a pit.

He went down a pit for virtually every day of his working life and he knew from personal experience that it was no place for his boys. His command became my mantra; for there, encapsulated in a single sentence, was a truth that both inspired me and saddened me. He went down the mines, putting his body through the toughest work imaginable, breathing the worst air possible; he did it all so I did not have to.

And when he got home after each shift, who was there to greet him and comfort him? My mam: our rock, our foundation, our fortress; the glue that held us all together.

So when I played in London for England against Brazil in 1956, alongside Stanley Matthews and Duncan Edwards, I thought of Mam and Dad. When I sang at the Southern Sporting Club in 1963, on the same bill as the Beatles, I thought of Mam and Dad. I've been hearing the applause ever since.

So much approval, so much praise. And I wish I could have transferred it all to them.

How could I not be inspired that their labours gave me a privileged childhood? How could I not be saddened that their labours caused them each a premature death?

When Daniel Grainger died in 1967, aged 73, I realised that he was one of the many thousands of good men who went the same way: victims of pneumoconiosis, a disease born of too much exposure to coal dust. He knew his day-to-day existence was unhealthy. A lesser man would have taken the easy way out, taken an easier job for much less money, but not my dad. He was a giver, not a taker.

Son, no way you're ever going down a pit.

He said the same words, delivered in his authentic Barnsley accent, to my three older brothers: John, born in 1924; Eric, born in 1926; and Horace, born in 1929. He wished he could have had the same words for my two other brothers, but they died of diphtheria when not even old enough to know the perils of growing up in a mining village. Leslie, born in 1920, died during his first year; George, born 1922, died aged four, around the time of the 1926 General Strike. I wish I had met them both. I wish I could have learnt from them just as I learnt from John, Eric and Horace.

I wish my parents had been spared such anguish. My mam, Lily Grainger (née Holliday), was a wonderful woman, hard-working and disciplined. Her toughness, particularly at those times of sorrow, made her an endearing character within the community and a beacon of hope for those of us who relied on her. I never spoke to her about Leslie and George, so I will never know how she dealt with the grief. Maybe she worked her way through the pain – using activity to avoid introspection – because she never seemed to stop. It would give me pleasure on clothes-washing days to help her put soaking trousers and shirts through the mangle to assist with the drying process. We all wanted to help her because she was a woman of action. It is amazing that she found the time to have seven children in just fifteen years.

She died in 1979 of what the doctor called 'a tired heart'. But we all knew that

5

she had the heart of an angel.

My mam's brother, John Holliday, was the same. He volunteered at age sixteen for service in the Great War, although he lied by saying he was eighteen, otherwise he would have been too young and told to come back in two years' time. My beloved uncle was a fine man, full of stories, full of vitality, and he lived to more than 100 years old.

The world of my parents was not much different from the world of my grandparents. In the late-Victorian era, the class system characterised British society. People had their futures mapped out for them even before they were born. Communal cultures and networks functioned in such a way as to undermine whatever passed in those days for social mobility. Blissfully unaware of a life beyond the village, my dad's generation had no idea that social mobility was even possible. The 1911 Census records my father as being a sixteen-year-old 'pit pony driver, belowground'. He was living at Dove Hill, Royston, Barnsley with his parents – Joseph Grainger, a 57-year-old Coal Miner Hewer, and Rose Grainger (née Timmingham) – and what seemed like myriad siblings.

I was born on Saturday 10 June 1933, a day that, beyond our tiny village, held little significance. In Europe, and especially in Germany, the political dynamics were changing ominously, but that did not yet concern me. West Riding was still suffering from the Depression, and the 30s was a strenuous period for miners.

I discovered from an early age that life in Havercroft, with its population of just 800, conformed to an orthodox pattern. The fathers worked the pits. The mothers held down domestic jobs and also brought up the children. And the children became a reflection of their parents. Some fathers would gamble too much or drink too much, and the children would suffer. Most fathers gave enough housekeeping money to their wives so the children could eat good food and want for nothing.

The Grainger children fell into the category that ate good food and wanted for nothing. That is why I regard my background as one of great advantages. Oh, sure, there was hardly a spare penny and never a hope of the family becoming rich. At Christmas, we had to make do with a bicycle between us, or a football between us. But we had privileges more important than possessions: kinship, identity, and loyalty.

I could see it in my dad's eyes that his days down the mines were tough but also that he delighted in his family and cherished us all. After a particularly arduous day, he would contort his aching body into the bath and immerse himself in the warm water. Bliss! As he was unable to clean his back, he would call me in, give me a sponge, and ask me to soap away all that sweat. The sweat of honest toil. The sweat of an industrious man. And how great it was for me to be involved, a small cog in the family wheel.

It was something that we even had a bath. I read recently that in Barnsley in 1946, for example, half of households lacked a fixed bath, and one in ten people actually shared a water supply or lacked piped water. Only one in four owned their own toilet. By those standards, we were better off than many.

And on most Sunday afternoons my mam would take that beef joint out of the oven to provide us not only with the best food, but also the focal point of some great dinner-table conversations. 'Pass me the pop,' someone would shout, and the bottle would go around the table, from brother to brother, like a Mexican wave.

Occasionally, my mam's main course, whether beef or salmon, would precede the luxury of ice cream. You did not get ice cream from the shop. You got it from the man who travelled around the streets on his horse and cart. You knew he was coming a mile off, for the horse and cart would make a distinctive rattling sound. Some kids would follow the horse on its round, patting it or stroking it. The kids who got ice cream had the widest smiles. Just as ubiquitous was the rag and bone man, who circulated the village on foot, looking for unwanted household items, which he would then sell on to merchants.

Funnily enough, there was a time when our house became the focal point of some excellent fast food – and all because of a toasting fork I made in school in 1946. It was just a simple thing, with metal wire, but it enabled me to make the finest toast in the village. There was no sliced bread in those days, of course. Instead, we would cut the loaf ourselves with a large knife, put slices of bread on to the toasting fork, stick it in the coal fire, and spread the Lurpak butter all over the hot toast. The butter would drip down your fingers. Then, having devoured the toast, we would run back into The Square and continue whatever game of football or cricket we were playing. That toasting fork survived in the family at least until 1970. I have not seen it since then, but it would not surprise me if I still had it somewhere.

Most things were a novelty in those days. But I was lucky. If I needed a pair of football boots, I got them. If I needed new laces, no problem. And we were always well dressed. Families acquired their dignity from hard work, good manners, and respectable clothes – even if, often, the clothes had been handed down. We had wealth, but not in the financial sense. Our wealth came in having good character and in our sense of community. People did not lock their doors because there was no need to. Community crime was virtually non-existent.

When we got our first television in 1950, a magnificent electrical operation from Cheetham's in Royston, we had everybody round to our house to watch the flickering monochrome images that in those days passed for entertainment. There was not much choice in those days but your expectations were low. You watched whatever the broadcasters decided. People would come in and out as if 10 West Street had turned into a mini-cinema.

A simple existence. An idyllic existence.

And if my memories appear to be those of somebody observing his past through rose-tinted spectacles, consider how many great and good footballers in post-war Britain emerged from mining communities. Our world was a football training ground, an academy; and although not everybody came out of the experience having flourished, those austere streets were a space in which enchantment became possible. We did not even need a football. A tennis ball would do. And, of course, four coats for goalposts. At virtually no cost, we had a game that could occupy and stimulate every boy in the village, week in week out, throughout our adolescence. Summer would bring a bit of cricket, which we loved, but it was our football ambitions that characterised our fantasies.

We played most of our football and cricket in The Square, which stood fifty yards from our house in West Street, and was the focal point for all the kids in the area; a hive of activity; a dwelling for our dreams. In winter, once darkness set in, we continued to play under the gas lamps.

The intrigue of those football matches in The Square was that I seemed to be related to most of the kids. There were my brothers, John, Eric, and Horace; then there were my cousins, Dennis Grainger, Jack Grainger, and Edwin Holliday. Big brother John was the best, because he was the oldest. He went to work at the pit, but he stayed strictly above ground. There was no way my dad was going to let him go down below, damaging his lungs with all that coal dust.

It followed that the first professional footballer I got to know was our John, who was most definitely a product of his background. Nine years older than I, he had the legs of a racehorse, with calf muscles that reflected hard work and good diet. He could sprint, he could run long distances, and all that ball practice in The Square gave him expert control and balance. All he had to do was put it altogether and he could turn himself into the type of winger that both he and I dreamt of becoming. In time, he would distinguish himself with Rotherham United, for whom he signed in 1947 from Frickley Colliery. He would acquire the nickname the 'Galloping Winger'.

As soon as my three brothers and I realised we could play football to a decent standard, we began to ask ourselves from where this physical prowess came. Some of it came from my dad's side, yes, but most from my mam's side. Lily Grainger had siblings who possessed the gifts of athleticism. Famous in the village for how they always seemed to be running, the Holliday brothers – my uncles – were paragons of perpetual motion. I delight in the fact that the fates brought together Daniel Grainger and Lily Holliday. When they married in late 1919, they made official in Royston, Barnsley, something that could easily have happened in Dudley, Staffordshire.

The Graingers and Hollidays were large families who originated from Dudley. Like many people in the late-Victorian era, they escaped unemployment by moving to the mining villages in Yorkshire, Durham and Cumberland. Royston seemed as good a place as any to start a new life. My dad, one of fourteen children (seven boys, seven girls), was born in 1894, my mam in 1900. After they married, they acquired a colliery house in West Street, Havercroft.

Havercroft-with-Cold Hiendley, to give its full original title, was growing in 1919, but not rapidly. According to the *Imperial Gazetteer of England and Wales* for 1870-72 by John Marius Wilson, the village's population was just 109 and there were 24 houses. You could buy swathes of land for a starting price of £1,563. Potential investors learnt that the 120-acre reservoir fed the Barnsley canal. It was mining that reconfigured the area but the population was barely more than five hundred when the Graingers turned up just after the Great War. In such a small place, you got to know everybody's name, and you made friends easily. However, once the mining industry took off, house building in the 20s became big business in Havercroft. Whereas in 1921, there were just 150 houses in the village, by 1930 there were four hundred houses. Number 10 West Street is still there, although now a different colour, with a different wall. And a different atmosphere. The Graingers have long since dispersed.

My dad worked at the Monckton Colliery, pits three and four, which, during his time, employed five hundred-odd men below ground and a hundred-odd above. The hardest work was to be found below, a laborious and dangerous arrangement that was fraught with uncertainty, both financially and physically. The threat of not making any money hung over every miner and his wife. No less significant was the fear of serious injury.

The most complimentary nickname that pit workers could bestow on a man was 'Gentleman Miner'. And that is what they called my dad. This sobriquet emphasised his personal attributes and the esteem in which his colleagues held him. He did not swear at home, never swore in front of women, never drank to excess, never boasted, and respected his fellow human being. He was a gentleman and a gentle man. He deserved better than to be unsure of his wages at the end of a backbreaking shift.

I will never know the true psychological effects on my dad of such an existence because he never grumbled. Not once. It gave him pleasure, I think, to know that he could give my mam enough money to run the household. And, after six boys, with two no longer alive, there was a new arrival in 1935: a girl called Lily, my baby sister. (Being female, she was never going to become a professional footballer, not in those days; but she got the next-best thing when she married Jim Iley, the brilliant left-half, then of Tottenham Hotspur, in 1958. But that is a story for the future).

Our house at 10 West Street had three bedrooms: one my parents shared, another that John, Eric, Horace and I shared, and another, the smallest, that young Lily occupied. In those days, sharing a bedroom meant sharing a double bed, so that, even when we were adults, Horace and I would sleep under the same covers in one double bed, with John and Eric sharing another. The bedrooms remained in constant use until way into the 50s because our John did not leave home until he got married at the age of thirty, Eric stayed at home until he got married at the age of 29, and Horace stayed at home until he got married at the age of 27.

Such closeness can make or break a family. For the Graingers, it made us. Those bonds enabled us to survive tribulations. As there was only a two-year gap between Lily and me, the two of us were particularly close, but the four brothers all looked after her. It seemed to fit the natural order that she developed, from a young age, a love of football.

Relationships flourished in those days. Our next-door neighbours were the Mays, who had a son in the Royal Navy. One day, he returned home with a monkey, which he kept in the kitchen. Whenever you went to their house, all you could see was this monkey running around wild amid the pots and pans and tables and chairs. Sometimes he would hang on the clothes line, which the Mays had in the kitchen.

These scenes were the types you would see in a film, or read about in a novel; not something to be located in a colliery house in Havercroft, West Riding.

We all felt immortal

My first school, which I began at the age of four in 1937, was Ryhill Junior. Ryhill was the next village to Havercroft, and although it might only have been a twenty-minute walk away, you had to cross the bridge over the railway line to get there. Neither the railway line nor the walk to school presented danger during those interwar years, so those mornings – big groups of kids walking, exploring the railway – became adventures that created distinctive personalities and established relationships.

At the age of eight, in 1941, I migrated to Ryhill Middle School, and then, from the age of eleven, in 1945, to Felkirk Secondary School, in South Hiendley. For me, school was one long sporting exploration. I was the captain of the football team but I also played in the cricket team, whose captain was George Dodd, one of my best friends, with whom I remained in touch until his death in 2014. Like me, he loved playing sport. Like me, he did what was necessary to enhance his athleticism.

When I think of him, my mind goes back to a cricket cup final we played against Cudworth in 1947. One of the Cudworth players was Michael Parkinson, later to turn himself into a successful television personality and journalist. Felkirk batted first but we ended up all out for just twelve. We were stunned but our teacher, a Mr Lawton, said, 'Grainger and Dodds, it's up to you to bowl them all out.' And we did. George got five wickets for zero runs and I got five wickets for four runs. Cudworth finished all out for nine. Somewhere among my personal memorabilia is the medal I won on that famous day.

The best word to describe my academic aptitude was 'average'. I was decent at English and maths, half-decent at history, but I could never quite appreciate the laws and cadences of science. I was interested enough in school to avoid censure from teachers, but I functioned – perhaps consciously, perhaps unconsciously – in the knowledge that I would play football for a living. And if not, perhaps cricket.

Had I been less athletically inclined, I would have given school more attention and probably would have done well. I knew dim and unintelligent kids when I saw them and I knew I did not fit into the same category.

I was fairly competent at gymnastics, especially at handstands; and those years at Felkirk represent a halcyon period in my life for it was there that sport became more than mere fun. It was character-building. How I throbbed with excitement. One does not forget those long summer evenings, swimming in the reservoir, and then eating the oversized but delectable sandwiches my mam made. Then there were those annual holidays to Blackpool with my school friends, playing football and cricket on the beach, shirtless, the sweat glistening, as the sun went down to reveal the stars. In Blackpool, there was a machine on which you stood to discover your height and weight. In the summer of 1947, I was aged fourteen, 5ft 3in, and 8st 6lbs.

What a world I inhabited. I was high on energy, intoxicated by adrenaline, and all that football practice in The Square of Havercroft, all those delicious beef joints, and even the daily dose of cod liver oil, had given me the legs of an adult. I could run, I could dribble, and I knew that, as a football player, I was catching up with my big brother, John Grainger. He welcomed my progress. We were friends as well as brothers. I always called him our John, even when everybody else called him Jack. But when it came to running, none of us were in Horace Grainger's league. He became a champion 100-yard sprinter. Early on, our John, Eric and I knew we would never be able to catch him. Horace had the Grainger surname but there was no doubting that he had the Holliday running legs.

Another of my close friends at school was a kid called Curly Worby. He was really Peter Worby but everybody called him Curly. It was the most inappropriate nickname possible, for not only did he lack curly hair, he had hardly any hair. He was one of the few boys who did not need to use the services of Sam Taylor, the local hairdresser, who did his work in a garden shed. Day in, day out, a queue would form outside his shed, people trampling all over his grass, as he proceeded to confer on his customers the same hairstyle – no matter what you requested. There must have been three hundred males in Havercroft at that time and every one of us looked identical. Well, everybody except for Curly Worby. He did not have enough hair. Just as I kept in touch with George Dodds until he died, so I kept in touch with Curly Worby until the letters and phone calls stopped coming and I heard that he had passed on.

There was another of my school friends with whom I wish I could have maintained contact. His name was Dennis Devonport, and, like me, he loved to play football and cricket in The Square at Havercroft. When I played for England against Brazil in 1956, he was there to cheer me on. By then he was a lorry driver, which was a tough job before Britain became a nation of motorways. After I returned to London in the summer of 1956, following an England tour of Sweden, Finland and West Germany, I heard that the folks at Havercroft were planning to put up flags everywhere to welcome me home. But there would be no flags. And rightly so. The day before my return, Havercroft went into mourning when the news emerged that Dennis Devonport had died in a crash in his lorry. He was driving some bricks to somewhere, but his lorry went into an embankment, and the weight of the bricks injured him enough put him in a critical condition. He died in hospital two days later at the age of 22. Ten years earlier, however, he was a happy-go-lucky twelve-year-old boy with his whole future ahead of him. We all felt immortal and, even then, felt privileged to be alive.

I was with Curly Worby when we listened on the radio to the 1946 FA Cup final, in which Derby County defeated Charlton Athletic 4-1 after extra time. I still recall the shock in the commentator's voice when he described how Bert Turner, that fine Wales international full-back, scored twice in the final few minutes: an own goal for Derby and then an equaliser for Charlton. There was something magical and mysterious about a commentator's voice in 1946. It would have been enough for me then to know that, one day, a BBC commentator would make reference to an outside-left called Colin Grainger.

No matter what we all did, Curly Worby seemed to be part of the group. At half-term holidays in school, we would be together picking peas in spring or potatoes in autumn, and would earn a few pennies for our troubles. Potato picking was hard work because by September the frost on the ground would hurt your fingers. But just like my dad down the pit, you were paid not for how many hours you put in, but, rather, for what you produced. Occasionally, we would go bird nesting, hoping to get an egg to take home. My parents kept hens and chickens, mainly for eggs, although, at other times, my dad would have to kill one of the birds for us to eat. Being a pigeon fancier, my dad must have found it tough emotionally killing a chicken. I did not like the process – it seemed a bit cruel – but I realised that the vagaries of our world forced a family to do what was necessary to eat.

When World War Two imposed itself on Europe in 1939, we all knew we would avoid the evacuation because we figured that nobody would want to bomb the tiny mining villages of West Yorkshire. Massive bombs did drop a few miles away, and the kids of Sheffield and other nearby towns were evacuated, but the war in a physical sense only came to Havercroft once when a small bomb fell near the mines. However, Havercroft did go to the war – in the shape of my brother, Eric, who joined the Army at the age of eighteen in 1944. Inexplicably, he went straight to the Front in Belgium. He had no training, nothing. We counted ourselves lucky that although he suffered injuries, he returned home safely in 1945. He damaged his ankle while abroad and the injury ended any hopes he had of becoming a professional footballer. Still, his circumstances could have been worse. Men of his age were dying every day at the Front. From 1939-45, you learnt to count your blessings.

The joy of Eric's return did not insulate me from the worst excesses of tragedy. Even today, people still recall the case of William Gledhill, aged eleven, who was walking near the pit at Ryhill, possibly looking for adventure. He turned into Pit Lane, went too close, and his coat got caught in the rope that manoeuvred the cage and dragged him down, cutting his body in half. The incident distressed our village. For a time, I could not stop thinking of him. A more horrific death you could not conceive.

The constraints of rationing provided a necessary sense of egalitarianism, and we all made the best of what we had. My mam would sometimes swap butter for sugar. We would cut up discarded jumpers and old coats to make rugs. There was no central heating, so in winter going to bed might be an ordeal because it was so cold. At night, candles would provide light. All fires were coal in those days, and once every four weeks the coalman would drop off a tonne bag outside your house. Then you had to get the coal into the coalhouse at the back by using buckets. The process took quite a while.

Our lives improved in 1946 when electricity arrived at the colliery houses. Suddenly, almost overnight, we had lights in the bedroom, whereas previously we could only use candles. The biggest beneficiary of electricity, I think, was my mam because she ran the household. She worked so hard that anything to ease the day-to-day burdens was something to be cherished. She would forever be putting irons in the fire, whether to warm the bed sheets at nighttime or to get the creases out of our clothes. And once a week, on a line in the kitchen, there would be twenty shirts hanging up ready to wear – five shirts each for four brothers. My mam had a simple philosophy: we all came first; she came second.

We took nothing for granted, not even shoes. My dad saved money by repairing our family's shoes, using a hobbing foot, which was a length of wood six inches in diameter and three feet high with a hole in the top to hold a piece of metal in the shape of foot. Better fixing shoes like that instead of an expensive trip to the local cobblers. When our shoes wore down too much, Dad would put leather in the soles if he could afford it, or cardboard if things were tight financially.

Electricity came at the right time. The winter of 1946-47 was horrendous and, for a time, brought the entire country to a standstill. The snow in Havercroft must have been three feet deep, which brought both benefits and pitfalls. Not until mid-March did the snow melt, which had knock-on effects for the football season. Not until mid-June were Liverpool confirmed as league champions.

In school, you learnt to grow up quickly. Throughout the war, we had already learnt how to use a gas mask and, eventually, we had to wear the things for real. If you wanted to use the telephone, you would have to go to the public one at the bottom of the street. And for what seemed like years, the sound of sirens would send children and adults scurrying in all directions. We would hide underneath the stairs until the perceived danger passed. For the most part, however, our world seemed exciting and adventurous, and the social changes brought about by the war helped bring people closer together.

At the age of ten, in 1943, I was part of a group of boys who took the bus to Oakwell every other Saturday in the football season to watch Barnsley's home matches. This was during the Wartime League, so the matches were only semi-competitive, and each team was full of guest players who only played because they just happened to be in the area. It was during these affairs that I watched some of the best players of the era: Raich Carter, Tommy Lawton, and Wilf Mannion, all three England internationals of distinction and great figures who lost the best days of their careers to the war.

Once the end of the war marked the return to competitive football, I delighted in the performances of Johnny Kelly, a Scot, whose dexterity on the left wing for Barnsley made the hair on the back of my neck stand on end. He did not just have pace and skill, he had a genuine love of the game. He was the type who would have played football for free; such was his passion for the game. And he was an outside-left, the same as me, which meant that I identified with him more closely than I did with any other Barnsley player of that early post-war era. In later years, when one or two newspapers called me the New Johnny Kelly, I took it as the ultimate compliment.

Another Barnsley player to enthral the spectators was Jorge Robledo, the Chilean inside-forward, whom everybody called 'George'. He grew up in Brampton, Yorkshire, began his working life by going down the pits, and would make a name for himself, first with Chile at the 1950 World Cup, and then with Newcastle United in the FA Cup finals of 1951 and 1952. Robledo was one of those players who always seemed to be sucking on a cigarette in the dressing room before the match or at half-time.

Attending football matches in the mid-to-late-40s was a strange if exhilarating experience. There was uniformity about it all. People would wear suits in one of three colours: black, grey or brown. Flat caps proliferated. Behaviour was almost always good. Conversation rather than singing was rife. People used to just stand there and observe in a constant state of deference. To get a feel for how British society changed from the late-40s to the mid-60s, consider how the comportment of the football spectator changed. Within twelve or fifteen years, every kind of fashion and every kind of colour and every kind of song could be witnessed on the terraces. I also developed a particular affection for Sheffield United after I attended a match at Bramall Lane in 1944 and saw at first hand the extent of the bomb damage.

I was one of 28,464 spectators at Oakwell on Boxing Day 1945 to see Barnsley defeat Liverpool 1-0 in the North Region War League match. Liverpool had Billy Liddell, that marvellously talented Scot, on the left wing, and Jimmy McInnes, the left-half, who would become the club secretary and would, so tragically, hang himself from the Kop roof in 1965. That 1945/46 campaign saw Barnsley reach the fifth round in the FA Cup, losing to Bradford Park Avenue over two legs. I attended the match at Oakwell against Park Avenue, who had an inside-forward of great style and panache; a visionary who seemed to play the game at his own speed. That was the first time I set eyes on Len Shackleton, an outrageously talented inside-forward whose personality made him a *bête noire* of the game's establishment. A decade later, he would enter my life as a teammate and, briefly, a confidant.

I was making good progress in my own attempts to distinguish myself as a player. I made the Barnsley boys' team for 1946/47, playing alongside Tommy Taylor, a youth-team player for Smithies United, his local colliery team. A centre-forward, Taylor's talent was obvious and there was no doubting he would not only make the grade but would probably play for England. Also in the Barnsley boys' team was a little kid called Harry Bird, whose attempts to play professionally fell foul of a knee injury. He turned to cricket, his second love, and played at the highest level for Yorkshire and Leicestershire. Eventually, going by the name of Dickie Bird, he became one of the world's most famous and beloved cricket umpires. Barnsley boys played Saturday mornings and we each received six pence for expenses – a not-inconsiderable sum for a thirteen-year-old in those days.

But I spent as much time watching football as playing. In 1947/48, Barnsley's average home attendance of 21,050 meant that nearly one in seven people from the catchment area of 150,000 attended matches at Oakwell. In some respects, Oakwell in the late 40s was a paragon of the game's social growth, for there seems little doubt that football helped to revive a nation still traumatised by war. My professional career coincided with dramatic changes in the social dynamics of football.

But it was not football that provided me with my first audience. I acquired my first taste of fame on stage. As a singer. And, naturally, it happened by accident. My dad was the concert secretary for the Havercroft Working Men's Club, and it was his job to ensure that the acts turned up on time and got paid. He even made the advertising posters. My mam worked behind the bar and my pals and I would often go back stage to listen to the acts. However, when on one occasion the scheduled act failed to turn up, I offered to perform my Al Jolson routine. 'Wait a minute!' I would shout to polite applause. 'Wait a minute! You ain't heard nothin' yet!' And then, to growing cheers, I would croon with a confidence that nobody knew I possessed.

I must have done well because the next time an act failed to show, some of the punters called for me to get up on stage and perform again. *Come on, Colin, give us a song* became a local catchphrase. It never crossed my mind that one day, way into the future, some of England's finest footballers would utter the same catchphrase. Then it would be Billy Wright, the England captain, shouting, 'Come on, Colin, give us a song.' Or Stanley Matthews. Or, most fondly, Duncan Edwards.

It would be nice to say that my ability to sing came from out of the blue. The truth is I had been practising in my bedroom for months, putting those old 78rpm records on a record player and singing Al Jolson or Robert Earl until my throat hurt. After each song, I had to wind up the record player before I could put on the next record. It was a laborious process but I loved it. I sang from the heart.

Our John signed for Rotherham United in 1947 at the age of 23 and went straight into the first team. That marked the end of my time travelling to Oakwell every other Saturday. Instead, the entire family – cousins, uncles, brothers – took a taxi with one of the Bingley drivers to Rotherham home first-team and reserve-team matches at Millmoor. On a few occasions, our John played against one of his school friends, Charlie Williams of Doncaster Rovers, a lovely black man of Barbadian and English mixed heritage who had a great personality, a quick brain, and a desire to become an entertainer. Royston-born, he was a decent player – 'I was never fancy, but I could stop them buggers that were,' he would say years later – but, as we shall see, he became a far more impressive, and more famous, comedian.

My dad would travel with us to watch our John, even though he much preferred boxing to football. Occasionally, I would travel to Millmoor alone, which involved four buses there, a two-hour journey, and four buses back. Our John turned himself into a fine outside-right, quick and fast, with great accuracy in crossing the ball. He would remain with Rotherham until 1957, making 352 League appearances, and he would also represent the England B team. The man who signed our John for Rotherham was Reg Freeman, who had been manager of the club since 1934 and was regarded in some quarters as a legend at Millmoor.

Our John would send a portion of his wages to my mam. Horace would also make sure Mam was all right when he secured a job on the railway. Consequently, my parents felt that little bit better off, which would enable the purchase of that first TV.

I scraped enough money together to attend a few of the days of the England-Australia cricket Test at Headingley, Leeds, in July 1948. I counted it as a privilege to witness the likes of Len Hutton, Denis Compton, Cyril Washbrook, Bill Edrich, Alec Bedser, Jim Laker and Jack Crapp for England, and Don Bradman, Neil Harvey, and Keith Miller for Australia.

But we were still not well off enough for me to attend the 1948 Olympic Games in London. The school arranged a trip to Wembley but my parents could not afford it. London involved a long trek in those days. And while I was disappointed, I understood completely. I listened to the events on the radio instead and I hoped that one day those cheers at Wembley would be for something I achieved.

The rapture of youth

School ended for me at the age of fifteen just before the Olympics, and I went straight with Curly Worby to work for Mr Beaumont's garage as a car mechanic for £1-1-2½ a week. Mr Beaumont was the brother of my woodwork teacher in school – the first teacher to give me the cane for bad behaviour. To save money, Curly and I would walk to school. For six months, I rubbed down the cars, five days a week, and then I joined a different garage in Wakefield and worked on the engines for Mr Hepplethwaite, which trebled my wages to more than three quid a week, and involved a short bus ride there and back. In accordance with family tradition and moral obligation, I gave a portion of my wages to my mam.

By now I was playing for the South Elmsall Boys in my preferred position of outside-left, and going by the nickname of Tal Grainger. I did not know what the nickname meant then and I do not know now, but for all my time with the team the sobriquet stuck to me like a tattoo. Although I was only fifteen, I did make the Ryhill Intermediate Under-18 squad in the Barnsley Intermediate League, which put me alongside grown men. I did not make as many appearances as I would have liked – perhaps the manager thought I was a bit too young – but I did play against Arthur Kaye, a Higham lad, who became a fine winger in the 50s and 60s for Barnsley, Blackpool, Middlesbrough and Colchester United. At that time, I felt I was better at cricket than I was at football.

But then in July 1949, just after my sixteenth birthday, came a telegram from a guy who signed himself Leslie J. McDowall. Was I interested in having a trial for Wrexham Football Club of the Football League Division Three North? The same club for which my cousin, Dennis Grainger, was playing first-team football? You bet!

My dad took me down there on the bus and we stayed at the Cambrian pub, which Dennis Grainger owned. It was only when I arrived in Wrexham that I realised it was he who had fixed up the trial. At first, I thought the session would consist of matches between 16-to-18-year-old boys, but then I learnt that the right-back marking me was aged 24. I must have done well because at the end of the week, Les McDowall – his more familiar name – asked to see me in his office. When my dad and I arrived, Cliff Lloyd, the club secretary, was also there. A good sign. We got down to business straight away. Wrexham were offering me £5 per week to join the ground staff as an apprentice professional footballer. Before I had a chance to speak, McDowall increased the offer to £5, 5 shillings.

When Mr Hepplethwaite in Wakefield learnt of my contract at Wrexham, and therefore my impending departure from the engineering works, he sent me an extra week's wages as a good-luck gift: £1-7-2½.

Les McDowall was unique and something of a visionary. Born in Gunga Pur, British India, in 1912, he was essentially a Scot who had distinguished himself as a half-back with Manchester City from 1937-49. He had just left Maine Road to take over as the Wrexham player-manager, so I was one of the first players to sign for him. He was a fine specimen, smart, upright, with a great presence about him and the kind of authoritative but benevolent manner that made you want to listen whenever he spoke. When he gave you advice, there was no ulterior motive. It was for your good, not his. He even encouraged me to play cricket in the summer for the Wrexham Boys Club, which I did.

There is an evocative photograph of McDowall on his first day as Wrexham manager in summer 1949. He is wearing his customary smart but slightly-out-of-date suit, exuding charm, while most of the first-team squad stand bare-chested and smiling on what appears to be a hot day. The grass is long, the terraces empty, but everything feels undefiled and unblemished, with no bad results and bad weather to spoil the ambiance.

Then came my first problem: finding a place to live. Dennis Grainger had sold the Cambrian and acquired a larger pub, called The Feathers, to where I moved. But it was difficult for his wife to look after me, as she also had a young child and was helping out in the pub. My cousin asked me to move out. Jack Jones, who worked for Wrexham as the reserve-team trainer and groundsman, came to the rescue by fixing me up in his house for three weeks. Then I stayed with a lady called Mrs Morton in a house next to the Wrexham railway station, but all I could hear was the commotion of the trains and the noise of footsteps as people came in and out of the station.

There was an art to finding the right digs and I had not yet mastered it. Mind you, I had it easy. One of the other players in digs had four children in Morton, Derbyshire, and after paying his £2 rent sent the rest of his money back home. For all the joy his young kids must have given him, he was never going to have it easy at Wrexham. He had pressures, financial and domestic. I had no pressures, which helped to make my existence thrilling and served to enhance my natural curiosity.

My domestic situation improved when I met a lovely lad called Percy Davies, an apprentice plasterer who was a year older than I, at the Wrexham Youth Club. We struck up a friendship and he suggested that I move in with him and his parents. Vi and Wilf Davies had a smart and well-appointed bungalow in a village called Rhosnesni. Percy Davies and I kept in touch with each other for 67 years – I never forgot to tell him how well and warmly his mother and stepfather treated me – and it was with deep regret in early October 2016 that I heard of his death. It was as if a member of my family had passed away. When his brother called me to tell me the bad news, all I could remember were the simple things about life in Rhosnesni: the food was quality, the company good, and I even had a bedroom to myself. At £2 per week, the arrangement seemed a bargain. Had he not invited me to stay with his mother and stepfather, I would surely have returned to Havercroft. I might even have given up football and instead gone down the pit, just as my father had. Consequently, I regard Percy Davies as one of the key figures in my playing career.

Sixteen might seem a young age for me to leave home but the truth is that life in a West Yorkshire mining village teaches you independence. I felt ready to go it alone. We still laugh about those times and how easily it was to be amused; how the rapture of youth turned every incident into our version of a cartoon strip. Indeed, I derived much joy from reading the *Dandy* or the *Beano*. Percy would read one while I read the other, and then we swapped. I would get match tickets for Percy Davies, so he could go to watch the likes of Liverpool or Manchester United.

Of course, I did miss my family, but I also felt no sense of loss and no homesickness in leaving Havercroft. Occasionally I would go home to see my mam and dad for a few days, but always in the knowledge that my brother, Eric, would take me back to Wrexham. Having my cousin, Dennis Grainger, around was a significant help. Born in Royston on 5 March 1920, he was thirteen years my senior, had joined Wrexham in 1947 after playing 37 League matches for Leeds United, and was always on hand to look after me if necessary. At his peak, he had been a fine outside-right with a breathtaking level of pace over fifty yards. I benefited from his experience.

Being an apprentice was no easy option. You went straight on to the ground staff, performing such mundane roles as cleaning the boots of the first-team players, marking the pitch, putting up the nets, making sure the fire in the dressing room was on, sweeping the terraces, painting the main stand, washing the kit –

everything designed to keep your feet on the ground. If you made the first-team squad, you knew you had got there the hard way, by serving your time.

Initially, I spent most of my time playing for Wrexham reserves in the Cheshire County League, which put me up against the hardened amateurs and semi-professionals of non-League clubs, or the talented youth-team players of Football League clubs. I have the programmes for the Wrexham-Macclesfield Town match on 24 December 1949 and the Wrexham-Chester match on 26 December, both of which reveal me at outside-left and my cousin, Dennis, as outside-right. The Macclesfield goalkeeper was Nat McKinstry, one of the best in their history. Having retired in the 50s, he became a regular supporter of the team and was still there, sitting in the stands, when I played for Macclesfield in the Cheshire League in 1966/67. The Chester goalkeeper was Harry Threadgold, who would later play for Sunderland and then became a legend at Southend United from 1953-63. The Chester inside-left was Tommy Tilston, who would sign for Wrexham in 1951.

Non-League football was a sobering experience for a seventeen-year-old kid, such as I was, but absolutely necessary. The opposing players might sometimes be bigger and tougher than those in the Football League. The attendances at places like Macclesfield, Runcorn, Rhyl, Altrincham, and South Liverpool could run into a few thousand. The pitches in non-League football could be muddy, the dressing rooms grim and damp, but this was part of my education. For me, the road to the First Division and to the full England international team went through the Cheshire County League.

I trained hard, played my best, and performed my duties on the ground staff with enthusiasm. And there alongside this group of wide-eyed teenagers was Jack Jones, leading us and inspiring us, and keeping our feet on the ground. The responsibility of keeping the Racecourse Ground in good condition proved particularly great in early March 1950 as Wrexham prepared to host the full international match between Wales and Northern Ireland. I swept the changing rooms, I swept the terraces, and I even marked the pitch. The significance of the match, of course, is that it was the day John Charles made his Wales international debut. It was also the last time an all-Ireland team competed in a competitive fixture. After that, for Irish players, it was either Northern Ireland or the Republic of Ireland but not both, as had been the case.

I would have liked to have met Charles afterwards but I was still aged sixteen – far too shy to impose myself on a legend. Still, it was nice to enjoy my first taste of international football. Wearing my Wrexham FC official blazer, I watched the match from the main stand, having shown guests to their seats before the kick-off. The goalless draw proved to be something of an anticlimax, with Danny Blanchflower, the Barnsley right-half, emerging as Northern Ireland's most accomplished player, overshadowing a rather subdued John Charles.

There was not a moment when I thought I had made the wrong decision in moving to the Racecourse Ground, even when there were options to join other clubs closer to home. The club was in good health, declaring a profit of £5,250 for 1949/50, and a good place for a young player to learn his job. I had no regrets even when the redoubtable McDowall left to replace Jock Thomson as manager of Manchester City on 1 June 1950. Thomson, who was best known for taking Bert Trautmann to Manchester City, went off to Dundee to run a hotel.

One of McDowall's first decisions at Manchester City was to invite our John and me to Maine Road in December to see if we would be interested in signing for the club. The manager said he wanted to build a team around the two of us, and he showed us around the ground, explained his plans for the future, and put us up for the night in a large club house. Essentially, McDowall was trying to poach us, which was strictly illegal. Had I tried to break my Wrexham contract, and had our John tried to break his Rotherham United contract, both of us would have faced *sine die* bans from the game. Word got out about McDowall's plans and two Wrexham directors travelled to Havercroft to speak to my mam and dad, to reassure them that the club would look after me and that I would move to a larger club eventually.

They told me I would enjoy working with the new manager at Wrexham, Peter Jackson. A former Stoke City and Southend United half-back, Jackson had never managed a team before and he did not quite inspire me as much as McDowall had. With Stoke, Jackson won the Division Three North championship in 1926/27 and the Second Division championship in 1932/33, but I never got the feeling he was going to be as successful a manager as he was a player. We shared Yorkshire roots – Jackson was born in Halifax in 1905 – but we never had much of a chance of developing a good working relationship. National Service called me in 1951.

I would spend my two years under the auspices of the Royal Air Force, stationed mainly at Odiham in Hampshire. I joined the RAF in the July and did the obligatory two days at Padgate, Warrington, to get kitted out. Then it was off for six weeks at Hednesford, Staffordshire, before the trek down south to Odiham. And I can say honestly that I loved every second of the RAF. The discipline – you had to be out of bed and in the shower at six o'clock every morning – seemed to suit my desire to fill each day with as much activity as possible. I played for the Fighter Command XI alongside some excellent players, such as Tony Marchi (Tottenham Hotspur) and Vic Keeble (later of Newcastle United), and I feel a certain irony in that my National Service did as much for my football as did my time at Wrexham. I worked as an admin orderly for the No. 247 Squadron, recording the times of the de Havilland Vampire flight sorties; an important job but a cushy one, too; a job I valued and performed to the best of my ability. A week later, I would serve food in the canteen; then a week after that, I would deliver coal (shirtless, so I could catch some sunshine); then a week after that, I would clean out the offices. The work was varied, which added to the experience and ensured there would be no boredom.

Doing National Service, you would forge friendships, solid friendships, which would last a lifetime. John Carter, from Cardiff, was one lad with whom I hit it off. In later years, once I had established myself as a professional footballer, I would always get him tickets for any matches I played at Ninian Park against Cardiff City. Another lad was George Forsett, from Halifax, with whom I would sometimes get the bus back home to Yorkshire. Occasionally, he and I would go for long-distance runs around the airport at Odiham. I found him an interesting character. He grew up on a farm with his grandmother, often slept rough, and loved the outdoors. Unfortunately, in later years, his penchant for existing in damp conditions caused him arthritis, which affected him greatly.

My biggest influence at the Racecourse Ground was Dennis Grainger. Like me, he was a winger, although he played on the right, with the No. 7 shirt on his back. And although we had similar styles, he was quicker than I could ever dream of becoming. Indeed, when I was under consideration for the Yorkshire Schoolboys Representative team, the main reason I failed, apparently, was that I was not quick enough for a winger.

My cousin Dennis, who had played for Southport once in August 1939 and then many times during World War Two, and for Leeds United just after it, told me that sprinting was as much about technique as it was natural, so he took me to a local cinder track and taught me how to sprint. We put on our spikes and spent hours sprinting up and down the track. 'For a winger, speed is a *must*,' Dennis would say, emphasising the word 'must'. And, of course, he was right. My speed improved dramatically after that and I felt I was a different player, as if running on air. I have no doubt that I got some of my speed from the Holliday side of the family. My maternal grandfather used to earn money by travelling to places in the north-east and Scotland for sprint races. People would bet on him, and if he won, he would do well out of it financially. Granddad Holliday, who was born in 1873, did not die until 1958, so he was still around to see all of his grandchildren excel in sport. Those sprinting sessions with Dennis Grainger converted me from a medium-paced player into a quick player, and, eventually, helped to make me an England player. But I am getting ahead of myself.

I signed professionally with Wrexham when I turned seventeen, receiving a £10 fee and an increase in weekly wage to £8. I made my first-team debut on 24 February 1951, at home to Hartlepools United, at outside-left. My parents read about it in the *Hartlepool Northern Daily Mail* the day before: 'Wrexham will bring in a 17-year-old outside left, Colin Grainger. He displaces [Billy] Tunnicliffe.' The right-back marking me was Joseph Willetts, who, being nine years older than I, was infinitely more experienced. But I had the advantage of mystery – Willetts knew nothing about me – and of my cousin's sprinting lessons. Eager to please but reluctant to make mistakes, I did the simple things well and absorbed all the advice that came my way. I had a good match and we won 1-0. Willetts shook my hand afterwards and wished me all the best.

One of the highlights of my first season with Wrexham was when the club gave me tickets to attend the 1951 FA Cup semi-final replay between Blackpool and Birmingham City at Everton. In those days, Goodison Park had that brilliant Archibald Leitch main stand, built in 1909, which made the whole edifice look stately. I was there, one of 70,114 spectators, standing amid the tumult of the paddock, just in front of the main stand, stretching on my tiptoes. And all to get a better view of Stanley Matthews. Whenever he got the ball, he made me think back to my impressionable years watching Johnny Kelly of Barnsley. A brilliant winger can have much the same effect on an audience as a singer. You could hear the gasps – the gasps of anticipation, the gasps of stimulation – all around the ground. Matthews was at his peak then with Blackpool and among the best players in the world. He so far ahead of anybody on the pitch that I felt sorry for Jack Badham, the Birmingham full-back marking him, who barely touched the ball all match. Was there a tougher job in football than trying to stop Matthews? Not in 1951.

Seeing Matthews in the flesh took me back to my days as a young lad – aged ten, perhaps – when I kept a scrapbook of newspaper cuttings. There would be Matthews photographs or Tom Finney photographs on most pages. Here were two players who defined the English game in the early post-war years. I used to study what the reporters wrote about the wingers. So when I was old enough to attend matches, it was always the wingers on which I cast my eyes – especially the wingers who could also score goals.

It was with my pal, George Forsett, that I attended as many football matches as possible at weekends. Odiham was not too far from Wembley, which enabled us to attend the 1952 FA Cup final between Newcastle United and Arsenal. Cliff Lloyd, the Wrexham secretary, got me a ticket. Newcastle won 1-0, and the scorer of the goal? Jorge Robledo, that talented Chilean-Yorkshireman, whom I had watched when he played for Barnsley in the mid-to-late 40s. We also went to the 1953 FA Cup final between Blackpool and Bolton Wanderers, and it was there that I witnessed Matthews in superlative form. Blackpool won 4-3 but we now know the occasion as the Matthews Final, for not only did he play with distinction but he also won his first FA Cup winners' medal after so many years of frustration. For me, this day was touched with pure magic. The Matthews performance was the true essence of football as art.

After the match, Forsett and I hung about London for a time, soaking up the atmosphere, appreciating whatever it was that made the city unique. But the cost of having so much fun was that we ended up skint and had to stay the night for free in a Salvation Army hostel. I dread to think of what we looked like the next morning, or what we smelt like, as we got the bus back to the RAF camp at Odiham.

Forsett and I were inseparable. Sometimes we would go to Arsenal matches at Highbury and Portsmouth matches at Fratton Park. Football grounds were unique places in those days. The hooliganism of the 70s and 80s and the sterility of the twenty-first century were phenomena of the future. This was football fandom in its purest sense. You paid at the gate and delighted in the communal experience. No need for segregation in those days. Strangely, although I was a full-time professional, I did actually watch more football than I played.

From Wrexham, I was close enough geographically to attend Liverpool matches at Anfield and Manchester United matches at Old Trafford. I never lost the excitement of walking through those terraced streets, absorbing the unmistakable proletarian aura, taking my place as part of a mass movement, as if visiting a cathedral. Travelling around the country gave me the opportunity to consider how different the regions were from one another. West Riding had its peculiarities, just as London did, just as Liverpool did, and Manchester did. Local populaces had their nuances, their vernaculars, but people seemed genuinely friendly and grateful to be part of a nation that had pulled through the war and had accepted rationing as a necessary consequence. It is hard to imagine now, in this era of cheap and convenient jet travel, how edifying and didactic it was in the early 50s to travel around Britain.

I would like to have played more football but National Service had to be the priority for men of my age. The important thing about the RAF was that I needed special permission to play first-team matches for Wrexham. You had to apply for a 48-hour pass and there was never a guarantee of acceptance. I do not recall any rejections because I knew that you only got so many passes. You learnt not to push your luck. I did not play at all for the first team in 1951/52, and only four times in 1952/53: away to Oldham Athletic, away to Halifax Town, away to Chesterfield, and at home to Crewe Alexandra.

(The Oldham and Halifax matches took place in February 1953, during which time Derek Dooley, the flame-haired Sheffield Wednesday striker, suffered the injury against Preston North End that would not only end his career but also cause the surgeon to amputate his leg. He invited me to play in his testimonial match in March 1955, a Sheffield XI versus an International XI who included Stanley Matthews, John Charles, and Tommy Lawton, but I missed it because of a minor injury. Years later, Dooley and I became friends and colleagues at Sheffield United.)

Wrexham drew 0-0 away to Halifax, but what sticks out for me more than the football was the unorthodox nature of my pre-match preparation. I took a bus from Havercroft to Wakefield, then from Wakefield to Halifax. I ended up in Halifax two hours before kick-off, so before I went to The Shay for the match, I ordered beans on toast and a cup of tea in the café at the bus station. Enjoying my solitude, I looked out of the window at the people passing and wondered how many of them were going to the match. Would they have been surprised if they discovered that the boy in the café was preparing to play? The truth is, nobody – apart, perhaps, the most enthusiastic of Wrexham supporters – would have known who I was. Whatever fame I had barely moved beyond my own private sphere.

Nearly 10,000 attended the home match on 11 April 1953 against Crewe, for whom Harry Catterick, later to manage Everton with much success, doubled up as the centre-forward and the manager. I found the atmosphere electric, partly because the Kop area behind one of the goals seemed to be a focal point for the masses. The noise would always increase, feeling tangible, sometimes reaching a crescendo, whenever the winger – Glyn Hughes hugging the right flank, me hugging the left – received the ball in a good position.

We had some fine players, like Tommy Tilston, an inside-forward from Chester who ended up at Crystal Palace; Tommy Bannan; a Scottish inside-right; and Ron Hewitt, a striker who would go on to represent the Wales national team. The regular outside-left in those days was Billy Tunnicliffe, who began with Port Vale in 1937, then moved to Bournemouth & Boscombe Athletic, but lost a large chunk of his career to World War Two. He gave Wrexham fine service, however, and he was still playing for Bradford City in 1955 – nearly two decades after he signed his first professional contract.

Being so much younger than everybody else on the staff, I did not make too many friends among the first-team squad. But I enjoyed training with them and I respected the talent and professionalism that these fine men displayed. More importantly, they all exuded humility: no boasting, no flash cars, and no disrespect for their colleagues. One or two of them liked a drink but that lifestyle was never for me. For the most part, I was too fearful of being caught with a pint in my hand by the manager, but I was also obsessed with health and fitness.

The Racecourse Ground, one of the oldest stadiums in Britain, was in transition in those days, with the club redeveloping the Kop the previous summer by laying down concrete, which, in turn, made the area more comfortable for spectators. I treasured the place. It had a sense of atmosphere even when empty. It was at the Racecourse on 4 April 1953, however, that one of our reserve-team players, Jock Kirkby, died. An American formerly of Stoke City, with a big physique and a strong handshake, he collapsed of a heart attack during the Cheshire League match against Crewe Alexandra and never woke up again. Footballers have such youth and vitality that when they die prematurely, there is something particularly shocking.

The incident cast a dark cloud over the Racecourse for the remainder of the season and the memory of this gentle giant touched all of us. Mortality is a horrible thing.

Ideal symmetry

My National Service was drawing to an end and I felt a sense of anticlimax, for some of the guys with whom I had experienced so many life-defining days I would never see again. It was different with John Carter and George Forsett. My friendship with each lasted well into the new century – until I stopped receiving Christmas cards from them and their phone numbers no longer worked. I miss them both.

I wanted to accept the offer of a role as a marker at the Queen's Coronation on 2 June 1953, but National Service took me instead to the north-east, where I helped with the transfer of sandbags.

The summer put me at a crossroads. With the 1952/53 football season consigned to history, I returned to Havercroft briefly. Not much had changed. The same faces potted around the village as if time had stood still. The horse and cart rattled around the streets, as it always did, selling its assortment of ice cream to the delight of the children, who now seemed so young. And I found it all so reassuring. My life had changed so much that it was nice to find an immovable environment that represented my childhood. But the greatest change was still to come – in the form of genuine romance. One night in the summer of 1953, I went to the cinema with a few friends. After the film, we noticed a couple of girls, and there was one in particular who seemed to radiate with joy and beauty. We followed them home and as we got closer, they giggled, presumably at all the attention. We caught up with them and I started talking to the girl who had attracted my interest. She was sixteen and smiled beautifully, with a confidence that belied her youth. I asked her name: Doreen Rowe.

'I am playing cricket on Saturday,' I said, a touch fretfully. 'Would you like to come and watch?' She said that she would be there.

Relief!

But on the day of the match there was no sign of her. I could not see her anywhere. She had stood me up.

Disappointment!

But then the fates intervened. I saw her that night at a dance. 'I must apologise for not coming to see you,' she said. 'But I have to tell you that I don't like cricket.' We both laughed and I could sense there and then that there was a connection between us. I found that I felt comfortable in her company. That night, I had the last waltz with her. Soon after we started dating and I knew early on in the relationship that I had met my future wife.

Doreen and I had a lot in common, for we shared a similar background. Her father, Harold Rowe, was a miner and his claim to fame was that he became the first man in Yorkshire to work a coal cutter. I valued hard work – I had seen how the intense labours of my parents had given me such a happy childhood – so I developed an instant respect for Doreen's father, who had many of the attributes that characterised my dad.

By that summer, our John had talked us all into setting up a bookmaking business. He knew his horseracing, as did Eric, who became the second in command. We did well out of it, particularly when the Grand National took place in Liverpool, and we learnt that success bred success. Many people in the village came to us to register their bets. Our headquarters was the shed and we always found it exciting at the end of each day when we counted the money and shared it with each other. On the odd occasion, we would be down financially, but we always knew we would make up the money the next day. Eric continued the business for a long time after the rest of us sold out. I gave up my share because I had something more significant with which to contend: a move from Wrexham to Sheffield United on 27 June 1953. The man who signed me for Sheffield United was Reg Freeman, who, as the manager of Rotherham United, had taken our John to Millmoor six years before. What ideal symmetry. Freeman told anybody who would listen that I could be as good a player as my brother, which embarrassed me, especially when I saw such quotations in the press, because I never saw myself in competition with our John. I feel sure that our John encouraged Freeman to sign me. Personal recommendations were a big part of the game in the days before player agents and television. Had I not joined Sheffield United, I might have joined Leeds United, who were also reported to be ready to make a bid for me. I seemed to have developed a reputation, with newspapers speculating about my next club. I had options but Sheffield United it would be.

Wrexham pocketed £2,500 from the transfer, a large sum for a team in the Third Division, and I never begrudged the club a single penny. Wrexham took the initial risk. I might have failed miserably. The club deserved to reap the benefit of the investment it put into shaping me. I was a better man and better player for my two years there.

Wrexham sent me a telegram telling me to get down to the Great Northern

Hotel in London, where Freeman would be waiting with the transfer forms for me to sign. He was an agreeable man and he had all sorts of nice things he wanted to tell me about the days when he managed our John at Rotherham. I had heard so much from our John about Freeman that no introduction felt necessary.

I was sorry to leave the Racecourse Ground, having made so many friends among the ground staff, having learnt so much from Jack Jones and Cliff Lloyd, and having developed such a good relationship with the Davies family in Rhosnesni.

Most of all, I knew that Bramall Lane, home of the new Football League Second Division champions, would provide the right context in which to take my career to the next level.

It was the First Division. It was Yorkshire. It was the big city.

And I had vindicated my dad:

Son, no way you're ever going down a pit.

CHAPTER II

Lines from the Pavilion
1953-57: Sheffield United,
Joe Mercer, Duncan Edwards, England

I could run as if on air

ON MY LAST DAY AT WREXHAM, I FELT TALL AND SANGUINE. ON MY first day at Sheffield United, I felt small and diffident. Something about Bramall Lane in the summer of 1953 had the effect of diminishing me, even if the sense of inferiority was all in my head and not based on anything tangible.

As befitting a newly promoted club, confidence permeated the place like a beautiful scent, and everywhere I turned I witnessed the symbols of significance: more players, bigger players, better players, bigger stadium, harder training, and more money. The club paid me a ten-quid signing-on bonus – I was far too naïve and reticent to ask for more – and the maximum twenty-quid-a-week wage as allowed by the rules. Such an amount scared me, for it came attached with great responsibilities and, initially, promoted a fear of failure. For all my insecurities, however, I could not wait to get started, but I could not take my place in the squad properly until October when my National Service ended officially.

Deciding to live with my mam and dad in Havercroft, I shared my old double bed with our John, who was still playing for Rotherham United. I paid my mam board, three quid a week, and I decided that I would not buy a car until I had saved up enough money to pay cash. The idea of a bank loan did not feel right. I went by simple principles: if you cannot afford it, you cannot have it; and if you want it, you have to work for it.

So while most of my new Sheffield United colleagues were driving to Bramall

Lane each morning in the comfort of their own cars (the more experienced the player, the more impressive the car), I was taking a more laborious route: the 8.05am bus from the The Square at Havercroft, two more buses after that, before arriving at the stadium at 9.50, just in time for training at ten. After a while, most of the passengers would recognise me and I would spend time talking about the previous match or the next match, or providing first-hand insights into the attributes of the other Sheffield United players.

Jimmy Hagan was always at the forefront of any conversation. He was a brilliant inside-right, obscenely talented with both feet, whom the press called 'a master strategist'; a player whose career had begun with Liverpool in 1933 when he was aged fourteen, included a spell with Derby County, before he flourished with Sheffield United from 1938. Hagan had the best car, attracted the most attention – and he did the least amount of training. He was in his mid-30s in 1953, contemplating careers as a chartered surveyor and a schoolteacher, and wanted to keep all his physical energies for the matches. You did not see much of him on the training pitch, and he only really came to the club in the week to work in the gym on his legs and upper body. He was effectively a part-time player then, but come Saturday afternoon he was never less than the consummate professional: skilled, cerebral, strong and inspiring. You learnt lessons just by watching him.

The joke about Hagan was that he would feign interest in Reg Freeman's team talks with exaggerated nods of the head, and then play matches off the cuff, making a virtue of spontaneity, as if the manager had never said a word. Freeman, of course, never had a clue. The thing that always stuck out for me about Hagan was that you only saw him usually for ninety minutes each week, yet he was somehow ubiquitous and imperious; the permanent elephant in the room; present even when he was not present, a bit like the first Mrs de Winter in Daphne du Maurier's *Rebecca*. In later years, once I became a student of Sheffield United's history, I formed the view that Hagan was the club's finest player of all time.

But he was not our only significant player in 1953. The dressing room was full of interesting characters and fine footballers, most of whom hailed from Sheffield and had been with the club since just after World War Two.

Joe Shaw, the inside-right and later a centre-half, for example, was eight years into what would become a 21-year career at Bramall Lane. Like me, he grew up in a mining community, but he was five years older than I, and he seemed like a grown man at a time when I felt like an overgrown boy. How he never played for

England, I cannot comprehend, for his powers of anticipation were of the highest standard, as if he had a sixth sense. The right-winger was Alf Ringstead, an Irishman, against whom I had played in the Cheshire League in 1950 when he was with Northwich Victoria and I was with Wrexham. Our goalkeeper was Ted Burgin, with his contorted hands, who was the joker in the pack, the frustrated comedian, always performing impressions of Al Read, a famous radio personality of the time. Not especially tall but remarkably agile, Burgin would go to the World Cup with England in 1954 as a member of the squad.

The player whom I had to dislodge from outside-left was Derek Hawksworth, formerly of Bradford Park Avenue and Bradford City, who had great pace, quick feet and a wonderful personality. Fred Furniss, the right-back, had been with the club since 1945 and was already considered something of a veteran. He kept himself to himself, rarely spoke, but became the object of our jokes when he failed his first six driving tests. In those days, it was harder to fail than pass, so quite what he was doing wrong was anybody's guess. We had Len Browning, a lovely lad from Doncaster, who began with Leeds United in 1946 at the age of 18 and averaged nearly a goal every two matches there. To much surprise, he signed for Sheffield United in 1951 and became an important part of the team that secured promotion in 1953. Two players whom I befriended were Tommy Hoyland and Graham Shaw, both from Sheffield, who had different personalities but seemed to complement each other during social gatherings. Hoyland, a wing-half, wore a permanent smile, emanating a joy that made him an attractive figure. He made up for his lack of pace with superlative ball control and he was always keen to tell people that he developed his game during regular matches while doing his National Service in Oswestry. Shaw was quieter, averse to hard training sessions, but he was a lovely lad; kind and genuine.

Cecil Coldwell, the full-back, believed that he flourished in his position partly because he had a good memory, which, to him, was as important as being able to kick well with both feet and being fit. 'You must be able to note the characteristics and styles of the wingers you come up against, and adjust your tactics accordingly,' he said once. Cec, as we called him, joined the club in 1951 from a non-League club, Norton Woodseats, and would remain a player at Bramall Lane until 1966.

And then there was Harry Latham, at one time a strong defender, whose career began with Sheffield United in 1937 and resumed after World War Two in 1946, before he hung up his boots in 1953 to become a popular and important member of Reg Freeman's backroom staff, with responsibility to run the reserve team. He had great inter-personal skills because he realised that players were more than just footballers; they were human beings, too, with the same insecurities and frustrations that afflict the miner, the schoolteacher, the policeman, the shopkeeper. Latham turned into something of a mentor to me and I valued the benefit of his experience and his attention at an important time in my career.

There was a distinct Yorkshire flavour throughout the entire squad, which helped to foster team spirit and friendship. No egos, no arrogance, no ulterior motives; just hard work and mutual respect, and all for the greater good. It takes a special manager to create such an ambience. We really were Sheffield *United*.

Given how hard we trained, I could hardly blame Jimmy Hagan for his absences. We slogged away in the Peak District, running up and down the hills until our lungs felt as though they would explode, and we never saw a ball until the middle of week. If the weather was bad, we did not see a ball at all. It was tough. It could be agony. But it was all designed to ensure that we were as strong in the final five minutes of a match as we were in the first five. Reg Freeman did not seem to care about Hagan's attitude to training. 'All we need is a Hagan in defence and we're all set,' he told journalists.

The exertions and pain did not bother me. I always enjoyed training, which, I think, gave me an advantage over those of my colleagues who seemed to hate the discipline of it all. Besides, I had spent the summer of 1953 playing cricket for Ryhill, so there was never a fear that I would put on weight or lose my physical edge. I retained the perception that I could run as if on air. And what did I do each weekday at four o'clock after the bus dropped me off at The Square? Why, more training, of course: at the Welfare Club, Ryhill, with my running spikes, doing hundred-yard sprints until my shirt became soaked with sweat and my thighs screamed for mercy.

I was going to earn every penny of that twenty quid a week . . .

The same values and ambitions

Or so I thought.

The truth is, 1953/54 was something of a write-off for me. I did not even appear on the official team photograph for the season because I was still in the

RAF, so playing in the opening First Division match of the season away to Portsmouth was out of the question.

I discovered quickly that there would be no easy route into the first team. Halfway through the week at training, Reg Freeman, the Sheffield United manager, would write out two teams on the noticeboard. If you were not in one of those teams, you knew you were not going to play for the first team at the weekend. You had a few days to get over your disappointment. It took me a while to discover what my name looked like on the noticeboard, or, indeed, in newsprint in the Sheffield newspapers. Although I liked Freeman, and got on well with everybody in the first-team squad, I felt like an outcast, an imposter, and no more sure of a decent playing career than when I signed on as an apprentice with Wrexham four years earlier. In many respects, I was now an apprentice at Sheffield United, and there were processes I needed to negotiate if I was going to become a first-team regular.

You learn a lot about yourself through times of introspection. You learn that even working hard does not guarantee success at the end of the week. It felt like when my dad came home from the pit during those terrible days of limited productivity to tell my mam: 'So sorry, Lily, no money today.' All that work, all that hope – all that anticlimax.

Eventually, after playing four reserve-team matches in the Central League, I made my first-team debut: home to Charlton Athletic on 14 November, with a 2.30pm kick-off, and a place on the left wing. I replaced Derek Hawksworth, who was averaging a goal every three matches, was flourishing in the top flight, and who was well on his way to becoming a Bramall Lane legend. Although he and I were competing for the outside-left position, we always got on well and I regarded him as a lovely lad; as kind-hearted off the pitch as he was quick on it.

With its cricket pitch and its pavilion, Bramall Lane was an aesthetically exceptional stadium in those days. From the air, it looked like one of those massive late-Victorian public parks, with its expanse of grass, glistening in the sun. At ground level, you wondered how such a large arena could provide the right acoustics for an intense football atmosphere. And yet, come the day of the match, with the crowds packed like sardines on the terraces, you realised that this place was special – especially for wingers and full-backs. When you were hogging the touchline next to the main stand, the pitch could be uneven and muddy, with the spectators almost on top of you; but when you were hogging the touchline on the opposite side, next to the cricket field, the turf was like a bowling green and you could feel lonely and peripheral.

But I should have known that my debut would turn into a personal nightmare. Just before my demob from National Service in early October, I had broken my wrist after falling over. As I prepared for the match against Charlton, portents were everywhere: the plaster cast around my arm; the muddy pitch; the lack of match fitness; Jimmy Hagan's absence through injury.

I should not have played. I was not ready; not even close. We drew 1-1 but I was far and away the worst player on display. The problem was psychological: the fear of falling over awkwardly and aggravating the damage to my tender wrist. Consequently, in trying to protect one part of my body, I destroyed my confidence. How I wished there was a plaster cast to protect my fragile emotions. John Hewie, the Pretoria-born Scotland international right-back, did not have to work hard to mark me out of the match. I did not come close to testing Sam Bartram, the veteran Charlton goalkeeper, and I felt embarrassed when I picked up my two quid bonus for drawing the match. Money for failure! An attendance of 27,661 witnessed my calamity.

Although nobody criticised me, and I continued to endear myself to everybody at Bramall Lane with my work ethic and enthusiasm, I had this feeling that Freeman was thinking: *Two and a half grand for this guy!*

To sum up my day of woe, my name did not even appear in the team line-up in the programme. I did not trouble myself to read any of the match reports on the Sunday and Monday. 'Don't worry,' our John told me before we went to sleep on the Saturday night. 'This is part of being a professional. Long term, this will help you. You will look back on this day and smile.' With more than two hundred first-class matches for Rotherham behind him, he had learnt how the vagaries of football can play havoc with the mind. So he could deal better with the frustration of Rotherham's 4-3 defeat to Lincoln City at Sincil Bank in the Second Division that day than I could with my wretched performance against Charlton.

(Most of the Grainger family were still attending Rotherham home matches in 1953/54, as it was easier to get there to watch our John in the Second Division than it was to get to Bramall Lane to watch me in the Central League. At that time, he was the more successful player, for not only did Sheffield Wednesday try to sign him in 1952, but he also played for the England B team against Scotland in Edinburgh in March 1953, a 2-2 draw in front of 25,000 spectators.

He was a fine player and should have spent more of his career in the top flight than in the Second Division).

There was much discussion at the time about Sheffield United's style of play, as if the move into the top flight had encouraged the players to dispense with the direct style of the promotion season and adopt more sophisticated methods. Additionally, the continental techniques became all the rage in the First Division, stemming from the match three weeks earlier at Wembley between England and a World XI, which ended 4-4. The likes of László Kubala, Giampiero Boniperti, and Joaquín Navarro, significant figures who all revealed their breathtaking tricks and stylish movement, seemed to delight the English football community. To my mind, however, Jimmy Mullen of Wolverhampton Wanderers and Stanley Matthews of Blackpool seemed just as impressive and dynamic. An article in the official Sheffield United programme ahead of our match with Charlton Athletic on 14 November 1953 made it very clear what our own style should be in the top flight:

> *To achieve success there's no need to be ultra-artistic. In the Football League's tense competition there's no stage available for ball trickery suitable for a music hall turn; no time either. It pays to be content to draw a man and beat him with a pass. No good purpose is served by beating a man by footwork once and then trying to beat him again two or three more. Our players showed last season the value of fast, direct action and prompt shooting. Why don't they stick to those methods regularly now? It seems a pity that players should handicap themselves and make their work harder than it need be.*

Ball trickery was not my style, of course, and I was more likely to want to sing in a music hall than display my juggling skills. And 'fast, direct action' was exactly what I wanted to execute – if only I could get another chance. Reg Freeman made it clear that he was 'looking round for reinforcements for one or two particular positions', with left-back and centre-forward particular problems. But 'there was no need for panic', apparently, even though the First Division table after the Charlton match revealed that Sheffield United were just two points off bottom place after seventeen matches.

For six weeks, during which time England lost famously 6-3 to Hungary at Wembley, to prove that the continentals might have had it right after all,

I familiarised myself with reserve-team football. And I had no right to complain because that was where I belonged. What I lost in job satisfaction, however, I gained in genuine friendships, most notably in the shape of Jim Iley, a fine left-half with strong legs and an engaging personality, who was still working as a miner at Frickley Colliery when he signed for Sheffield United. With our regular conversations touching on all subjects (sometimes even football), it became clear early on that we shared the same values and ambitions. I was a Stanley Matthews man; Jim Iley was a Tom Finney man. I did not know then, of course, that we would become part of the same extended family. Looking back, I find it inconceivable that there was ever a time when I did *not* know the redoubtable Jim Iley.

On Boxing Day morning 1953, I was expecting to play for the reserves against Manchester City at Bramall Lane, but Reg Freeman selected me for the first-team match against Manchester City at Maine Road. No longer constrained by the plaster cast on my arm, I performed relatively well in freezing conditions. Although we lost 2-1, I recall giving Ken Branagan, the City right-back, a difficult time – executing the very direct style that the Sheffield United programme had been advocating. After the final whistle, he congratulated me on my performance.

I remember looking at the personalities that characterised the Manchester City team: Bert Trautmann, the former German prisoner of war, in goal; Jimmy Meadows, a fine outside-right; the Welshman, Roy Clarke, at outside-left; and Johnny Hart, the mercurial inside-forward.

And, then, of course, there was Don Revie: that splendid auteur, who was making a name for himself as a deep-lying centre-forward since he watched Nándor Hidegkuti perform a similar role for the Hungarians at Wembley. Eventually, Les McDowall, the Manchester City manager, and Revie would reconfigure the system into the 'Revie Plan', with no small amount of success. With his great control and inherent strength, Revie cut a fine specimen on the pitch. The closest I got to Revie that Boxing Day was when we shook hands after the final whistle. Interesting, then, that three years later, McDowall, previously my manager at Wrexham, would try to take me to Maine Road for a second time, only here the plan would see Revie moving to Bramall Lane as an exchange.

Buoyed by my performance at Maine Road, unencumbered by the insecurities I had felt earlier in the season, I now knew I could hold my own in the First Division. I had overcome a barrier. The top flight was my milieu. At last I could now stick out my chest, feel self-assured, and look fans in the eyes as

I met their requests for autographs.

I had to wait until 20 February for my third match, away to Wolves, which we lost 6-1. Boasting three players – Billy Wright, Jimmy Mullen and Dennis Wilshaw – about to go to the World Cup with England, Wolves were then one of the best teams in Europe and they would win the league by four points ahead of West Bromwich Albion. Pleasing on the eye and excellent going forward, Wolves provided all the signs of how far we were from that standard. They were also tough, and I recall an incident in which Eddie Stuart, their powerful South African defender, knocked me into the crowd in an attempt to win the ball. This was the beginning of Wolves' golden era, and as I nursed my bruises, and as I took stock of the defeat, I looked on with a mixture of admiration and jealousy.

The 1953/54 season was a troubled one for Sheffield United and as winter gave way to spring, there were fears of a swift return to the Second Division. A 2-1 victory at home to Aston Villa on the final day of the season, coupled with Middlesbrough's 3-1 defeat away to Arsenal, ensured that we avoided relegation. Joining Middlesbrough in the Second Division were Liverpool, who had been First Division champions seven years earlier. How quickly the world was changing. Billy Liddell, their brilliant Scottish outside-left, and somebody whose career I had followed with interest, was far too good for the Second Division. It seemed anomalous to me that I was likely to spend 1954/55 at a higher standard than Liddell. Such was the nature of football in the mid-50s, Liddell did not even consider leaving Liverpool to remain in the top flight with another club. His loyalty to Liverpool eclipsed his professional ambition. I liked that.

For all the concerns at Bramall Lane over results and tactics, there were significant occurrences and historical novelties for Sheffield United in 1953/54. There was the arrival from Worksop Town of a young goalkeeper called Alan Hodgkinson, a part-time butcher, who made his debut in a friendly and was evidently destined for greatness. Enthusiastic and hyperactive, he was only 5ft 8in but he had the agility of a cat and a sixth sense for spotting imminent danger. I had no doubts, from the first time I saw him in training, that he would become an England international. His time at Bramall Lane would come.

We won the Sheffield & Hallamshire County Cup twice in the same season: first with a 5-0 victory over Rotherham United in the final held over from the previous season and then with a 4-2 victory over the same opponents seven months later. Then there was the first match at Bramall Lane under a permanent set of floodlights: against Rotherham on 16 March – 75 years after the stadium staged the first-ever floodlit match in the history of the world.

My domestic situation was changing. Eventually, our John married his fiancée, Margaret Jackson, and left home, which gave me the double bed all to myself but deprived me of some great nighttime conversations about the game. The only consolation was that I was now the best footballer living at 10 West Street, Havercroft. Better still, I was seeing more of Doreen as my relationship with this delightful young lady blossomed. We began to talk about the future, about settling down together, even if there were no guarantees at that point that I would make the grade at Bramall Lane. I might have been earning more money than ever before but contracts in those days were short – one year at a time, with no promises of more – and the uncertainties great. I found out in March that I would be signing on for Sheffield United for 1954/55, but I dreaded a repeat of 1953/54. Three first-team matches in one season was less than I had hoped for, and life in the Central League, with the low attendances and minimal press coverage, lacked glamour and novelty. To play in the reserves was to encounter anonymity. I was even booked once, against Bury reserves when, according to the referee, I refused to go back ten yards for a free-kick. Sheffield United paid the fine on my behalf.

But even at difficult times one must contextualise situations to find meaning and to inspire analysis. Firstly, there was the first team's fight against relegation, which no doubt made Reg Freeman reluctant to take risks on young, unproven players.

Then there was the tale of poor Len Browning. He developed tuberculosis that season – we knew something was wrong when he started to feel weak during matches – and had no choice but to retire in 1954. The diagnosis came as a shock to him and to all of us, and it emphasised not only the ephemerality of professional football but also the randomness of adversity. The disease could have afflicted any of us. I counted my blessings.

Cultural experiences

It was without Browning that we went to West Germany in May 1954 for an end-of-season tour, which taught me not only about different styles of football but also about how Europe was recovering in this early post-war period.

The speed with which the Germans rebuilt their country after the horrors and destruction of World War Two impressed me greatly; but more than that, the friendliness of the locals, whether in Cologne, Hamburg, or Berlin, made me realise that we, as Englishmen, had no enemies here. Everywhere we went we enjoyed German enthusiasm and hospitality.

The food – mainly veal, which I had never tasted before – was of a high standard, as was the coffee, and what pre-war buildings remained inspired in us a genuine appreciation. Cologne Cathedral was a particular treasure, although there was still evidence of the damage it had suffered during the aerial bombardments. I played twice in West Germany, against Karlsruher SC and Hessen Kassel, but I remember the tour more for the cultural experiences.

I do believe, however, that the most resounding signs of West Germany's recovery from World War Two came six weeks later in Switzerland when the national team won the 1954 World Cup, defeating Hungary 3-2 in the final in Bern.

For all Hungary's style and panache, which they had revealed at Wembley eight months earlier on that momentous November afternoon, I found something enchanting about West Germany's new status as champions of the world.

The future of English football

My first match of 1954/55 was against Chelsea at Bramall Lane on 20 September: a 2-1 defeat. I saw some of the signs of Chelsea's prowess, with Roy Bentley excellent up front, and Ron Greenwood, with his thinning hair and serious demeanour, solid at centre-back, but I had no idea that they would end up winning the First Division championship. At that stage in my career, I did not know what a title-winning team looked like. The right-back marking me was John Harris, a 37-year-old Glaswegian, who had begun his career with Swindon Town in 1932 – the year before I was born. I had all the pace in the world but he had all the experience, in addition to being part of a better team.

Football was not as fluid in those days, so an outside-left would always come face to face with a right-back, a predictable subplot within the main event. I learnt quickly the names of all the full-backs in the First Division likely to mark me. On 30 October, when Tottenham Hotspur came to Bramall Lane, the right-back was Alf Ramsey, who had played for England in the 1950 World Cup and also against Hungary in 1953, and won the League Championship in 1951. With a spring in my step and a determination to make a name for myself (and Doreen watching from the stands), I produced the best performance of my career at that point, using my pace to full advantage and using the direct style that Reg Freeman had demanded of us. I found Ramsey slow, and, surprisingly for a player of his experience, lacking in confidence. 'Ramsey never ever attempted to match [Grainger] in speed,' one journalist wrote. I scored in a 4-1 victory, in which Alf Ringstead was superb, scoring twice, and I sensed immediately afterwards that Ramsey's playing career was drawing to a close. He had the lines of defeat engraved all over his forehead. The arrival of Danny Blanchflower at White Hart Lane that year seemed to confirm as much, for Tottenham, under Bill Nicholson, were beginning a rebuilding programme that would pay dividends at the end of the decade and beyond.

For now, however, if I wanted to see what class looked like, I only needed to cast my eyes towards Jimmy Hagan, who always seemed to dictate the pace of Sheffield United's play. Our supporters appreciated him so much that they invented new words to an old tune. Instead of *Wonderful, Wonderful Copenhagen*, they sang 'Wonderful, Wonderful Jimmy Hagan'. He deserved the attention. He was that good. I could run at great speed – as quick with the ball as without it – but Hagan did not need pace. With his sharp brain and the ability to see opportunities before everybody else did, he had an advantage over most players in the First Division. He was a thinking man's player who did not receive as many headlines as he deserved. After that match against Tottenham, Ringstead and I took the plaudits. 'Soccer fans are saying . . . keep eye on Colin', was one such headline. 'The speedy Grainger showed Tottenham Hotspur what he could do . . .' But Hagan was the heartbeat of the Sheffield United operation. What little footage exists from those days at Bramall Lane does not do justice to his significance and talent. To appreciate his ability, you needed to be there in person.

We were now enjoying a spell of good form, and we even brushed aside Manchester United at home on 13 November, winning 3-0 as I put my name on the score sheet again. We were superb that day, stylish and strong, but I could see even then the signs of the Manchester United team that would flourish the season after and beyond. Indeed, one newspaper report suggested that 'the losers should have had the points in the bag pre-interval'. I more than held my own against Bill Foulkes, the Manchester United right-back, as we pegged our opponents farther and farther back in the second half. It would be an exaggeration to say that Manchester United collapsed in the final twenty minutes, but they never came close to matching our 'never-say-die spirit that gained its reward with three second-half goals in thirteen minutes, two of them the most remarkable ever seen at Bramall Lane'. We were now, the report stated, 'the most improved team in the First Division'.

The most significant element of the day, however, was that I came face to face with a young player who was attracting a lot of attention: Duncan Edwards, an eighteen-year-old left-half, who seemed to have all the attributes – strength, style, zeal, intelligence, composure – to make him world-class. A force of nature, Edwards possessed a childlike charm on the pitch and a genuine love of life, which provided an intriguing contrast to his muscular physique and breathtaking athleticism. He was an endearing boy inside the body of a powerful man. I overshadowed him that afternoon but I knew I would never do so again.

He was the future of English football. He could look forward to a decade and a half at the top of the game and almost certainly develop into one of the finest players the British Isles has ever produced. Edwards and I came nowhere near each other during the match but we did shake hands afterwards. The start of a friendship? Yes – but I could not have known that at the time; and it would be another eighteen months before fate conspired to put us together in the type of intense environment designed to enhance male bonding.

For now, I was content merely to keep my place in the team and to learn the intricacies, minutiae and procedures of life in the top flight of English football. It was no secret that my style of play owed almost everything to speed – all that sprinting practice with my cousin in Wrexham was paying dividends – but I also developed a level of comfort with the ball. My passing improved, as did my eye for goal, and I felt I was entering a period of good, consistent form.

My reputation improved and the football journalists took note. But the extra attention in newspaper reports came at a cost. Eager to stop me by any means possible, right-backs seemed to take pleasure in autographing my shins with their jagged leather studs. After every match, as I lowered myself into the bath, I could feel the stinging sensation when my lacerated legs became immersed by hot water. I could never count on protection from referees. Their interpretation of the rules did not extend to protecting wingers from hard tackles. Just as centre-forwards could still shoulder-charge goalkeepers into the goal, so defenders could kick wingers into the crowd. You would be on the floor, writhing in agony after a foul, and the best you could hope for was a wet sponge from the well-intentioned but wholly unqualified trainer – hardly the required treatment on a freezing cold day.

Everything about the game in the 50s seemed designed to cause discomfort, up to and including the ball itself, which was heavy at the best of times, never mind when it absorbed rain, became horribly misshapen, and assumed the characteristics of a kettlebell. If you were unlucky, you would head the ball on the laces and end up with lace marks on your forehead for a few days. Many a defender – usually Howard Johnson, one of our centre-backs, and probably our bravest player – would turn up for training on a Monday morning with the indentation still evident, as if, like livestock, a cowboy had attacked his forehead with a branding iron. You laughed, but always in the knowledge that you could be the victim next week.

Manchester United exacted revenge on 2 April when they defeated us 5-0 at Old Trafford. There was no Duncan Edwards on show that day, but there was Tommy Taylor, who scored twice and looked every inch the England international centre-forward he had become. I had a particular interest in Taylor, for he grew up just a few miles from Havercroft, and I had known of him long before he had signed for Barnsley in 1949. He first came to my attention just after World War Two when he emerged as one of West Riding's most talented teenagers. Newspapers called him a prodigy, and now he was fulfilling his potential – on this occasion, at our expense. There was still a fear of relegation when we went into our match away to Blackpool on 30 April, but I scored in a 2-1 victory that secured our place in the First Division for 1955/56. While 'Grainger and Ringstead required a lot of watching', Stanley Matthews of Blackpool 'was not allowed to weave much magic'. I scored in our final match, a 5-2 victory at home to Portsmouth, which saw us climb to a final position of thirteenth.

We went on a tour to The Netherlands and West Germany in good heart. How could we have known that this trip would represent our final experience of working with Reg Freeman; that his permanent smile, which helped to perpetuate the image of a charming man, concealed a distressing secret?

Coaching as a science was still in its infancy in England

For weeks, we had grown used to seeing Reg Freeman rubbing his back against the frames of the wooden doors at the training ground; his personal massage system, designed expressly to provide relief from pain. Sometimes he would get

Harry Latham, his trusted lieutenant, to help him. Back trouble was not unique among men of a certain age – especially those who, like Freeman, had been involved with the game since time immemorial – so I thought nothing of it.

But when I discovered the horrific news that Freeman died on 4 August 1955 after returning home from West Germany, I connected the dots and realised that the signs had been staring me in the face for quite a while. He had cancer. He was suffering. And the worst part of it was that he knew 1954/55 would be his final season in charge of the team. He went straight from West Germany to hospital to live out his final few days. The sense of shock was acute and cast a dark cloud above Bramall Lane. The beginning of pre-season training in July 1955 was not a happy time for the Sheffield United players and, for a few days, as we tried to make sense of this cataclysm, we all felt disorientated.

We shared our Reg Freeman stories and celebrated his attributes as a man – his charm, his refusal to criticise his players, his honesty, his integrity, his unique lack of ego – and as a manager. But such appreciation and respect came amid the backdrop of genuine grief. I had known him and his wife since his days as manager of Rotherham United; since our John introduced me to him in the late 40s. To my knowledge, none of the Sheffield United players went to Freeman's funeral. It was a low-key, private affair in Rotherham, just as he would have wanted. The sense of loss affected us. One day he was a significant part of our professional lives, the man to whom we looked for inspiration. The next day he was gone. Understandably, his wife stopped coming to Sheffield United matches and I never saw her again.

Amid the turmoil, E. Senior Atkin took over as the caretaker manager, adding the position of chairman to his curriculum vitae a week later. Ernie Jackson took charge of training, with help from Harry Latham, but for all the great team spirit and family atmosphere, there was uncertainty in the air and a ubiquitous sense of insecurity among the players.

And then, on a suitably hot day, 18 August 1955, two days before our opening match against Newcastle United at St James' Park, Atkin revealed to us the identity of the new manager: the incomparable Joe Mercer.

We all remembered Mercer as a dazzling left-half with Everton before the war and with Arsenal after it. I had seen him play when I attended the 1952 FA Cup final with my pal, George Forsett, and also in many matches at Highbury during my National Service days. I delighted at Mercer's intelligence at Wembley and his capacity for leadership, even though Arsenal lost. But having hung up his boots, he became a journalist and a grocer in Wallasey and seemed to have turned his back on the game. I did not expect I would ever see him again, never mind work for him. The fates intervened, however, and I would grow to adore this most charming of gentlemen.

With his trademark smile and enduring good nature, he arrived at Bramall Lane, aged 41, to begin a career in management that would bring him success – eventually – with Aston Villa in the early 60s and with Manchester City in the late 60s, and would see him take the England job in 1974. But to reach the top he first had to learn vital lessons, and I counted it as a privilege that he chose Bramall Lane as his *de facto* university.

After our 4-2 defeat to a Jackie Milburn-inspired Newcastle United, a match in which we never got going but could still have secured a draw, Mercer made it clear that he had his own ideas and wanted his own people around him. This policy meant the end of Ernie Jackson's employment at Bramall Lane. While I was sad to see Jackson leave, his replacement, George Smith, proved to be an important part of the backroom staff. He was a coach rather than a trainer and had distinguished himself with the Football Association as one of the English game's brilliant thinkers. Whereas Jackson had put the emphasis on fitness and running, Smith was more interested in ball work and tactical planning. Not all of the Sheffield United players liked this new policy – coaching as a science was still in its infancy in England – but I welcomed it because I knew learning different ways of playing would make me a more accomplished professional. Besides, if a greater emphasis on ball work was good enough for Joe Mercer, it was good enough for me. I was pleased to discover that Jim Iley thought the same way. To sum up his philosophy, Mercer used a simple analogy: 'How could Joe Davis have reached snooker perfection without the use of snooker balls?' During his early playing days, Mercer resented it when the trainer would not allow the players the use of a football. Now a manager, he did not want his Sheffield United players to feel the same way about training. He encouraged us to cherish the ball, to treat it with respect. He would stage regular team meetings, lively and cosy sessions, which he called 'talk-ins'. It was during one such session that he announced a new tactical plan: a sweeper system, with Joe Shaw, far and away our most versatile player, tidying up at the back. Always keen for balance, Mercer would have a creative player performing alongside a tough-tackler; an artisan to complement a labourer.

But it would take time at Bramall Lane for everything to click into place.

We only secured a solitary point from our opening five matches and, by early September, the First Division table look liked a car crash from Sheffield United's point of view. We improved. I scored both goals in a 2-0 victory against Tottenham Hotspur at Bramall Lane on 5 September, a result that elicited such headlines as, 'The Joe Mercer plan comes off'. The key quote from Mercer – 'Wingers must be mobile' – seemed directed at me, and I was happy to take the advice on board because I knew I had found a manager who could make me a better player. I was, one journalist wrote, 'beginning to show the form that made Reg Freeman once say he would be every bit as good as brother Jack at Rotherham'.

Then, five days later, I performed well in a 1-0 victory against Manchester United, in which, one newspaper reported, 'the points went to the better-balanced side'. The defeat was one of only seven United would suffer all season as they marched impressively towards the League Championship. Duncan Edwards did not play that day. He was a last-minute absentee through illness, an intervention that accounted for their 'disorganised' performance, and, ultimately, for their 'sad sort of match'.

One particularly pleasant memory is the 2-0 victory away to Preston North End on 24 September, a match in which Tom Finney returned to the Preston team after a spell out. 'The truth was,' one newspaper wrote, 'that Preston were just not good enough against this rejuvenated Sheffield United side.' Another newspaper recorded: '[Bobby] Howitt and Grainger were a formidable left wing for United, whose attack made Preston's defence look very ragged. Preston's best players were right-half [Tommy] Docherty, who had more drive and method than most of his colleagues, and George Thompson, whose goalkeeping stood between Preston and a more decisive defeat.' Although this was only our first away victory of the season, there were signs that Mercer's philosophy of accurate passing through midfield and great speed up front were having a great effect. More significant than the return of Finney for Preston was the presence in our team of Jim Iley, then aged just nineteen, and already mature enough to 'give the forward line plenty of support'. He seemed to be a born leader, free of nerves; the type of man you would want in the trenches alongside you. For such a young man, he was relatively experienced, having played at Wembley in 1951 for the National Association of Boys Clubs. Football was in the blood; his grandfather had played for Crook Town, a leading amateur club, before the Great War.

Jim Iley and I played together for Sheffield United against Sheffield Wednesday in the Sheffield County Cup at Hillsborough on 2 November 1955, with 16,158 – 'a poor attendance', according to Ross Jenkinson of the *Sheffield Telegraph* – watching our 5-2 victory. Under normal circumstances, such an occasion would be forgotten by the time of the next match, but it was here that I felt I had truly mastered my profession. The delightfully named Monty Marston seemed to agree. In the *Sheffield Telegraph*, he wrote: 'Left winger Colin Grainger played a leading hand in three of [the] goals, and undoubtedly gave his best performance this season – a display which surprised Mr Peter Jackson, who was Wrexham manager when Colin moved from his club to Bramall Lane, and caused manager Andy Smailes to remark ruefully: "No one had a better chance to sign Grainger than Rotherham United."' On the same page, Jenkinson referred to me as 'dashing' and 'beautifully balanced'.

And even in defeat, for me, there was praise. We lost 3-1 at home to Portsmouth on 5 November, but one newspaper noted that the Moscow Dynamo players, attending the match during their tour of England, 'clapped the display of Sheffield United left winger Colin Grainger'. One headline went: 'Grainger schemes in vain.' As a team, we really were poor that day, and I found it embarrassing to be singled out for praise on a miserable day.

Keen to please, I felt I was developing a great working relationship with Mercer. After training, he would take me on to the pitch at Bramall Lane and give me what amounted to private coaching sessions. 'When we're attacking like this,' he would say, making exaggerated movements with his hands, 'you should be running here.' He would advise me on where to position myself, when to cross, and when to attack the penalty area when the ball was coming in from the right. He would bring Jim Iley, too, and offer him tactical guidance. And then, afterwards, the three of us – or sometimes just Mercer and I – would go over to Mrs Crook's café across the road from the stadium for egg and milk, and some instructive conversations about the game. Mercer was manager, tactician, and father figure all rolled into one, and I could see why the club directors were so keen to employ him. He presented an image of what football in the 60s might look like.

So what that 1955/56 turned into a fight against relegation? Sometimes you have to take a step backwards in the present to take two steps forwards in the future, an axiom Joe Mercer knew only too well. His response to our indifferent results was to ensure that we spent the majority of our training sessions practising our shooting: shots from outside the penalty area, volleys inside the penalty area, penalty-kicks, free-kicks, right foot, left foot. We mastered all of the arts – until it came to the matches, which is when our natural anxiety kicked in; the natural anxiety that comes with being involved in a relegation battle; the natural anxiety that makes it easier to miss than score. As one of our unnamed defenders told the journalist, Monty Marston of the *Sheffield Telegraph*, 'I shall be glad when we've won this relegation fight. It's a terrible strain, and, so far as I am concerned, it's taking all the pleasure out of football.'

A symbol of security

I married Doreen Rowe on 3 January 1956. I wore my best suit, which I had made especially for the occasion by Barney Goodman, an ebullient Jewish tailor, who was famous in Sheffield for the quality of his craftsmanship. He did not come cheap. The suit cost me twenty quid, a week's wages, but it was still in perfect condition ten years later when one of my brothers owned it. Class is permanent, of course, and the Barney Goodman business was still flourishing sixty years later – as was my marriage. When I celebrated my sixtieth wedding anniversary on 3 January 2016, I could reflect with absolute certainty that marrying Doreen was the single best decision I have ever made. Sometimes I even think about that time she stood me up in Havercroft on what would have been our first date – *I must apologise for not coming to see you. But I have to tell you that I don't like cricket* – because my efforts to make her my girlfriend were worth it. I only have to look at the photographs of my children and grandchildren to realise how blessed I am.

My wedding day was a day of significance for Jim Iley, too, for it was then that he met his future wife – Lily Grainger. And, I can say most assuredly, I could not have wished for a better man to marry my baby sister and for a better woman to marry my great friend.

Our afternoon reception doubled up as the shortest honeymoon on record. My brother, Horace, delivered a touching and amusing best man's speech and everybody went home happy. The day after, I joined my Sheffield United colleagues in preparation for the FA Cup tie at Bramall Lane against Barrow, whose manager, Joe Harvey, I had watched at Wembley for Newcastle United in the 1952 FA Cup final. My teammates had a surprise for me: a shower of confetti and a photographer to record the scene for posterity. I scored the fifth in a 5-0 victory. 'Grainger's ability as a winger is undisputed,' Monty Marston of the *Sheffield Telegraph* wrote, 'but such goal-getting intentions will certainly make England's selectors lift their eyebrows.' Joe Mercer expressed surprise that Barrow were at that time sitting at the bottom of the Football League Division Three North. 'They must be in a false position,' he said. 'I applaud them for trying to play good football.'

The victory gave Sheffield United a fourth-round away tie against Bolton Wanderers and already we began to think of Wembley. The romance of the FA Cup? Try telling that to the new Doreen Grainger. In the week of her wedding, she had different ideas of what romance meant. Until we could buy a house of our own, Doreen and I lived with my mam and dad at No. 10 West Street, which continued to impart the aura of permanent activity. Except that it was no longer No. 10. At some point in the mid-50s, the authorities altered the numbering in the street, and our house became No. 12. Moving house without moving house...such were the peculiarities of living in an infinitesimal village that was metamorphosing into a small village.

I barely had time to adapt to married life. Joe Mercer sent the first-team squad to Lilleshall in Shropshire on 9 January for a three-day coaching course, in the hope, he said, that the education would 'infuse more confidence into the players'. We had become what one newspaper described as 'the puzzle of the season', playing better football than our First Division position suggested. We went from Lilleshall to Manchester to prepare for the match away to Manchester United, which we lost 3-1. Taffy Williams, the journalist, described me as easily Sheffield United's best forward, and Jim Iley's performance 'on a par with that of Duncan Edwards'.

Events were moving quickly. We defeated Bolton 2-1 in the FA Cup at Burnden Park to secure a fifth-round tie against Sunderland. And then I heard that Arthur Turner, the brilliantined, muscular Birmingham City manager, contacted Joe Mercer with a view to signing me. Turner had apparently been impressed with my performance when we defeated Birmingham 2-0 on Christmas Eve. The Turner-Mercer telephone conversation did not last long and, so I was told, did not end amicably. 'Clubs can ask forever about Colin,' Mercer told the press. 'The answer will always be the same: no!' He tipped me for a place in the England team. A rare halcyon period for the club, Birmingham ended the season playing in the FA Cup final, losing to Manchester City, but I never regretted it that Mercer kept deterring potential suitors. I was happy at Bramall Lane.

Indeed, by early spring, I knew Sheffield United would keep me on for 1956/57 because I had learnt to read the signs. For example, if the club agreed in February to buy you a new pair of boots, you knew you were okay for another season. If the club had no intention of keeping you on, the directors would deem a new pair of boots a waste of money. As it happened, Harry Latham took me across the road to Jack Archer's sports shop and said, 'Choose your boots, Colin.' As a newly married man, I found the guarantee of another year at Bramall Lane financially and psychologically significant. Suddenly, the pay packet became more important than it had been when I was a bachelor. And a brand new pair boots became a symbol of security; a prelude to the offer of a new contract.

Every Friday after training, Arnold Newton, the club secretary, would appear with a shoe box full of brown envelopes, each stuffed with cash. With a smile on his face, in one movement he would shout a name and throw an envelope to an eager player. 'Hey, Arnold, you've underpaid me,' somebody would say. 'I played for the reserves last week and didn't get my appearance money.' With the maximum wage still in force, a football player was particularly sensitive to being short-changed. The club would use low-denomination notes to give the impression of a healthy pay packet but nobody was falling for it. If you made thirty quid in a week you were fortunate. And grateful. Little wonder that players sometimes took part-time jobs outside the game to boost their income.

Not that we at Sheffield United could complain about the wages. When you lose more matches than you win, you keep your mouth shut about money. After losing 1-0 in an FA Cup fifth-round replay to Sunderland (a 'shot-in-a-million' from forty yards by Ray Daniel in the 83rd minute; a shot that hit the iron stanchion of the net and whizzed back into the field of play), our First Division campaign became a rage against the dying of the light. From that moment on we only picked up ten points from our remaining thirteen matches and slid down the table at an alarming speed.

It was amid another poor run of results that Jim Iley and I discovered we had made the Football League representative team for the match against the Irish League in Belfast on 25 April. As was often the case in those days, we were among the last to find out about it. We read about it in the *Sheffield Telegraph*. We also noted other members of the team: Jimmy Armfield of Blackpool, Roger Byrne of Manchester United, Tommy Taylor of Manchester United, Albert Quixall of Sheffield Wednesday, and Johnny Haynes of Fulham. A veritable feast of talent. 'If Mr Reg Freeman had been alive at the present time he would have been very proud,' one newspaper reported, 'for two of the players he signed for Sheffield United as lads have made the grade and gained representative honours. Left winger Colin Grainger and left-half Jim Iley have been selected to play for the Football League against the Irish League, and though still in the grip of the relegation struggle, United have sportingly agreed to release the players.' Joe Mercer did not see any risk in allowing us to play in Belfast. 'I am proud,' he said. 'And thrilled.'

Before Jim and I worked out how we were going to get to Manchester for the flight over to Belfast, we received a message from Quixall that he was offering to drive us to the airport. I always liked Quixall. He gave the impression of being cocky and overconfident but he was nothing like that at all. A Sheffield lad, he was modest and humble, and the opposite of what people perceived him to be. The most notable of the Irish League players was George Eastham of Ards, a Blackpool lad, who would earn fame in 1963 for his involvement in the court case that became a landmark in improving freedom of players to move between clubs. In front of more than 20,000 spectators, the Football League XI, worth £250,000, apparently, lost 5-2. 'This was the worst team to wear an England jersey,' Malcolm Brodie of the *Belfast Telegraph* wrote. Ouch!

After returning home on the Thursday, I joined the Sheffield United bus for the trip on Friday down to London for the weekend match against Tottenham Hotspur at White Hart Lane. The tension was growing, for relegation was staring us in the face. It was while we were enjoying dinner in the hotel that somebody shouted out, 'Telephone call for Mr Grainger.'

Surprised but full of anticipation, I made my way to the reception to take the call.

'Hello, Colin. This is Ross Jenkinson from the *Sheffield Telegraph*.'

'Now then, Ross. How are you?'

'Congratulations, Colin. You're in the England team for the match against Brazil at Wembley next week.'

'Eh – is that right? You're pulling my leg.'

As I placed down the receiver and thanked the receptionist, I considered the irony of it all. There I was, receiving confirmation that I was now an international player, all while preparing for a match that could, if the result went against Sheffield United, turn me into a Second Division player.

The blood must have drained from my face, because when I returned to the dinner table somebody shouted, 'Have you seen a ghost, Colin?'

'I've just been selected to play for England.'

Part of my surprise was born of being told three weeks earlier that I would not be part of the England team for any of the spring fixtures against Brazil, West Germany, Finland and Sweden. I had made the eighteen-man squad for a Football Association tour to South Africa, a low-key affair involving eighteen matches that seemed designed to give players experience and officials the chance to have a good time on expenses. 'I am surprised to see Colin Grainger among [the South Africa tour squad],' one journalist wrote. 'Not because I don't think he's good enough. On the contrary.

'I thought he might be under consideration for the full international trip to Sweden and Germany.' It seems I was. And, consequently, instead of playing against the likes of Southern Transvaal, Natal, Griqualand West, Southern Rhodesia, and Border in South Africa, I would play for England against Brazil at Wembley, with the likelihood of going to West Germany and Scandinavia. I would even miss out on the Sheffield & Hallamshire County FA Cup final between Sheffield United and Doncaster Rovers at Belle Vue.

Suitably enthused, I was determined to play the match of my life at Tottenham on 28 April, and we began well. I scored with a header and I felt confident that we would secure the victory to remain in the First Division. But then Howard Johnson, our centre-half, went off injured – no substitutes in those days – and we fell apart. Bobby Smith scored a hat-trick and Tottenham won 3-1. 'Sheffield Go Down: Handicapped By Injury' went the headline in *The Times*, which rather summed up our tale of woe. It was an 'undistinguished match, vital only to the statistician'.

We might have won with eleven fit players, and thus avoided relegation; but the truth is that we had been playing brinkmanship all season, and especially in the final month. For all the excitement that Joe Mercer brought to the team, and for all the novelty of a new tactical approach, which I enjoyed, the balance in the team did not feel right. We had the results to prove it. We did not concede the most goals in the First Division or score the fewest, but our away form had been poor for the most part.

Frustratingly, we lost twelve matches by the odd goal. If we had converted only two of those defeats into draws, we would have survived and sent Aston Villa down. Instead, we finished bottom, two points from safety. There was no concealing the gravity of the situation. This was a poor season.

As if to sum up the dichotomy of my existing between pain and pleasure, I received a handful of telegrams after the match, including one from Ted Forshaw, my pal from National Service in Odiham, who had been a professional with Everton and was set on a career in rugby league:

> Greetings = Mr. C. Grainger, c/o Tottenham Hotspur FC Whitehart Lane Tottenham London-N17 = Congratulations on your selection for England. Ted Forshaw +

Too famous and far too talented to be one of the lads

I joined up with the England squad at Lancaster Gate on Monday 4 May, five days before the match, and I felt as small and as insignificant as I had when I turned up for my first day as a professional with Sheffield United. I was only just over the injury that had ruled me out of the match against Wolverhampton Wanderers the Saturday before, but the burden of my new surroundings rendered my legs jelly-like.

When I presented myself to the receptionist at the FA headquarters, she said, 'Ah, yes, Mr Grainger – you'll be sharing a room with Mr Matthews.'

'Mr Matthews?' I replied, my voice rising an octave.

'Yes, that's right.'

'But I can't do that.'

'Sorry, Mr Grainger, it has already been decided. What are you worried about?'

'Stanley Matthews is a star, one of the greatest players in the world. I shouldn't be sharing with Stanley Mathews.'

I wish I had taken the trouble to check the facts. The 'Mr Matthews' with whom I would share a room was Reg Matthews, the goalkeeper for Coventry City in the Third Division South, which came as a massive relief. The other Matthews – the legendary Stanley, whom I idolised – never shared a room with any player. He was far too famous and far too talented to be one of the lads.

The players to whom I introduced myself first were the lads from Manchester United: Tommy Taylor, Roger Byrne, and Duncan Edwards, who were all seated together, each wearing a smile that could only have come from the confidence born of their new status as champions of England. I had no such confidence. To me, the environment was alien.

'Hello, I'm Colin Grainger of Sheffield United.'

I had met them all before, of course, during the trip to Belfast a week earlier, but I did not want to assume they remembered me. I was famous locally, in Sheffield and in Barnsley, but still not a national figure.

'Come and join us, Colin,' Edwards said in a thick Black Country accent that must have been how my grandparents spoke.

The England manager was Walter Winterbottom, whose reputation was that of a grammar-school headmaster, but he was nothing of the kind. He was quiet, extremely polite, never given to shouting at people, and always eager to perpetuate the sense of team spirit. We trained at Highbury, the home of Arsenal, but all we did was mostly run around the pitch. When we had a meal, I noticed that Stanley Matthews was nowhere to be seen. 'He eats on his own,' somebody told me.

Matthews had only just returned to the team after a spell out. John Atyeo, the prolific Bristol City striker, also returned. I was surprised to discover that Nat Lofthouse and Bill Perry, two fine players, had been dropped, while Tom Finney had been ruled out through injury.

The day after, when we had some free time, Duncan Edwards asked me if I fancied walking into the West End with him. We cut through Hyde Park and shared stories about our backgrounds. He was interested to learn that the Graingers and the Hollidays hailed from Dudley, Staffordshire, the town where he was born in 1936. We spoke about Joe Mercer, who was not only my manager at Sheffield United but also the man who, as the coach of the England Schoolboys team, recommended Edwards to Manchester United in 1952. Edwards might otherwise have signed for Wolverhampton Wanderers or Aston Villa.

As we strolled around London, Edwards and I enjoyed our anonymity, taking in the sights like wide-eyed tourists, and even going shopping. It was Edwards' idea to go to a lingerie shop. A gift for the lady, he said, picking up a saucy pair of knickers with that childlike charm of his. The lady in question was Molly Leech, to whom he was engaged. I was a bit more self-conscious when I selected something appropriate (i.e., less risqué) to take back to Doreen in Havercroft. It required no small amount of dexterity to get these gifts into our rooms back at the hotel in Lancaster Gate without any of the other players noticing.

Edwards was something of a paradox. He was shy in social situations, yet he had the most endearing personality. For example, whereas most of us conformed to protocol and addressed Walter Winterbottom as 'Mr Winterbottom', Edwards always called him 'Walter' – in that thick Black Country accent that we all liked to imitate. Nobody else would have got away with such informality where Winterbottom was concerned but, then, nobody else had Edwards' attractive disposition off the pitch or magical exuberance on it. Although I was aged only 22 at that time, Edwards made me feel like I was of an older generation.

As my relationship with Edwards seemed to develop quickly into a friendship, I felt a part of the England structure. I woke up on the morning of the match feeling good. I read the newspapers.

'Stan's back: England need him again,' went one headline.

'Colin Grainger beats brother Jack to first family cap,' went another.

Apparently I was 'the fastest footballer in England'; quicker aged 22 than I was three years earlier when I could sprint 100 yards in 10.4 seconds. Journalists noted that I was now earning 'top money' at Sheffield United – twenty quid – and that my speed and direct style could find gaps in the 'square Brazilian defence'. Everything I read seemed designed to make me feel great. But when the time came to get on the bus to Wembley, the nerves kicked in, and everything around me – the players on the bus, the spectators outside walking to the stadium, the discordant sounds – turned into an overwhelming assault on the senses. Trembling and sweating, all I could think of was the members of my family who had come down for the match to form part of a 100,000 capacity crowd. What were they thinking? Would they get their tickets okay? Would I let them down? Was I really of the required standard for a career at international level?

In the dressing room, I found myself changing next to Stanley Matthews, which, I think, Walter Winterbottom arranged deliberately, possibly in an attempt to calm my nerves.

'Do you still get nervous before these big matches, Stanley?' I asked him, partly out of curiosity, partly out of the need to fill an uncomfortable silence.

'Nervous? I am as nervous as you, Colin.'

And then he swigged something from one of those new Babycham bottles. I did not ask him what it was but he was shaking so much that some of the liquid spilt all over the floor. He was nearly twenty years older than I and had been a professional since before I was born. He was an idol of mine. He was above sharing a room and the dinner table with his colleagues. And yet, on that blissful afternoon, as Matthews' hands juddered, I realised that there was something wonderfully egalitarian about the Wembley dressing room.

Walter Winterbottom had given us some information about the Brazilians. They were great on the ball and technically superb, but not good at closing you down when you had the ball. Our plan was simple: do not let them have the ball and they will fade away. At that time, Brazil had never won a World Cup, and, while there was an aura about them, it was not an aura of invincibility. I formed the impression early on that they had more to fear about England than we had to fear about them. One of the first things I noticed was that the Brazilians wore boots like slippers, made of fine leather. Our boots had improved from ten years earlier but were still heavy and cumbersome.

Tommy Taylor scored to give England the lead inside three minutes, which was long enough for us to realise that the Brazilians were limited when it came to the art of defending. This was easier than I expected, and confidence engulfed my being, replacing the apprehension that had made the pre-match countdown so debilitating. When we had arrived at Wembley two hours earlier, it felt as though my veins contained cement, but now they contained rocket fuel.

In the fifth minute, Stanley Matthews received the ball near the corner flag and then, as a loud cheer circulated the stadium, he flicked it between Canhoteiro's legs to feed the England right-back, Jeff Hall. Hall's pass forward found Taylor, who beat Pavão. The ball went across the goal from Johnny Haynes, and there I was, drifting in at the far post, in perfect position to side-foot the ball home from four yards out.

As England debuts went, this was perfect: five minutes of action, my first touch, and already I had engraved my name on the list of England goalscorers.

Brazil responded by scoring twice early in the second half, through Paulinho and Didi, and then John Atyeo missed a penalty for England just after the hour mark. Tommy Taylor restored our lead in the 65th minute, before Roger Byrne missed a penalty two minutes later. The match continued to excite, with Brazil pushing forward in search of an equaliser but leaving gaps in midfield and at the back. Billy Wright in defence and Duncan Edwards in midfield were superb, as was Stanley Matthews on the right wing. I was always impressed with Wright's timing in the air, which enabled him to out-jump taller men. In the 83rd minute, I picked the ball up on the halfway line, laid it off to Johnny Haynes and kept running. Haynes passed wide to Stanley Matthews, who made light work of Nilton

Santos' attempted tackle, and I continued my run towards the left of the penalty area. Matthews' cross to the far post was accurate and clever, forcing Gylmar, the Brazil goalkeeper, out of position. I darted towards the six-yard box, jumped as high as I could, and met the ball a split-second before Gylmar got there, and the roar of the crowd confirmed that my header was nestling in the back of the net for a 4-2 lead.

Not in my wildest dreams did I envisage such a debut, but it was a fine victory for a fine team on a day that those present were unlikely to forget for a long time. After the tribulations of the matches against Hungary in 1953/54, and the anticlimax of the 1954 World Cup in Switzerland, the England team had reclaimed its lost horizon.

I discovered later the reason why Stanley Matthews was so keyed-up: apparently Brazilian journalists were writing that he would be no match for Nilton Santos. As events unfolded, the opposite proved to be the case. Matthews was world class, even at the age of 41. Whatever was in that Babycham bottle was doing him good.

Afterwards, I was at the back of the bus with Roger Byrne, and as the Twin Towers of Wembley faded into the distance, he turned to me and said, 'Colin, look at that. Just look at that. Once you've played at Wembley, you've done it.'

Antithetical to the conservatism of the English game

One match, two goals, and suddenly – having begun the week by feeling inconsequential – I felt now part of the England set-up. The fifty quid match fee added to the sense of unreality. I would have paid fifty quid to play for England.

When we flew to Copenhagen, Denmark, on 14 May on our way to Stockholm for a match against Sweden, I noticed how eager Duncan Edwards was to sit next to me on the flight. I still have the photograph of us both smiling, two young men on a new adventure, each with a look of anticipation engraved over our youthful features.

When we arrived in Sweden, Reg Matthews and I shared a room again. On our first free day, he asked me if I fancied going to visit the Sweden manager, George Raynor, a well-respected Yorkshireman, in the centre of Stockholm. Raynor had played for Rotherham United under Reg Freeman in the mid-30s and had made a name for himself coaching teams in Italy, Sweden, Iraq – and Aldershot. He led the Sweden team to gold at the London Olympic Games of 1948 and to third place at the 1950 World Cup, so he already boasted a reputation for being a visionary and an inspirer of dreams. Matthews had played under Raynor at Coventry earlier in 1956, so it seemed natural that they should want to meet up under these markedly different circumstances.

Considering Raynor was the Sweden manager, he did not live in the lap of luxury. His apartment was neat and well appointed, but scarcely what one might expect from such a significant football figure. The Swedes were largely amateur in those days and Raynor had to supplement his income by coaching in schools.

The three of us consumed copious amounts of tea and a few biscuits, while Matthews and Raynor shared stories of their time together at Coventry. Occasionally, I would chip in with some observations of my own. It was all pleasant, but I formed the opinion, based on some of the things Raynor said, and the way he said them, that he regretted deeply his failure to make the grade as a manager in the top flight of English football. Perhaps his problem was that he was a man ahead of his times, a radical, when such revolutionary thinking was, arguably, antithetical to the conservatism of the English game.

When Matthews and I returned to the England hotel in Stockholm, we did not say a word to Walter Winterbottom that we had been socialising with the Sweden manager. I suspect Winterbottom would have been less than impressed and rather suspicious. Instead, we went to our room and wrote to our families back in England. Matthews had not done so well in school and struggled with his writing, so much so that he dictated his letters and I wrote them down for him. I grew to like him and we felt an affinity for each other, partly because we shared a room, but also because we began our England careers at the same time.

The match itself at the Råsunda Stadium, Stockholm, lacked the excitement of our encounter against Brazil, but in many respects provided more of an education. The Swedes were fit and efficient, with a more patient style of play. The fierce wind seemed to affect them less than it did the England players. 'Sometimes a goalless draw has character,' *The Times* reported. 'Quite often it produces excitement in the furnace of a fierce struggle. Yet somehow here was a match lacking these qualities. It was without poise and for long stretches even a melancholy silence fell on the packed Råsunda Stadium between the bursts of the national cry *heja* that swirled around the ground in an effort to breathe some fire into the battle.'

Matthews was the busier of the two goalkeepers, and the Swedes certainly impressed with their neat passing in midfield, but I think we suffered for our direct style. Sweden did not allow us anywhere as much time on the ball as had Brazil at Wembley, and they even stopped Duncan Edwards from storming through the middle with his trademark runs. It was not a day for wingers, and I saw as little of the ball at outside-left as Johnny Berry of Manchester United did at outside-right. Given the circumstances, the goalless draw felt like a more-than-decent result for England.

We flew on to Helsinki for the match against Finland, and again I found myself sitting on the plane next to the ebullient Edwards, whose enthusiasm for life was beginning to make all this travelling feel to me like such an attractive feature of international football. Flying was a novelty in those days, and Edwards did not conceal his love of it.

We defeated Finland 5-1 at the Helsingin Olympiastadion, although it was only two goals by Nat Lofthouse – a substitute for Tommy Taylor just before half-time – in the final fifteen minutes that gave the scoreline a semblance of respectability. I was involved in the intricate exchanges of passing that contributed to our third goal, by Gordon Astall in the first half, and I enjoyed far more time on the ball than I had in Stockholm. In status, the Finns were as amateur as the Swedes, but not as efficient or as talented. Indeed, the Finland substitute goalkeeper, Aarre Klinga, who played the latter stages, was as much a basketball player and an ice hockey player as he was a footballer.

Evidently, the match must have been more fun to play than to watch. *The Times* reported, rather grandiloquently, '[A]ll one longed for was the arrival of Father Christmas from Lapland behind a train of reindeer bearing some gifts, out of season perhaps but more appropriate than the football, to the beauty of the northern day.'

The singing winger

As I had learnt after the match at Wembley against Brazil, scoring two goals for England has an intoxicating effect; as if providing the benefits of alcohol without the detriments. This time, after the Finland match, it was Nat Lofthouse's turn to feel drunk on success, and it was impossible to avoid his joviality as we went to a bar to ease some of the pressure of the previous two weeks. He had just become England's joint all-time leading goalscorer alongside Vivian Woodward on 29 after his two strikes in Helsinki.

Late in the evening, as laughter and music filled the air, Lofthouse approached the pianist, who earlier in the day had played centre-forward for Finland, and said words to the effect of, 'One of the England players has a voice like Al Jolson, so you should get him up to sing.' Unbeknown to me, the word had got around the England players that I had performed as a crooner in the Havercroft Working Men's Club and that I liked to sing in the bath after matches.

There are three things Lofthouse did not expect: first, that the pianist would invite me up on stage; second, that I would agree to perform; third, that I would actually sing as if I had been practising all my life for this moment.

'Wait a minute!' I shouted to warm applause, re-enacting the opening words of my act in Havercroft. 'Wait a minute! You ain't heard nothin' yet!' And then, to growing cheers, I would croon with a confidence that nobody knew I possessed. It was just like the old days at Havercroft when I was a teenager.

And here my routine was the same. First, I attempted Al Jolson, and I could see each of the England players wearing the same bewildered expression; as if to say, 'I didn't expect *this*'. Then I attempted Nat King Cole. And then Billy Eckstine, Frankie Laine, Johnnie Ray, and Billy Daniels. And afterwards the intensity of the applause took me by surprise. What should have been Nat Lofthouse's night became my night. *Come on, Colin, give us a song* became the catchphrase among the England players, just as it had among my pals eight years earlier. Unlike my days as a teenager singing in Havercroft, however, journalists were there in Helsinki to witness my stagecraft.

The best part was that the pianist did not know any of the songs, so he stopped trying to play. I sang without any music.

The story about the 'Singing Winger' made the newspapers back in England.

We went nowhere near East Berlin

We moved on to West Germany to face the winners of the 1954 World Cup – England's most important match since losing in the quarter-finals in that tournament.

The trip to Berlin crystallised once and for all the positive feelings I had developed for West Germany during the tours of 1954 and 1955 with Sheffield United. The place and the people intrigued me. By now, eleven years on from VE Day, my perception was the German people felt as if World War Two was in the past, and that it was no longer the dominant cultural influence and political issue in West German society. The Germans no doubt felt differently because the past was still part of their present. But insofar as the viewpoint of an outsider is valid, I felt that I was visiting a country obsessed with creating an exciting future. The German public seemed extremely friendly and happy to see us. There was certainly no feeling that the two nations had been enemies from 1939-45. We were now in a time of peace and that was how it felt. Everywhere we turned we could see a nation in transition, rebuilding the infrastructure, with as much work going on at night as in the day – as if the country was impatient, trying desperately to meet a deadline to finish the work. Consequently, my own attitude to the Germans was one of admiration. Having grown up in a mining village, I learnt the importance of a good work ethic, so I was impressed by how hard the Germans grafted. I could see at first hand the improvements in the West German infrastructure. By 1956, the improvements were even greater. There was still a lot of rubble, of course, but at no time did the Germans present to us the face of defeat or of insecurity. My prevailing views of West Germany were of charming friendliness and admirable determination.

I liked Berlin even in 1956, when it was evolving and still disfigured by scaffolding. But we only saw the parts of Berlin that were deemed by the Football Association to be politically appropriate. Our tour to West Germany was organised strictly; far stricter, in fact, than when we visited Helsinki and Stockholm. We could never go out in Berlin without any form of supervision. Every trip – whether to Belsen, which was sad, or through the Black Forest, which was wonderful, or in our bus around the city, which was interesting – was planned to keep us under control. In one sense, we were ambassadors for our country. But we were also young men excited by the novelty of being so far from home. The FA officials impressed upon us the need to behave respectfully at all times. We prepared at the West German State football school in Barsinghausen, near Hanover, and enjoyed facilities of the highest standard – certainly far better than those we had experienced at Lilleshall.

Once in Berlin, we found our movements controlled by well-dressed civil servants based in the British sector. We went nowhere near East Berlin because there were obviously political sensitivities. We were therefore unable to appreciate the differences between the Soviet sector and the rest of the city. There was no Berlin Wall then, of course, and I never felt that we were in a divided city. I do not recall seeing anything that resembled a border between West and East Berlin, although a barrier obviously existed. Our schedule was so controlled that we only really saw what the FA officials wanted us to see. The one thing I do recall was that there were British and American soldiers everywhere; thousands of them, or so it seemed.

It was certainly a privilege to play against the world champions in their own stadium. The Olympiastadion was inspiring, and, of course, there were historical connotations, too – not least those grainy images of Jesse Owens that survived from the 1936 Olympic Games. There were ninety-odd thousand people there for our match and the noise was deafening when we walked around the track before entering the pitch at the halfway line. Naturally the Germans were full of enthusiasm, but the stadium also had large sections full of British, American and French soldiers, so there were cheers for us when we took to the field. It was easy to spot the British soldiers: they were the ones sporting oversized hats, carrying rattles and banners. By and large, the soldiers looked after us and were always keen to talk football.

Each England player had his own motivations that day. While I saw the value in playing the world champions, and knew West Germany would provide a yardstick for where England stood in the pantheon of international football, I had greater concerns, like playing well enough personally to keep my place in the team and ensuring that I did not let my family down. I wanted to maintain the form I had shown against Brazil. Against the Germans, I think I produced one of the best displays of my career. Afterwards, somebody showed me a German-language newspaper report about the match, which said that I was England's best player. I could have scored twice early on but I did score just after the hour mark to put us two goals up. We won 3-1 and the West Germany players were genuinely riled at losing the match. West Germany had some fine players, most notably Fritz Walter, their inside-forward, who was their captain when they won the World Cup in 1954. But there was the sense that already they were in decline. It was hard to imagine that they would win a World Cup had a tournament taken place in 1956. England, by contrast, might have had a chance. Afterwards, however, there were no pleasantries. Unlike the Brazilians, who hung around to talk to us at

Wembley, the West Germans melted into the Berlin night. In the language of those times, the headlines made interesting reading:

'Tommies give Berlin Soccer Sector: Colin Grainger is in Wright class'.

'Grainger best, say Germans'.

'It's Sunday! Young England put us on top again'.

'Colin Grainger stole the show'.

'England a match for anybody'.

With typical bombast, Tony Stevens, reporting from the Olympiastadion, wrote:

> *Oh! It's great to be in Berlin now that England's here! For Berlin, the sector city, is a piece of England this glorious day. The two-toned town – bright lights in the Western part, and that dreary old tombstone city past the Brandenburg Gate and into the Russian sector – has had itself a week-end spree. The leather-jacketed police have been indulgent. Sweeping-up operations did not start until early this morning. Now small knots of deliriously happy British soldiers are on their way back to camp all over Germany, after celebrating in the old-fashioned way after yesterday's famous 3-1 victory in the Olympic Stadium here . . . At last English soccer has something to be happy about.*

Roy Peskett, a doyen of the game, described my 'smooth speed and goalscoring ability', which reminded him of no less a figure than Cliff Bastin, that supremely gifted Arsenal star of the 30s. The German newspaper, *Zeitung*, awarded me its man-of-the-match. Walter Winterbottom, not usually one to highlight individual performances, said, 'I was extremely pleased with Colin Grainger.'

Overall, the experience was a lot to take in for a relatively young man. There we were, a group of young lads, going to face the world champions, and defeating them in their own stadium. But it was more than a football match. It was an education that taught me all about the fortitude of the German people. Although the presence of foreign soldiers provided permanent reminders of external political influences, West Germany was already offering images of what the 60s might look like.

No hiding place

As soon as I got home, I fixed myself up with an agent: Len Young, who had been an entertainer since the mid-40s and now represented the Kaye Sisters, a delightful trio of women who were not sisters at all but looked so much like each other they could have been triplets. Young saw the marketing potential in my impressions of Al Jolson, Nat King Cole and Billy Eckstine. I had the mid-50s look and the mid-50s hairstyle. And I had a level of fame that now, at last, went beyond West Yorkshire.

I met Young in Piccadilly, London, and we ate salted-beef sandwiches as we got down to business. Would I, he asked, fancy doing some singing gigs in my spare time: pubs, clubs, that sort of thing? I did not need asking twice. He pulled out a contract and I signed it quickly, without reading any of the details.

But my first gig happened by pure chance, when a quartet of chirpy male Americans, who called themselves the Hilltoppers, arrived in Sheffield to prepare for a concert at the Empire. While staying in the city centre, they paid a visit to Bramall Lane, since their leading singer, Jimmy Sacca, had played semi-professional football – soccer or American football, I was never sure which – in the United States. Sacca had a conversation with Joe Mercer, who mentioned to him that I had done some singing on tour with England. Sacca came to watch the players train, after which he introduced himself to me. He asked me how I felt about appearing in the first house on the Friday night. I agreed, without really thinking of the implications or bothering to ask if I would be paid. Sacca's logic was simple: the Hilltoppers, who created harmless, easy-listening music, were not necessarily to the taste of a hardened Sheffield audience. My presence would make everything feel familiar. In a sense, they were trading off my local fame.

I played for Sheffield United away to Swansea Town on 13 September 1956, a match we lost 4-1 on a mild evening. We did not arrive back at Bramall Lane until three o'clock the next day, a Friday afternoon. I had no time to lose, as I had to get home, put on suitable attire, and get to the Sheffield Empire at half past five. Joe Mercer was there to meet me, which helped to settle my nerves. 'Good to see you, Colin, son,' he said. 'I know this is a big moment for you. So, if you confine your singing to the summer, you have my blessing.'

Then Jimmy Sacca arrived. Perpetually tanned and super confident, he shook me by the hand and said, 'Quick, we have to get you made up.'

'Made up?' I asked, somewhat perplexed.

'Yes, I'll put make-up on your face.'

'I don't need any make-up on, Johnny.'

'You had better wear it,' Sacca said, 'because the lights will make you look pale, like a ghost. The make-up will ensure you look healthy. It's the way of things, Colin.'

The mid-50s was an era of inflated masculinity, so the thought of wearing make-up in front of Joe Mercer horrified me. Conversely, I had to be professional – and I was earning fifty quid for my efforts, so I could hardly tell Sacca what I thought was right. It was his environment, not mine.

The compere announced the next act. 'It's the England international . . . the Sheffield United player . . . the Singing Winger . . . the one and only . . . Colin Grainger.'

To great applause, I walked on to the stage to discover that some of the Sheffield United players had high-price seats in the front row. Seeing my pals should have made me more nervous, but, actually, I felt my nerves disappear completely. I felt as relaxed as I would have done playing in the Football League. The first thing I learnt about singing for money was this: there is no hiding place. In football, you are one man of eleven. In singing, you are one man of one.

I performed three songs – numbers by Al Jolson, Nat King Cole and Billy Eckstine, just as I had in Helsinki – and I produced just the kind of warm-up that Len Young, my agent, craved. As I walked off the stage to deafening applause, I noticed I was drenched in sweat. But I ensured that the Hilltoppers sounded palatable to the Sheffield punters, and everybody went home happy. The next day, photographs of my performance were all over the local newspapers. I had aroused more attention than the Hilltoppers, whose own performance had been overshadowed completely. They did not care. They were happy that the night had been successful. I still have the press cutting of the Sheffield United players in their seats, displaying golden smiles, evidently enjoying the performance. Under the headline 'Singing footballer', one report seemed to welcome my performance on stage. 'Sheffield teenage girls swooned over a crooner at the Empire Theatre, Sheffield, last night. He was none other than England and Sheffield United left winger Colin Grainger. Fair-headed, 23-year-old Colin was on the stage at the invitation of the America vocal group the Hilltoppers. The audience liked him and so did the Americans. Jimmy Sacca, leader of the group, said: "He was wonderful. He could join us any time he likes." Watching Colin were the Sheffield United team and a very astonished manager, Joe Mercer.'

I was embarrassed at the press coverage. I certainly do not remember anybody swooning over me. The most surprising element of my Sheffield Empire debut, however, was that it only took me twenty minutes to earn fifty quid. In football, I had to work for nearly three weeks to earn that kind of money, always with the fear lurking at the back of my mind that an overenthusiastic right-back would try to autograph my left leg with his studs. I purred like a cat when Len Young handed me a wad of cash. 'There'll be plenty more of that,' he said.

Surprised that my singing had aroused such a response, Joe Mercer told me: 'I have never seen anything like it.'

And nor, it seemed, had the Hilltoppers, for they asked me if I would move to the United States to become their permanent opening act. I could earn, Sacca told me, the equivalent of five grand a year. The Hilltoppers comprised of Sacca, Donald McGuire, Seymour Spiegelman, and Billy Vaughn, who had met at Western Kentucky State College in 1952 and had enjoyed a big hit in the UK in 1955 with 'Only You (And You Alone)'. Their problem was that, while they were big in the United States, they were struggling to crack the British market. With an eye to ticket sales, Young took the view that my presence would provide publicity and novelty, attributes that, in a northern English city, the Hilltoppers seemed to lack.

But I never considered going to the United States, not even for five grand a year. I was a footballer and would remain so until my legs gave up on me. Besides, I was happy in England, and Doreen – soon to leave her job as a machinist in a shirt factory – was now pregnant. It was a good job I turned down the offer. The Hilltoppers never did crack the UK market, and they folded up a year later, with Billy Vaughn branching out alone and making a considerable success of his status as one of the most versatile American musicians. I was saddened to discover in 2015 that Jimmy Sacca had died aged 85. He had inspired me and educated me and entertained me. I admired his professionalism and his talent. I wish I could have worked with him more often.

At that time, I sang purely on instinct. I had never had any lessons or any training. Whatever gift I possessed, it was purely natural and spontaneous, not from hard work. But I knew that if I wanted to take up singing seriously I needed lessons, commitment, and proper support. Perhaps my greatest asset was my confidence. I was never self-conscious. The desire to sing emanated from me like sweat. In early November, Len Young fixed me up with an appearance on ITV. I was injured at the time – I missed the match away to Huddersfield Town, a 4-1 victory – so I had time to practise. I do not remember my TV fee, but it was more than I would have earned from Sheffield United.

I sold my Sheffield Empire story to the *Sport Express*, whose leading correspondent, Brian Glanville, that doyen of the game, phoned me up to configure my words into an intelligible article. It was the start of a long friendship. And of a regular column at £3 a time.

Even for an England international, football was not easy money in the 50s. Singing was.

If only I could combine the two roles . . .

Life would never be the same again

Actually, *three* roles.

A few months earlier, at ten-to-five on the morning of Tuesday 3 July 1956 – just weeks after I had returned from my first tour abroad with England – in St Helens Hospital, Barnsley, Doreen had given birth to a healthy baby, whom we called Colin junior. In those days, the prospective father did not attend the birth, so I spent the entire 48 hours of Doreen's labour waiting nervously for a phone call. When the news came that everything went according to plan, I was the happiest man in the world.

I was now a professional footballer, a semi-professional singer, and a dad. Life would never be the same again.

Pulled out a penknife

Sheffield United kicked off the 1956/57 season in the Second Division with a match away to Rotherham United. Our John was playing for Rotherham and, although he was never less than the consummate professional, I formed the impression that he was playing within himself, as if to put the spotlight on his younger brother. I scored twice in a 4-0 victory. The newspaper took particular interest in our playing against each other.

'The two brothers travelled together from their home near Wakefield to Millmoor,' Derek Hodgson wrote. 'Inside the ground, they separated. The crowd chuckled later when they met again – Colin, Sheffield United outside-left, had fallen back to challenge Jack, Rotherham's outside-right. The day's honours went to the younger Colin. The Sheffield express, a Master Cutler at defence-slicing, wrecked Rotherham in the closing minutes and his two goals turned what would have been an honourable defeat into a 4-0 near-rout.'

Afterwards, both managers – Joe Mercer of Sheffield United, Andy Smailes of Rotherham United – used the same phrase to describe the match: 'It wasn't a fair test.'

Having played four matches for England during the summer, I found the Second Division relatively easy. I scored twice in a 5-2 victory at home to Fulham, then once in a 4-2 victory against Port Vale. And then, on 1 September, I scored the first hat-trick of my career, in a 6-1 victory away to Barnsley. I actually got the bus to Barnsley that day, among the Barnsley supporters, because the Oakwell stadium was not far from my home in Havercroft. Later on, members of my family would travel in the same direction, on the same bus, to take their seats in the main stand.

The stars aligned for me that Saturday afternoon. Every pass went where it was intended. Every dribble came off to perfection. Every time I found space, I received the ball. Barry Betts, the Barnsley right-back, was the wrong man in the wrong place on the wrong day. A talented defender rather than a clogger, he was usually a left-back but Barnsley switched him the other side of the defence to mark me. I tore him to pieces. The Barnsley goalkeeper was Harry Hough, who, in the 70s, would return to my life with an offer to keep me playing at non-League level.

While I received a lot of attention for my hat-trick, the best player on the pitch was Jim Iley, my future brother-in-law, who used his strength and intelligence to great effect. 'Speedy Blades rip Barnsley to ribbons,' went the headline on Stanley Ford's match report. He wrote: 'How the crowd revelled in the brilliant unorthodoxy of defence wrecker Hagan and breathtaking bursts of match-winner Grainger! The United outside-left must be a certainty for England this season.'

A certainly for England? I read that line over and over again and quite liked the sound of it.

What must Joe Richards have thought? A chirpy man with a permanent smile and a thin, David Niven moustache, he was the Barnsley chairman but also a member of the England selection committee, which helped Walter Winterbottom pick the national team.

I had now scored eight goals in five matches. However, as if to emphasise the unpretentiousness of football in the 50s, I took the bus back to Havercroft by myself, stopping on the way home to buy a copy of the *Green 'Un* Saturday Final newspaper to read the reports. I was an England international. I was a semi-professional singer. I had just scored a hat-trick. But I had to use public transport to get home just like most other men in Havercroft. Just as I found the dressing room at Wembley agreeably equitable (juxtaposing me alongside Stanley Matthews), so it was with the Barnsley-to-Havercroft bus (juxtaposing me alongside Barnsley supporters).

Much to the chagrin of Frank Blunstone, the outside-left who was having problems at Chelsea, I made the England team for the match away to Northern Ireland on 7 October 1956. I performed well and might have had at least a couple of goals had it not been for some excellent saves by Harry Gregg, the Northern Ireland goalkeeper, who really was superb that day. 'Luck Deserts The Irish', the headline in *The Times* read, somewhat soberly. 'English footballers scramble a draw in Belfast.' And perhaps we did well to draw. You could see even then that these Northern Ireland players, such as Danny Blanchflower, Billy Bingham, Jimmy McIlroy, and Peter McParland, had the makings of a good team.

And then, suddenly, for no discernible reason, my form dipped, and so did that of Sheffield United. I did sustain injuries, but they alone do not explain my malaise. Perhaps I was tired after the excesses of the summer months with England. Worse still, rumours filtered around the dressing room that the club was struggling financially. A good run in the FA Cup would certainly have boosted the bank balance, but we lost in a third-round second replay to Huddersfield Town at Maine Road, Manchester City.

I played for the Football League XI against the Irish League at St James' Park, Newcastle, on 31 October – a dour match after which Henry Rose, the journalist, described our performance as 'deplorable'. In front of 34,000 people, a colossal attendance for what was essentially a friendly, I scored in a 3-2 victory (Nat Lofthouse and Johnny Haynes scored the others). Don Hardisty wrote that, 'The only concrete success in the English attack was Sheffield United's super speedman Colin Grainger, who managed to score a goal although he was rationed to a bare half-dozen passes in ninety minutes' play.' But I was suffering pain throughout. The big toe on my left foot had gone septic and had swollen up. So great was the swelling, I could barely put on my boot. Afterwards, Bill Ridding, the trainer for the Football League XI, who doubled up as the Bolton Wanderers manager, told me he could help. He came to my hotel room, pulled out a penknife, and twisted it into the toenail. The pain made my eyes water and I was in constant agony on the train home from Newcastle to Sheffield. Unable to put on my shoe, I took a taxi home from the train station. The damage ruled me out of the match away to Huddersfield Town on 3 November.

By the time England played Wales at Wembley on 14 November, I was fit and again made the starting line-up, which gave me the opportunity to face John Charles, whose international debut I had witnessed at Wrexham six years earlier. Our paths crossed during the interim period when we played cricket together in a benefit match for Willie Watson, that icon of Yorkshire sport, who had represented England at both cricket and football. By 1956, Charles was one of the best and most versatile players in the world.

In the run-up to the England-Wales match, I used my column in *Sport Express* to express my concern about the 'difficulties' of the Wembley pitch. A portent, alas.

After England's 3-1 victory against excellent opposition, *The Times* summed up the real story with its headline: *Injuries Spoil Wembley International.* Jack Kelsey, the brilliant Wales and Arsenal goalkeeper, suffered concussion after diving at the feet of Tom Finney and had to go off the pitch. The player to replace Kelsey in goal was Alf Sherwood, the Newport County right-back, who fancied himself as a goalkeeper and had famously saved a penalty from Billy Liddell to consign Liverpool to relegation in 1954.

Kelsey's woe was merely the prelude to a nightmare of my own; an injury that would change my entire career, although I could not have known that at the time. Early in the second half, I stretched to reach a pass by Johnny Haynes, the Fulham inside-left, and twisted my left ankle. In spite of the noise of the capacity crowd, I could hear the crack of my ankle to confirm the damage. My eyes watering, my mind scrambled, I hobbled off the pitch. It was now ten players apiece, with all the intensity of the occasion long since gone.

And so journalists revived the story of the Wembley curse, Peter Lorenzo writing:

Wembley's danger corner claimed another victim yesterday. Sixteen minutes after half-time in this injury-ruined international, England and Sheffield United 23-year-old left winger Colin Grainger was carried off with a suspected fractured right ankle. This self-inflicted injury happened almost on the goal-line about twelve yards to the right of the dressing-room goal. Four yards from this spot in the 1952 FA Cup final against Newcastle, Arsenal and Wales full-back Walley Barnes received the injury to his right knee – ligaments and cartilage – which kept him out of the game for more than a year. Fifteen yards from this spot, in the 1955 Cup final, also against Newcastle, Manchester City and England right-back Jimmy Meadows was helped off with injured right knee ligaments. Meadows hasn't played a game since. Coincidence?

Joe Mercer claimed that the Wembley pitch was *too* good. Players had become so used to muddy, uneven pitches in the Football League that the bowling green of Wembley presented its own challenges. The unsuspecting player would find that his studs would sink into the perfect turf. As I said afterwards, 'I stopped the ball with my left foot, and as I tried to turn, the studs of my right boot got stuck ... and I heard my ankle go crack.'

The debate continued. Joe Mercer then claimed that the new, low-cut 'continental' football boot, with its 'plunging neckline', was causing problems. 'I should have been against these boots all along the line. Now I think they should be barred. I have had a talk with Grainger and feel certain the boots caused the trouble.' There was, Mercer said, no broken bone in my ankle but, rather, torn ligaments. I would miss important England matches against Yugoslavia and Denmark. I also missed a friendly match between Sheffield United and an All Stars XI that included such luminaries as Bill Shankly, Sam Bartram, Peter Doherty, and Willie Watson.

I would not taste action until late December – a reserve-team match against Derby County, after which I would play for Sheffield United against Lincoln City at Bramall Lane on Christmas Day 1956. It was the worst possible situation, for the pitch was frozen – hard, slippery and unforgiving – and likely to give my ankle all sorts of problems. I played well within myself, refusing to take any risks, and I expressed relief when I came off the pitch at the final whistle free of injury. We won 2-0. It was the first of eight matches I would play in heavy conditions within a twenty-day period.

Three hundred quid! In white fiver notes!

It was in late January 1957 that Joe Mercer called me into his office. I remember the conversation clearly because not only could I see the regret in his eyes, but I could feel a sense of disorientation immediately. I wish I'd had the time to prepare for what was coming:

'Colin, the directors regard you as an asset and they want to sell you. Simple as that.'

'But I don't want to leave. I am happy here.'

'Colin, they're not going to give you a choice. They need the money. They want to sell.'

'That's not my problem, boss.'

'Colin, the directors have said if you don't leave, you will never play for the first team again. You will be in the reserves for the rest of your career. You don't want that, do you?'

'They can't do that, boss.'

'Sadly, Colin, they can – and will.'

For the first time in my career, I realised how external forces can influence a manager's decision-making. Mercer did not want to sell me any more than I wanted to leave. But he had to act in accordance with the wishes of his employers. And the directors gave him an ultimatum:

Sell Grainger.

For the best price.

As quickly as possible.

I could not control the desire of the directors to sell me and I could not control the offers that might come in from other clubs. But even with my limited power, I could stall, play for time, and make it difficult for any deal to go through; or, in the patois of American politics, I could try to filibuster the club into submission. But that was never going to work.

Mercer and I agreed to meet Bill Murray, the Sunderland manager, at The Fox pub in Brotherton, just off the A1. Murray did a decent enough job selling Sunderland to me – which, to be fair, was not a difficult task – and I found him an extremely charming man. But I kept putting him off. I made it clear that I wanted to remain at Bramall Lane, and any move away would be against my will. The three of us met again in York, this time with Bill Ditchburn, the wealthy Sunderland chairman, who owned a furniture warehouse; and, again, I said I would think about it. I was in no rush to make a decision. While the fine reputation of the Sunderland fans impressed me, the club's nicknames – Star-Spangled Sunderland seemed a common one at the time – told me a different, less attractive side of the club.

Aware of my penchant for making money as a singer in my spare time, Murray told the press: 'We don't want to run the risk of signing [Colin] only to lose him after a few months. We have had experience of that sort of thing.' At the end of the report came a line that, at the time, meant nothing to me: 'Sunderland directors are likely to have an important matter before them at Wednesday's session – the League's examination of their books. Developments may follow.' Indeed they would.

During this period, Wolverhampton Wanderers came in with an offer of £23,000 to sign me. The Wolves scout, Mark Crookes, who made his name developing talented young players with Wath Athletic, even came to my house to tempt me. But the Wolves offer came with a caveat. The club, although relatively wealthy by the standards of the day, could only pay half of the cash immediately, with the other half to be paid at a later date. Sheffield United needed the money quickly to stave off the creditors. Birmingham City and Bolton Wanderers also showed interest but, again, neither could not pay the entire fee up front. The best Sunderland could offer was £17,000 in cash plus Sammy Kemp, their reserve-team winger, whose valuation of £6,000 meant that Sheffield United received the equivalent of £23,000.

I was dealing a lot with Brian Glanville, at that time a young novelist and talented football writer, who ghosted my regular column for the *Sport Express*. In the strictest of confidence, I kept Glanville informed of developments concerning my transfer, which probably did him more harm than good. He was sworn to confidentiality. Other journalists, who might have discovered information from different sources, were under no such restrictions and could publish what they wanted.

'I see your transfer is in the news,' he wrote to me on 24 January from his home in Sloane Avenue, London SW3. 'Naturally I would not ask you for any information before it takes place – if it does! But if and when it does happen, do please send me an article as soon as possible about how you find your new club, teammates, manager, style of club play.' Off the record, I told Glanville how much I resented the way the Sheffield United directors threatened me – a great story that, alas, he was unable to use. I did not want my feelings about the directors to go public, to overshadow the affection I had for the club's supporters, for my soon-to-be former teammates, and – of course – for Joe Mercer.

I played my last match for Sheffield United on 2 February, a 2-0 defeat to

Blackburn Rovers at Bramall Lane, and then I was off to Sunderland, with all the complications of finding new accommodation for what was now a young family of three.

In later years, I discovered that Stoke City were trying to sign Graham Shaw, the Sheffield United full-back, and that had Shaw agreed to the move, then I would have remained Bramall Lane. Shaw was not interested, however. It would have been better for me if he was.

It was in the Royal Station Hotel, York, that I signed the forms to became a Sunderland player. A press photograph shows me well-dressed and smiling. The smile was fake. Inside, I was full of remorse and regret. When I went back to Bramall Lane to pick up my belongings, Mercer called me into his office. Dichotomised and frustrated by the events of the previous few weeks, he made no secret of his disappointment at the circumstances surrounding my move. 'You do know I want you to stay,' he said, more than once, and you could see it in eyes that he meant every word.

'I want to stay, boss,' I replied.

'I know, son. I know.'

Then, in the style of a casino cashier, he pulled out a thick wad of those large £5 notes – the famous 'white fivers' that had been in circulation since time immemorial. (No £10 notes in the 50s, of course). Mercer licked his fingers and started counting the money with exaggerated hand movements, never once making eye contact with me. He then handed me the notes, smiled, and said: 'Here's three hundred quid for you. I get expenses from the club, so I want you to have this. You're getting nothing from the move so this is the least I can do. You deserve it.'

Three hundred quid! In white fiver notes!

Tax free!

My heart raced. But I could not let my excitement show. Not here. Not in front of Mercer. I was supposed to be feeling remorse at my move away from Bramall Lane. This was not the time to celebrate. This payment was illegal, of course, but I did not care. Illegal payments were part of football prior to the lifting of the maximum wage in 1961. Almost every player received backhanders or some form of forbidden benefit, and everybody, up to and including the Football Association, knew it and turned a blind eye.

What mattered most to me – even more than the money – was what this gift symbolised. It summed up the essence of Joe Mercer. Three hundred quid was a lot and he had no obligation to pay me a single penny. But pay me he did, from his own pocket, money he probably could not afford, to ensure that I left the club on good terms and had some compensation for my troubles.

As we shook hands, he seemed reluctant to let go, as if, for him, parting company would signal the end of an era. I regretted it that our working relationship was over but I hoped that the fates would conspire to reunite us in the future.

For me, the truth is immutable: in the history of British football, there has never been a nicer man than Joe Mercer.

CHAPTER III

With the Millionaires
1957-60: Sunderland, Len Shackleton
Alan Brown, Empire theatres

Aloof, perpetually overdressed, stiff upper lip

MY FIRST IMPRESSIONS OF BILL MURRAY WERE THAT HE HAD A LOT in common with Joe Mercer and exuded common decency. Dapper and intelligent, a man existing permanently in a state of middle age, he would have earned more money had he avoided professional football and instead stuck to his original plans. Born in Aberdeen in 1900, he was studying to be an engineer just after the Great War when Cowdenbeath offered to employ him as sophisticated full-back. Murray did well enough to attract interest from Sunderland and he moved to Roker Park in April 1927, winning a League Championship medal with the club in 1935/36, alongside the delightful Raich Carter. Murray went to St Mirren briefly – missing Sunderland's FA Cup final victory in 1937 – but returned to Roker Park as manager on 24 March 1939. And so began the longest managerial career in Sunderland's history.

None of us really knew how much influence he had on team selection or on which players the club signed, but it suited the board of directors to have him as manager because he was the consummate diplomat; at his best when creating unity out of division and calm out of chaos. I liked him immensely, even if his pre-match team talks were so clichéd and hackneyed that he might have been reading them from the backs of cereal boxes.

How could I have known that when I arrived at Sunderland in late January 1957 that Murray was entering his final weeks in charge? As soon as I arrived at the club I heard the hints that not everything was right. The chairman, Bill Ditchburn, had been spending so much money on players, trying to turn the team into the best in England, that Sunderland earned various nicknames: The Millionaires being one; the Bank of England Club being another. By 1948, the squad boasted the likes of Len Shackleton, Fred Hall and Willie Watson, with Trevor Ford, Billy Elliott, Stan Anderson, Billy Bingham and Charlie Fleming joining later on. Ditchburn gave Murray unlimited funds, although the lack of success created a sense of anxiety within the boardroom, which, in turn, trickled down to Murray. Such was the attitude of underpaid top-flight players in those post-war years, we did not much concern ourselves with the minutiae of Sunderland's balance sheet.

But it did not take long to see that I had taken a step forward. The gym was better, the dressing rooms larger, and there was a billiard room to help players avoid boredom in the afternoon. It all felt that little bit bigger than Sheffield United.

Roker Park was a fortress.

But it was an illusion.

A fortress built on quicksand.

Until Doreen and I could buy a house, the club put us up at the Seaburn Hotel, Bywell Avenue, with its stunning views of the North Sea. The situation was not ideal. Our baby son, Colin junior, remained at my parents' home in Havercroft, which meant that Doreen, still only nineteen, travelled backwards and forwards to see him. I went back to Havercroft as often as I could, and, initially, I did most of my training at Sheffield United.

There were benefits to living at the Seaburn, however, not least the presence of Don Revie, who was there with his wife, Elsie. Revie had moved to Sunderland from Manchester City two months earlier for £22,000, a colossal sum for a player on the verge of his 30s and seemingly in the twilight of his career. Revie could still play but was more reliant on his cerebral attributes than his physical ones. Having long respected him from afar, I grew to like him. In the evenings, he and I would sit in the bar talking nothing but football. Doreen and Elsie would often meet up to go shopping or to check out what the local estate agents were offering. Often, the four of us would meet for an evening meal. The vibe was reassuring.

Revie was a complicated character and, in those days, something of a religious man. I went into his room once to find him kneeling down at the side of his bed saying his prayers. I am not even sure if he noticed I was there. I walked back out, somewhat embarrassed, and never mentioned the incident. I cannot say that I saw, in 1957, the signs of a man who would become one of the game's all-time great managers, but hindsight tells me now that his intelligence certainly set him apart. He was a brilliant thinker and tactical innovator, always coming up with ideas and schemes. For him, football was as much about the mind as the body. But although he was great company in social settings and was never less than charming, he could be withdrawn in the dressing room, often keeping his thoughts to himself. He had a strong presence on the pitch but not off it. I formed the impression that Revie was two men, each complementing the other but also providing mystery to the onlooker. Perhaps Revie wanted it that way; as a kind of shield to stop people from getting too close to him.

I met the entire Sunderland first-team squad on 8 February 1957 at the Great Northern Hotel, Kings Cross, the day before the match away to Tottenham Hotspur. One of the first things I learnt was how many of the Sunderland players had other work interests outside of football. When I arrived at the club I found that Len Shackleton, George Aitken and Billy Elliott already ran their own businesses, while Ray Daniel was in the process of raising money so he could make investments of his own. Daniel had a decent singing voice and, being a Welshman, liked to show it off during long coach journeys to away matches. I remembered him from when he scored the freak goal from forty yards for Sunderland that knocked Sheffield United out of the FA Cup a year earlier. I, of course, had a few fingers in a few pies, so it was interesting to share stories about our extra-curricular activities and our plans for post-playing careers. Everywhere I turned in the bar, I could see talent, personality, and professionalism. Billy Bingham called us the Crazy Gang – long before the Wimbledon team of 1987/88 earned the sobriquet.

I liked the look of Aitken. Dark-haired and quick-witted, with a cheeky smile, he was from a mining background and he had distinguished himself with East Fife in Scotland, after which he turned down attractive offers from English clubs to sign for Third Lanark of Glasgow in 1950. But Third Lanark were short of money and were never likely to keep hold of Aitken for long. He told me the story of how he joined Sunderland in November 1951. Alex Ritchie, the Third Lanark manager, arranged for a policeman to knock on Aitken's door in the middle of a cold night.

The policeman had a message: 'Meet Mr Ritchie in Glasgow tomorrow morning.' When Aitken arrived at the appointed hotel, Ritchie and Bill Murray were there with the news about Sunderland's interest. Murray proved so persuasive that not only did Aitken sign for Sunderland in the afternoon but he also agreed to make his debut two days later – away to Fulham in the First Division. 'I barely had time to break the news to my family because I had to go to Cathkin Park [Third Lanark's ground] to pick up my boots,' Aitken told me.

There was nothing as onerous about my Sunderland debut, which took place at White Hart Lane. Aitken made the starting line-up but Revie did not. As I looked around the players in the dressing room – seven internationals – and took stock of my surroundings, I realised that I had joined a club of great significance and confidence. I put on my Sunderland shirt for the first time and then Len Shackleton sat down next to me to offer encouragement and advice: the usual clichés and axioms. And then, as if to force home his points, he put his right hand on my right shoulder and said: 'Colin, this is the greatest club in the country.'

Yes, of course.

My debut went well from a personal point of view but not for the team. In front of 52,104 spectators, after a goalless first half, Tottenham won 5-2, with Shackleton and Fleming scoring the Sunderland goals. The result was not entirely unexpected. Tottenham were at that time fighting hard with Manchester United for the First Division title, while Sunderland were sitting uncomfortably in third-to-bottom position. I played well in the first half but Tottenham stepped up the pace thereafter. Given Tottenham's superiority, I barely touched the ball in the second half, but it was not a match for a winger. The chief subplot was the battle between those two Northern Ireland greats: Billy Bingham of Sunderland and Danny Blanchflower of Tottenham. But the man who did the most to destroy us that afternoon was Alfie Stokes, a super-quick inside-forward, who had made his name with the England Schoolboys team just after World War Two then drifted into non-League football with Clapton. Arthur Rowe signed him for Tottenham in 1953 and the player flourished. You could see in 1957 the signs of a Tottenham team that would go on to win the Football League and FA Cup Double in 1960/61.

A week later, Sunderland defeated Sheffield Wednesday 5-2 at Hillsborough. Ross Jenkinson of the *Sheffield Telegraph* reported: '[The] only club which has never played in any other than the First Division is the proud claim on the front page of Sunderland's official programme. On this form they will keep the boast, especially if they are to be helped so much by the mistakes of opponents. All the skill and life Colin Grainger and Don Revie brought to a team which started with that doomed look could have been brought to nought if Wednesday had been consistent.' We were probably no better against Wednesday than we had been against Tottenham but sometimes you need – and deserve – the breaks. I delighted in being mentioned in the same sentence as Revie, for it gave me the sense that, even this early on, I had already become part of the Sunderland system.

So vast, so lush, so open

I prepared to make my seventh appearance for the full England team in the British Championship match against Scotland at Wembley on Saturday 6 April 1957. Making his international debut in goal was Alan Hodgkinson, my former teammate at Sheffield United, who had become the goalkeeper I had been predicting since he was a teenager in 1953. In his preview of the match, Peter Wilson of the *Daily Mirror* wrote:

> *This Saturday's clash of the Auld Enemy takes on even greater significance for England and their manager Walter Winterbottom . . . The likes of [Alan] Hodgkinson, [Duncan] Edwards, [Jeff] Hall, [Roger] Byrne and Grainger promise much. We shall have a clearer idea of how far such promise will be fulfilled come quarter to five on Saturday . . . Walter Winterbottom, who instigated and has presided over a deft revolution of English football these past four years, will see England's encounter with a skilful and resolute Scotland as the litmus test to the chemistry he has created.*

It was interesting that this journalist saw Scotland, rather than the likes of Brazil and West Germany, both of whom we defeated in 1956, as the yardstick for how far England had progressed since the cataclysm against Hungary in 1953.

As we approached the stadium in the bus, we saw men in kilts and heard the noise of bagpipes in the distance. The sights and sounds made for a unique atmosphere. Inside Wembley, there seemed to be more Scots than Englishmen, which gave the impression to the England players that we might as well have been playing in Glasgow or Edinburgh.

After the kick-off, Scotland dominated. Tommy Ring, then of Clyde, later of Everton and Barnsley, put Scotland ahead within sixty seconds of the start, and we barely had a significant move for the rest of the first half, with Willie Fernie, the Celtic forward, and Jackie Mudie, the Blackpool forward, particularly impressive for the visitors.

At half-time, Winterbottom impressed upon us the need for subtle changes. He said to me words to the effect of, 'Colin, isn't about time you demonstrated what a good crosser of the ball you are? I want early crosses, Colin, but not into the middle of the Scotland penalty area. I want you to cross deep, to the far post.' He then told Derek Kevan, the West Bromwich Albion forward, to make late runs from deep to benefit from my crosses to the far post. Everything was designed to take advantage of George Young's lack of mobility, although we all knew his reputation as one of the finest Scotland players of all time.

Just after the hour mark, Tom Finney found me on the left of the penalty area with a square pass. Eric Caldow, the Scotland and Rangers right-back, tried to close me down but my first touch gave me time and space. All I could think of was Winterbottom's advice; and so, instead of dashing towards the byline as I usually would have done, I checked back, switched the ball to my right foot, and crossed deep to the far post. And who should be there but Derek Kevan, launching himself forward to head home beyond the flailing arms of Tommy Younger. The prototype England goal. A goal straight out of Winterbottom's half-time team talk.

Scotland responded well, with Tommy Docherty and Bobby Collins superb, and Jackie Mudie growing in stature. But with six minutes remaining, I made a run wide, which gave Duncan Edwards, by now a dominating influence, the space to dash through the middle and score with what *The Times* called a 'shattering bang' from twenty yards out. And so 'the cloak of victory was stripped from Scotland'.

We won 2-1 to secure the British title, but the headline on the match report in *The Times* summed up the poverty of our overall performance: 'England Recover in The Second Half: Unimpressive Wembley Win.'

If the match was unsatisfying, and Scotland unfortunate to lose, my personal performance did not satisfy me, in spite of my involvement in both England goals. I lacked the confidence that had characterised my displays against Brazil and West Germany in 1956 and the pace that had made me an international player in the first place. I learnt that the Wembley pitch, so vast, so lush, so open, can bring both the best and worst out of a player, depending on his state of mind and the condition of his body. Ten months earlier, Wembley was my perfect milieu; now its goldfish-bowl intensity exaggerated my insecurities. This was the first time I had ended an England international feeling worse emotionally than when the match began. What a difference an injury can make.

Still, I was a British champion. I waited for a medal that never arrived.

Shorts becoming tighter

For all their talent and tactical brilliance, Tottenham would not win the League in 1956/57. Manchester United, with Duncan Edwards in supreme form, were not only the best team in England but also one of the best in the world. They were halfway through their two-legged European Cup semi-final tie against Real Madrid when Sunderland went to Old Trafford for a First Division match on 20 April 1957. Manchester United played the game with such control and speed that although we lost 4-0 the scoreline could have been anything. Edwards was devastating that day, scoring once but also involving himself in everything United did. He was the fulcrum, the heartbeat of the operation, and the ball seemed attracted to him. It was much easier playing with him than it was against him. Worse still, United had a player of whom I knew little but who had beautiful touch and balance and a devastating left foot: Bobby Charlton. He was still a teenager then but, like Edwards, had the appearance and confidence of a fully grown man. United played spontaneously, assuredly and without fear, as if to reject the science – and constraints – of conventional football tactics. Nothing, it seemed, could stop them dominating the domestic game, although they did lose 5-3 on aggregate to Real Madrid in the European Cup.

It felt to me as if football was entering a new era. European competition had given us a glimpse of what was happening in the outside world. Suddenly, the stars of the global game seemed familiar, even if, for the most part, they had foreign accents and mysterious expressions. We learnt about Alfredo Di Stéfano, Real Madrid's deep-lying forward, who at that time was arguably the most complete player in the history of the game. I took a particular interest in Real Madrid's outside-left, Francisco Gento, who was famous at the time for breaking eleven seconds over 100 yards. Just as there was a magic about the Hungarians of 1953, so there was about Real Madrid in 1957. Harold Macmillan, the British prime minister, might have been a man of his times – aloof, perpetually overdressed, stiff upper lip, conservative hairstyle – but the elite football players were already evoking the social emancipation and laissez-faire attitudes of the 60s. The balls were becoming lighter and players' shorts becoming tighter. And in another nod to the future, John Charles of Leeds United, that supreme competitor, blessed with an exceptional physique, always making sure the ball worked for him, agreed to join Juventus of Italy for a fee of £65,000.

In 1956/57, Manchester United had more in common with Real Madrid than Sunderland did with Manchester United. From the day of my arrival in January to the end of the season, we never moved out of the bottom four. On one occasion, after losing 4-1 at home to West Bromwich Albion in March, we slipped into the bottom two – the relegation zone. Although we ended the season with three successive defeats, Cardiff City suffered for their failure to score goals, and they went down into the Second Division alongside Charlton Athletic.

The last straw

Survival for Sunderland – just. But there would be no celebrations, and only a mild sense of relief. The clouds that had been hanging over Roker Park were now black and menacing. And then, on a miserable 10 April 1957, the Football Association found the club guilty of making illegal payments to players. The Bank of England Club, for all its cultural charm, history and wonderful supporters, was steeped in corruption, and had been at least since 1953.

The Football Association fined Sunderland £5,000, the largest financial penalty the game in England had ever seen. Bill Ditchburn, the chairman, was banned from the game for life (rescinded in 1962), while other directors suffered indefinite suspensions. Six players were known to have received illegal payments: Trevor Ford, Ken Chisholm, Willie Fraser, Johnny Hannigan, Billy Elliott, and Ray Daniel. Ford, by now playing for PSV Eindhoven in the Netherlands, had left Roker Park in 1953, which gave some idea of how long Sunderland had been playing fast and loose with the rules. Between them, the six players had received more than £5,000 in crisp one-pound notes, distributed in brown paper envelopes.

The story of how the scam went from being a private affair to a public scandal is worth repeating here because it says something about the way football functioned in the 50s. The trouble started at Roker Park just before I arrived when a mysterious man calling himself 'Mr Smith' wrote to the Football League providing details of Sunderland's illegal payments. Officials at the League and at the Football Association were not dumb. They were aware that clubs were using all sorts of innovative ways – free holidays, jewellery, free accommodation, cars and cash *et al* – to circumvent the rules about illegal payments. But the letter from 'Mr Smith' forced the game's establishment to intervene. At first, the officials from the League and Football Association could not find anything incriminating. The Sunderland directors appeared to have covered their tracks – but they did not consider the over-enthusiasm of the League's new secretary, Alan Hardaker, who, eager to please his bosses, wondered why Sunderland had spent £3,000 on straw. 'To protect the pitch from frost,' one of the directors told him. Hardaker then contacted his brother, Ernest, the chairman of Hull Rugby League Club. According to Alan Hardaker, the conversation went like this:

> Alan: *How much does it cost to cover your ground with straw in a normal sort of winter?*
> Ernest: *It would depend on how many Saturdays were involved.*
> Alan: *Well, if I gave you £3,000 would you be able to manage for a season?*
> Ernest: *Blow me! For that we'd manage 25 seasons.*

Sunderland might still have avoided censure, but Alan Hardaker noticed on the club documents an incriminating note added in pencil: 'Where do I post this?' Sunderland's cover was blown. Essentially, the club had placed orders for straw way in excess of what was required. When the suppliers came to deliver the items they gave credit notes to the club for the amounts returned. In turn, Sunderland cashed the credit notes and used the money to pay the players.

So, who was the mysterious 'Mr Smith'? A disgruntled director, perhaps, for there were all sorts of power struggles going on behind the scenes at Roker Park. Or maybe 'Mr Smith' was a jealous Sunderland player who had missed out personally on the illegal payments. Whatever, Bill Ditchburn took full responsibility for the con. He thought he would get away with it because, as he stated, 'every other club was doing the same'. As one journalist wrote at the time, for Mr

Ditchburn, it really was the last straw. Perhaps the saddest part of the whole sordid affair was when the Football Association fined Bill Murray £200 for his role in the scandal, although the word 'role' exaggerates his involvement. An honest man with great integrity, Murray was crestfallen by the news and he tendered his resignation at the end of the season. With the exception of a brief spell playing for St Mirren in Scotland, Murray had been at Roker Park since 1927. It was hard to conceive of a more anticlimactic ending for a genuine football man who had given the club far more than he had taken out. He was never the same after that. He passed away four years later, just before Christmas 1961, at the age of 60. He aged quickly, going from a middle-aged man to an old man seemingly overnight, and died of a broken heart. He never lived to see his vindication or have his money refunded.

I always liked Bill Murray. He was, like many people of that time, a gentleman; a paragon of humility and charm. He never lost his temper, never shouted, and he had such a stable personality that no matter what life threw at him, he never changed his demeanour. If he sometimes seemed overshadowed by Sunderland's star players, he probably liked it that way. Even when he left the club he behaved as if it was just another incident on just another day. Inside, however, he was hurting. You could see it in his eyes. You could see it in every line that disfigured his forehead.

Sunderland had broken the Eleventh Commandment: *though shalt not get caught*. Other clubs were also making illegal payments to players – no mitigation, of course – but it seemed to us that we suffered for our reputation as the game's biggest spenders. Sunderland's sobriquet, the Bank of England Club, was a marketing slogan that became a burden; a burden that weighed on us heavily. It was not so much the perception of wealth that made Sunderland a target for the authorities but, rather, that the directors boasted all the time about money. Boasting about wealth in the early post-war years was considered vulgar and un-British.

For my part, I can say honestly say that I never received anything illegal from Sunderland. By the time I arrived at Roker Park, the Football Association was already delving into the club's books, which seemed to make the Sunderland chairman and directors paranoid and sensitive. In 1957, the directors were playing by the rules, but still an atmosphere of distrust suffused the boardroom like a rancid miasma. Would I have turned down money had it been offered to me?

Probably not. Football players were so undervalued and underpaid in those days that the distinction between what was morally right and morally wrong became blurred. We could justify backhanders – boot money from the club or payments from journalists for stories – on many levels. The problem was not that players and clubs broke the rules over illegal payments but that the rules were inherently flawed and iniquitous. It all reminded me of the exchange between Sherlock Holmes and Watson in *The Hounds of the Baskervilles*:

> *Watson: Because it's not actually possible for the victim to have done it, Sherlock, that's why!*
> *Sherlock Holmes: It was the only possible solution!*
> *Watson: It's not in the rules!*
> *Sherlock Holmes: Well then the rules are wrong!*

Tell me, was I delirious?

Summer 1957.

It was a relief to be away from the paranoid atmosphere at Roker Park for a few weeks. I attended the FA Cup final between Aston Villa and Manchester United on 4 May with a press ticket procured by Brian Glanville, who was ghostwriting my weekly column for the *Sport Express*. Aston Villa won 2-1, and while I was disappointed for my friend, Duncan Edwards, I found myself impressed with the performance of Peter McParland. '[He could even be the match-winner [for Villa],' I had written a few days earlier. And so he was, scoring twice to deny United the League and FA Cup Double.

The Sunderland directors had arranged a tour of the Soviet Union only to pull out just a few days before the scheduled 29 May journey from London to Riga via Stockholm. Stanley Rous, the secretary of the Football Association, asked West Bromwich Albion to take Sunderland's place.

Pleased that I would be staying in Britain, Len Young, my musical agent, arranged a season of gigs for me at Empire theatres and variety clubs all over the north of England and Scotland: Sunderland, Sheffield, Leeds, Liverpool, Middlesbrough and Glasgow. Tough places, full of working-class, salt-of-the-earth types. At fifty quid a night, I would make more in two months than in the entire

1956/57 season playing football. I got myself the finest suit I could afford from Savile Row. I arranged singing lessons through an agent, Joe Collins, to take any rough edges off my voice. When I arrived at his house in Maida Vale, London to stay the night, he introduced me to one of his daughters. 'I'd like you to meet Joan,' he said. She was a strikingly pretty actress, aged 24, like me, with more than a dozen films already on her curriculum vitae. Joseph Collins would play the piano as I sang, and he would offer suggestions about improving the strength and tone of my voice. My lungs became as powerful as my legs.

I practised singing in much the same way as I practised sprinting during my Wrexham and Sheffield United days: obsessively, relentlessly, as if nothing else mattered. I could no longer insulate myself with the knowledge of being the charming football player who crooned harmlessly as a novelty act. I was now a semi-professional, whom punters paid money to watch, which meant every performance had to be as close to perfection as possible. Goodwill had to be earned. One bad night could ruin an entire summer. A ruined summer could mean a ruined career. Margin for error: zero.

The Sunderland and Sheffield shows benefited from my name-recognition, and my spirits soared. My mam and dad came to see me at Sheffield, which must have evoked memories for them of when they heard me singing in the bath as a teenager. I still have the poster advertising the Sunderland night, and there is my name, positioned prominently, alongside Betty Driver, the singer of 'The Sailor with the Navy Blue Eyes', who would later make a name for herself as an actress with Ealing Studios and on the television soap, *Coronation Street*.

The Leeds City Variety club was different because I felt I had to prove myself. At Middlesbrough, my connections to Sunderland, a rival city with great implications in the football world, added an interesting dynamic, but I seemed to go down well. I heard afterwards that the first Middlesbrough and Sunderland shows amassed record takings. Liverpool was unique because I felt the entire city was full of singers and quick-witted comedians. I feared my crooning might have appeared antediluvian, but the audience responded well. While there, I went to see my cousin, Dennis Grainger, the former Leeds United and Wrexham outside-right, who owned a club in nearby Birkdale, straight up the coast.

I did a week at the London Metropolitan, opening for Max Miller, the self-styled 'Cheeky Chappie', star of the 20s and 30s, and it was there that he recorded his LP, 'Max at the Met'. But I could see that he was not well, and it did not come as a surprise not long after when he suffered a heart attack.

The only time I felt fear was when I went to Glasgow for a gig on Monday 7 July. Len Young had arranged for a friend of his to meet me there. He was John McPhail, a journalist for the *Daily Herald*, who had played international football for Scotland from 1949-53 and more than two hundred Scottish League matches for Celtic from 1945-56. He had been particularly active in business during his playing career – on one occasion going bankrupt – and now he was working for Young to supplement his income as a writer. McPhail drove me around Glasgow to give me a feel for the place. The Gorbals, a densely populated district on the south bank of the River Clyde, was a particular treasure. You could feel the pulse of the place; constant activity, authentic atmospheres, the smell of cooking food hanging in the air. McPhail knew about my playing career but less about my singing. 'You'd better be good,' he said to me. 'The main act last week, Bobby Thompson, was jeered off. If you're useless, the patrons won't take any prisoners. They'll just throw stuff at you until you get off the stage, like they did with Bobby.'

Thompson was a comedian, not widely considered handsome, and he delivered his material in a thick Durham accent, which the locals could not understand. He could have been the funniest man in the world and nobody in Glasgow would have known. Apparently, his performance was so bad that the Glasgow Empire paid up his contract early and sent him on his way. I did not even attempt to conceal my reaction to this sample of information. The blood drained from my face. For the first time in my life, I felt disconcertingly out of my depth – and I had not even reached the Glasgow Empire yet. I had visions of being booed, abused, and thrown out of the theatre by two thousand unforgiving Glaswegians. I could see the headlines about the clean-cut England international wearing a Savile Row suit running away from Sauchiehall Street with a baying mob in pursuit. But there were no jeers, no abuse and no rotting fruit – just friendliness and respect. The applause that greeted the end of my performance provided the ultimate relief. Glasgow gave me a confidence in my singing that, hitherto, had not been there.

Television came next. I performed with Jack Hylton and his orchestra on the *After Hours* show on ITV, presented by Hughie Green, which we filmed at studios in Birmingham. The Hilltoppers got back in touch to see if I would reconsider their offer of a contract in the United States. I did a television show with Winifred Atwell, Eric Robinson and Matt Monro on the BBC. Atwell was a genius on the piano and she even insured her fingers for £40,000, an arrangement made by her husband, Lew Levisohn. The agreement precluded her from ever washing the dishes. She sang as well as she played piano and, to my eyes and ears, appeared to be the consummate professional. Monro was less experienced than Atwell and in the dressing room before we all went on air he seemed nervous and unsure of himself, even though he was already established as a featured performer with the BBC's famous Show Band. I was nervous, too, but I realised from my career in football that once you are performing, the nerves disappear. Monro was a lovely man, who, like most people involved in the entertainment industry in those days, exuded humility off stage.

My television appearances led to the offer of a HMV recording contract, which meant I had to have voice coaching early on a Monday morning from an Italian bloke at eight quid a session – nearly half my weekly wage as a football player. Once my voice reached the necessary standard, I cut two tracks – the Charles Canwell composition, 'Are You'? and 'This I Know', both of which would be released in 1958 – in two intense, four-hour sessions on Denmark Street, London.

The main man at HMV was Wally Ridley, a record producer, who made his name on the EMI label with such stars as Alma Cogan, Donald Peers, Anne Shelton, Ronnie Hilton, Joe Loss and Benny Hill. He was responsible for guiding the early career of Vera Lynn and it was his decision that EMI should acquire for British release Elvis Presley's 'Heartbreak Hotel'. There was an aura about Ridley and I found that just being in the studio with him was an education.

I started to socialise with theatrical and musical types, like Toni Dalli, the Italian singer, who loved football and once played at outside-left for a Showbiz XI alongside Sean Connery at Arsenal; and Ronnie Hilton, the Yorkshire singer. Hilton had enjoyed a great run of chart success in the 50s and I wished to bask in the reflected glory.

And then, as if to validate the perception that my celebrity had moved way beyond football, I joined Joe Collins and his other daughter, Jackie, for the premiere in London of Joan Collins' latest film, *Sea Wife*, a romantic drama set in the Pacific, which co-starred Richard Burton and Basil Sydney. There is a quote in the film in which Sister Therese says, 'Tell me, was I delirious?' Given my state of mind, I was just as likely to ask myself the same question.

I purred like a cat.

What could possibly go wrong?

The Clown Prince of Soccer

Everything could go wrong. And his name was Alan Brown.

He was the new Sunderland manager, appointed on 30 July 1957, by Colonel John Turnbull, the new Sunderland chairman. I should have seen the signs. Brown arrived wearing an old-fashioned suit, a forced smile, and seemed keen to reveal his ominous penchant for revolution. If Sunderland wanted the complete opposite of Bill Murray, the club could not have done better than Brown.

A sergeant-major type with piercing eyes, he liked to promote himself as a paragon of morality and he made it clear that part of his job was to clean up the club from top to bottom. A good idea – in principle. But only if he knew what he was doing. He had been a moderately successful defender with Huddersfield Town and Burnley, for whom he played in the 1947 FA Cup final. A good friend of the Football Association secretary, Stanley Rous, Brown stayed in football as a coach with Sheffield Wednesday but also benefited from the proceeds of his restaurant in Burnley. He became the Burnley manager in 1954, against the wishes of some senior players, but did put in place the foundations for what would become a successful youth policy. Burnley would benefit from his work long after he moved to Sunderland.

The problem with Brown was that he seemed to have a suspicion of senior players. He did not even attempt to conceal his dislike of Don Revie. I felt that Brown resented Revie's reputation, experience and natural intelligence. Brown preferred to work with impressionable young players, whom he could bully and shape into his own image, as if chiseling away at stone in search of his ideal sculpture.

Established professionals, by contrast, presented a threat to his authority. And as we prepared for the 1957/58 season, there was no Sunderland player more established than Len Shackleton. Although a brilliant player with a great reputation, Shackleton's fame transcended the game from the moment he published his autobiography, *Clown Prince of Soccer* in 1956. Famously, he entitled Chapter 9, 'The Average Director's Knowledge of Football' and left the page blank. The establishment despised Shackleton and he despised the establishment. It seemed to count against him, certainly in the corridors of power, that he had so much talent, for in those days there was often a great mistrust for maverick players.

His control was prodigious. No matter how you passed the ball to him, he would have it under control in one movement. His dexterity was such that he did not have to do much running. 'Len played to the gallery,' Stanley Matthews said, but the gallery loved it.

I count it as a privilege that I played alongside Shackleton, although I never actually got close to him as a person. I do not think any of us did. He was the opposite of his reputation; the classic dichotomy between the reality and the legend. The Clown Prince of Soccer? I found him introverted and reticent, almost shy, and not the type with whom you could have a long, intense conversation. I never saw anything resembling a clown. Some Sunderland players could not work him out. He would train in the morning with the rest of us, say as little as possible, and then dash off to work in the shop that he owned. The rest of us would go off somewhere for a coffee. Shackleton gave the impression of a man planning a future outside of football. But on the pitch, where it mattered most, he was a class act. He could think that little bit quicker than most other players and there was a mystical aura surrounding him, as if he inhabited a different space from the rest of us. He conformed to my sense that truly great players in the 50s, like Shackleton and Stanley Matthews, had different characters from the merely good players; as if their talent had reconstructed their personalities to enhance them as men and as athletes.

Shackleton and Bill Murray had got on well; so much so, in fact, that Shackleton invited Murray to write the introduction to *Clown Prince of Soccer*. When Murray called him '*the* most controversial player of his generation', he meant it as a compliment. When Murray referred to Shackleton as 'a player who seems to be promoted by an imp of mischief', he was blurring the distinction between opinion and fact.

I wondered how Shackleton and Alan Brown would get on. They did not like each other – their personalities clashed like a set of cymbals – and Shackleton hated Brown's archaic training methods. Pre-season gave new meaning to the word *tough*. Brown, still only 42 when he joined us, and fitter than some of his players, had us on the beach for weeks, pushing us so hard that we feared having no energy left for when the season began. At Roker Park, he would have us leapfrogging all over each other non-stop for twenty minutes and then running up and down the terraces, which, in those days, given the size of the stadium, was an arduous task. We had no doubt that players should work hard, especially in pre-season, but Brown's training risked injury and forced us to use muscles that we would never use in matches. I did not mind these tough sessions so much, but, then, I was still only 24. The players nearing their 30s or beyond should have been encouraged to train in a different way, with more ball work and more five-a-sides.

I remember Billy Bingham laughing about the prospect of Brown having Shackleton doing this kind of training for a full season. 'Imagine Shack buying into all Brown's running stuff,' Bingham said to anyone who would listen. Bingham rated Shackleton highly and as a better dribbler than Stanley Matthews.

I liked Bingham. There was a wonderful spontaneity about the way he acted off the field and about the way he played. His style on the pitch was all about improvisation, a strategy that would stand him in good stead in later years when he became a successful manager. It did enter my head in 1957 that Bingham might become a great leader of men, for he spoke with authority and never had a bad word about anybody. He could inspire. He could make you feel comfortable. He certainly had intelligence and a great curiosity about the game itself and about the vicissitudes of the human condition. I socialised with him often – usually a coffee after training – and enjoyed his company immensely. Perky, vivacious, always smiling, he was a more endearing person than Shackleton, who, though charming, was something of a mystery; an individual never likely to flourish under an inflexible authoritarian like Alan Brown.

But nature intervened on a warm Saturday afternoon. During the first half of our match against Arsenal at Roker Park on 24 August 1957, the opening day of the season, Shackleton injured his right ankle and did not appear for the second half. On the Monday after, he drove in his Humber Hawk car to a hospital in Barnsley, which was not far from where my parents lived at West Street, Havercroft. Coincidentally, I was at West Street, visiting Colin junior, so Shackleton popped in to see me. He was with John Watters, the Sunderland physiotherapist, a pipe-smoker par excellence, whom I knew well and trusted implicitly. Preoccupied with my baby son, I did not consider why Shackleton should feel the need to visit me.

'Keep this to yourself, Colin, but I'm going to pack it in,' Shackleton said. 'I haven't told Sunderland yet, so your discretion would be welcome.'

'You're *quitting*?!' I said, not even attempting to conceal my surprise.

'It's my time, Colin. It's over.'

And so it came to pass that in the house where I grew up, the legendary Len Shackleton, aged 35, called time on his illustrious playing career. It was nice to know he trusted me with such important information. Indeed, it was the longest conversation he and I ever had. But I would have preferred it if he carried on playing. We needed his celebrity in a dressing room that was becoming increasingly dull. I wished then I knew him well enough to offer some advice; something along the lines of, *if you quit now, you will regret it for sure.* In those days, when players, even those at the highest level, had no guarantee of a successful post-playing career, retiring was not something to be undertaken lightly. Perhaps he did not enjoy the game as much as I did.

Not until Tuesday 3 September 1957 did *The Times* report, 'Shackleton Not To Play Again'. Apparently, the right ankle 'would no longer stand up to maximum strain' and the surgeon advised him to stop playing. To my eyes, Shackleton did not look particularly upset about the news. I formed the view immediately that his retirement had less to do with his ankle than his frustration at the thought of playing under Brown. The ankle injury was not *that* bad. I had seen players with worse injuries resist retirement and carry on. Rumours emerged within the dressing room that Shackleton had cut a deal with the club, one that would give him a full year's salary as a severance payment and the club insurance money for losing an important player to injury. I was not sure. There was not enough evidence with which to make a definitive judgement. I knew that Shackleton resented Brown and would never have flourished under him.

Having thought he was surviving only on pure natural ability and that Brown's philosophy of fitness above skill would negate the value of that natural ability, Shackleton realised that football at Roker Park could no longer be about random acts of poetry. Life under Brown would be painful and boring. Why risk becoming a cripple to play for an unpopular manager who made a virtue of prosaic pragmatism? If football could no longer be fun, why not try something else?

The next time I saw Shackleton he was a journalist, writing about the game in his own eloquent, inimitable way, and annoying the establishment as people like him were wont to do. He was a one-off and way ahead of his time; a 60s player, arguably, long before the 50s had ended.

Change was in the air. Our John, having performed with distinction for Rotherham United since signing professional forms in November 1945, left Millmoor to sign for Lincoln City in June 1957. He played 352 Football League matches for Rotherham, scoring 112 goals, and presented himself as one of the most beloved, loyal, and most talented players in the club's history. While he always loved the club, I think he resented it that the directors never offered him a testimonial for twelve years' service. Shackleton, meanwhile, was only granted his testimonial at Sunderland when he hinted he would reveal to the press details of the clubs' illegal payments to players.

A decline commensurate with our results

The scandal of the illegal payments cast a shadow over life at Roker Park. On pure reputation, we had a squad good enough to challenge for the First Division championship. On the pitch, where it mattered, we soon realised that 1957/58 would become a laborious fight against relegation. Away from Roker Park, there was not much sympathy for us, and critics expressed delight when our bubble burst.

Charlie Hurley, a talented central defender from Cork in Ireland, made his Sunderland debut away to Blackpool on 5 October – a 7-0 defeat. 'I could not have played worse if I tried,' he said. He probably wondered if he had been better off staying at Millwall, where life for him was more serene. He certainly had to be persuaded to sign for Sunderland, and I understand it took Alan Brown two long meetings and a decent lunch to convince him. Hurley took his time to flourish with Sunderland, but I do not think he helped himself by travelling back to London after each home match to see his girlfriend before travelling back to Sunderland on Sunday night. Big mistake. If you do not put down roots quickly your career can suffer. And, yet, in time, after many months of 'moping' – his word – Hurley would develop into one of Sunderland's all-time great players.

It was with him that I developed a system to win money at the bookmakers, based on what I had learnt during my time in Havercroft running a betting operation with my brothers. Hurley and I did well and banked a decent amount of money, but this was hardly a time to celebrate. Personally, I already began to feel that my career had reached a plateau, while Hurley told me that he hated moving from the life he loved in London.

We lost our next match, on 12 October, 6-0 away to Burnley, after which Hurley gave an interview to the local press. 'I'm no flop, says Charlie Hurley,' went the headline, and I felt sorry for him. Ron Routledge, Fred Chilton and Allan Graham would never again play for the club as Alan Brown decided that changes should be made quickly. Ambrose Fogarty, a slick midfield player from Limerick, made his debut away to Birmingham City on 9 November, a match we won 3-2 with two goals by Don Revie and one by Billy Bingham. At the turn of the year, however, the First Division table looked to everybody at Sunderland like a suicide note. We occupied 21st position in a league of 22 teams. Not that I looked at the newspapers much during the latter weeks of 1957. Match reports had nothing of value to a player suffering from defeat after defeat. We also lost 3-1 to Everton in an FA Cup third-round replay after extra time at Goodison Park.

The prevailing view within the dressing room was that Alan Brown's presence had created discordance out of harmony, anxiety out of tranquillity – but he and his strange ways were only part of the problem. The truth is that the balance was all wrong. It all felt so transitional. Both the financial scandal and Brown's methods had more effect on the team than they should have done.

The supporters had a right to feel disillusioned. But, for the most part, the fans who followed us regularly were exemplars of passion and loyalty, even if attendances did start to plummet. There really was a Roker Roar – a noise that could, on good days, send a shiver down your spine and give you an extra yard of pace.

Off the pitch, the players got along well. The poker sessions among us, especially on long away trips, became legendary. The stakes became higher and higher and some of us could lose an entire week's wages during a single away trip. When debts became really high, something like fifty quid or more, players would write IOUs and pay up in instalments. Don Revie always seemed to do well out of poker, Billy Bingham and I not so well.

Catalogue of imperfections

The Sunderland directors, more interested in stability than in success, seemed to absolve Alan Brown of any blame for our plight. The older players had a different view. It was obvious to me how little respect the likes of Billy Bingham and Don Revie had for the manager. Their experiences, personalities, seniority and modes of discourse were a threat to the obviously insecure Brown, but he was the man with the power. Although still only 24, I regarded myself as one of the more senior players, so I always felt I could never be a long-term solution for a manager keen on younger, more impressionable players.

Few of us could ever work out Brown. The first time I met him, when he strolled like an odour into Roker Park on his opening day in the job, he called me to one side and quizzed me about the other players in the squad.

'What do you think of Revie? Tell me about Shackleton? What do you think of Bingham?'

How else to answer but to extol the virtues of these extremely talented players?

I have no doubt that Brown asked other players the same questions. He seemed keen to spread the very anxiety that he was feeling personally. He seemed to walk around with a permanent smirk on his face, an arrogant smirk; a ploy, I believe, to impose himself on the senior players. He was sizing us up all the time, breeding tension and mistrust, dividing and ruling; treating adults like teenagers and teenagers like adults. I could not face working with him or playing for him. Suddenly, football felt like work and training felt like prison.

Perhaps his biggest mistake came in his first week when he asked four experienced players – Don Revie, Billy Elliott, Ray Daniel and Len Shackleton – to round up all the practice balls and bring them to the training pitch. Usually, the ground staff and youth-team players performed such tasks, but Brown had other ideas. He was asserting himself, sending out a signal about where the likes of Revie and Shackleton fitted into the new hierarchy at Sunderland.

Less than a month into the 1957/58 season, having found myself in the reserve team against Annfield Plain, I decided it was time to move on. I wanted a transfer, preferably to a club in the First Division but, more importantly, to a place where the atmosphere was conducive to good football. I discovered, too, that Willie Fraser, our Scotland international goalkeeper, also wanted a move. To make matters worse, Ray Daniel, our Wales international centre-half, admitted to feeling depressed that his career had ostensibly stalled. He was nostalgic for happier times at Arsenal. No doubt Brown could have dealt easily with two rebels and one unhappy player, but when nearly the entire first-team squad demanded a meeting with him, he must have realised that the grievances could no longer be ignored. I still have the *Sunday Express* press cutting from 9 September 1957 about the 'New Sunderland Sensation', with a somewhat overwrought report by Alec Johnson. 'Players see manager – two want a move', went the sub-heading:

New sensations come today from Soccer's most sensational team of them all – Sunderland. 1: Two of Sunderland's top-priced stars – Colin Grainger, the £23,000 England left winger, and Willie Fraser, the Scottish international goalkeeper, tell me they will ask for a transfer. 2: All the first-team players marched into manager Alan Brown's office last week for a showdown. They wanted to know if they would soon be forced to give way to the youngsters in Mr Brown's plan for the team's future. Manager Brown told them: 'Nothing like that is going to happen . . . for the moment.' And there the talks ended.

I told Johnson: 'The way things are at the moment, I do not feel happy at Sunderland and I shall ask for a transfer. The atmosphere among our players is more strained than it was during the trouble last season. I've been with Sunderland about six months and I still haven't got a house. The hotel is alright, but when you're married this set-up is no good. I have to travel all the way to Wakefield to see my wife – when I can. I've had a private talk about my housing problem but don't seem much nearer getting one. There's a young player on the first-team left wing at the moment and now that I've got over my injury maybe a move would be the best thing.'

I was the last person who wanted confrontation. Trouble, or even the hint of it, was not part of my nature. But Sunderland in 1957 was a club in transition, lurching from one crisis to another, and it was the seasoned professionals – those of us acquired at great cost, with big reputations – who seemed to pay the price for all of the uncertainty in the dressing room and mismanagement in the boardroom.

A week later, I gave an interview to Henry Rose of the *Daily Express* in which I made it clear that reserve-team football in the North Eastern League was anathema to me. 'I am disappointed at not being in the first team,' I said. 'It's no good to me being in the reserves. I haven't asked for a transfer and don't want to make any trouble, but I shall see what happens for the next match and maybe the one after. If I'm still fit and out of the First Division side, I shall have to do something about it in my own interests.' Rose's report described Brown as a 'stern disciplinarian', and quoted him as saying, 'I thought it best to give [Colin] a run out with the reserves', because he believed I had not had enough training after a spell out through injury.

In my mind I was still an England international – I did not know then that my international career was over – so to be playing in the North Eastern League was sobering and worrying. But my concern was not born of arrogance or of a blow to my ego; on the contrary, it was born of a feeling that playing under Brown could only do my career and my private life harm. I returned to the first team for the match at home to Bolton Wanderers on 18 September – a 2-1 defeat.

What little respect most of the older players had for Brown disappeared on a Friday morning in January 1958 when our groundsman decided that the Roker Park pitch was too frosty for training. Brown told us, 'I want you to follow me in your cars to the beach.' On arrival, he forced us to change into our underwear and beckoned us into the North Sea. For twenty-odd minutes we swam in the coldest, least inviting water known to mankind. One of the lads caught a particularly bad dose of flu, which, for reasons unknown to us, Brown found amusing. On another occasion, a Friday, he told us to follow him in our cars to a field in Durham. He ordered us to go for a walk for twenty minutes, after which he said, 'Right lads, that's it. See you tomorrow.'

I could just about cope with a North Sea swim in January and a useless walk in a Durham field. But my relationship with Brown all but disintegrated when I went into his office one afternoon and found his secretary sitting on his lap. Suffice it to say she was not typing up one of his letters. Worse, they did not even attempt to conceal their intimacy. Both of them just smiled, their pride at being caught serving only to exaggerate my embarrassment. I walked out of the office, shaking my head, and came to the conclusion that Brown could never have enough human qualities to compensate for his catalogue of imperfections. It was not so much the affair with his secretary that bothered me. Affairs were widespread in the game, especially among many older players. It was the juxtaposition of Brown's infidelity alongside his constant moralising that I despised. Such hypocrisy never sat well with me.

And yet, often inadvertently, occasionally deliberately, Brown could provide humour, or at least find himself at the centre of it. In this golden age of smoking, he was the consummate anti-smoker who banned anything relating to tobacco. By contrast, John Watters, the club physio, was rarely to be seen without a pipe. He was a source of smells and you could tell a mile off when he was coming into the dressing room because a cloud of smoke would precede him. Once, after training, Watters was puffing away out of the dressing room window when somebody shouted, 'Quick, Johnny, Alan Brown is on his way.' Acting with too much haste, Watters put the smoking pipe inside his tracksuit pocket and tried to act all innocent when Brown arrived. There was no concealing the smell and there was no concealing Watters' discomfiture, which created a humorous tension. Clearly realising what was happening, Brown kept Watters talking, asking questions to which he had no interest in the answers, while the pipe burnt away in Watters' tracksuit pocket. Eventually, Watters disappeared under a cloud of smoke and everybody, even Brown, fell about laughing. It was a rare moment of camaraderie between the manager, his coaching staff, and his entire first-team squad.

To compensate for Brown's dourness, we had, as first-team coach, George Curtis, a former Southampton, Arsenal and Valenciennes inside-right, who went by the nickname of 'Twinkletoes', apparently because of the way he played. When we did ball work in training, it was with Curtis, who loved his five-a-side matches and often played in them. It was he who organised golf days, often on a Monday, at the South Shields club. Stan Anderson and Don Revie were excellent, playing off low handicaps. Curtis would manage the Norway national team in the 70s, without success. He spent the last years of his life living alone in a Chelmsford trailer park, until dying, aged 84, in 2004.

I counted it as a privilege to play alongside Anderson and Revie. Anderson was already well on the way to becoming a Sunderland legend but he was more than a good football player. He was, like Revie, a natural leader and a man of great curiosity. Always looking to the future, he trained to become a joiner in case his playing career never took off. He also played the piano to a high standard. One evening, Doreen and I had a meal with Anderson and his wife, Marjorie, at their house. He begged me to sing for everybody. I only agreed if he accompanied me on his piano. I sang 'Two Different Worlds', the Frisch-Wayne number that had been a popular hit in 1956 and was part of my professional repertoire. Later in the evening, Anderson told me of his plans to set up a new business based on his favourite hobby: a golfing range. 'Do you fancy coming into it with me, Colin?' Yes, I replied, and I was serious. I was willing to invest my own money into his passion but he never mentioned the idea again. Perhaps the uncertainty of life at Roker Park precluded risk.

Once I had alerted Alan Brown to my frustration at living in a hotel, in autumn 1957, I rented the club house at No. 1 Bywell Avenue, Sunderland for £1 per week. For the first time, Doreen and I, plus Colin junior, were living together as a family.

The arrangement provided a sense of personal security and well-being and a welcome retreat from the tedium of life under Brown. Football was still a fantasy world for me, but now I was beginning to see and feel harsh realities around every corner. I realised, however, one immutable fact: if I wanted to see the rainbow, I had to experience the rain. A true professional cannot divorce the joy of playing at Wembley for England against Brazil from the frustration of playing in the North Eastern League for Sunderland reserves against Annfield Plain. Two extremes – and perhaps the essence of my career lay somewhere in between.

My right ankle was starting to hurt; and although I continued to do extra sprint training in my spare time, nature was revealing to me for the first time the benefits of rest and preparation. Physiotherapy was useless and rudimentary in those days, and the heat lamp and massages did little to ease the swelling in the joint. Only time could heal. But I was impatient. Young men always are.

I guess I just miss my friend

'Colin! Colin! It's Malcolm.'

6 February 1958. Another relaxing afternoon. Another phone call. Another journalist at the other end of the line.

'Colin. Have you heard the news about Manchester United?'

It was Malcolm Usher, a Newcastle-based reporter whom I knew well and to whom I would often pass on little tales, snippets of inside news, in exchange for three or four quid at a time. But this time his quivering voice, so unlike him, portended bad news.

'United's plane has crashed on take-off after refuelling in Munich. Some of the players have died.'

At unnatural speed, the blood drained from my face, and I considered the implications of this beloved team – the Busby Babes, one of the best in the world at that time – disintegrating in the worst possible way. I thought of the injustice. I thought of the horror. I thought of my two friends: Duncan Edwards and Tommy Taylor. Had they survived?

Taylor died instantly; Edwards would battle on for a short time.

I struggled to reconcile Taylor's demise with the charming boy I remembered meeting on a cricket pitch in Barnsley in the 40s; I struggled to reconcile my mental image of Edwards, lying in a hospital bed, hovering between life and death, with the endearing young man whom I'd got to know so well on England international duty. I cast my mind back to that time when he and I went into a lingerie shop in London, drunk on happiness, when he held up a saucy pair of knickers and said, 'A gift for the lady.' I wanted to laugh. I wanted to cry.

Legend has it that while recovering at the Rechts der Isar Hospital, Munich, he asked Jimmy Murphy, the United assistant manager, 'What time's the kick-off against Wolves?' Such was his thirst for life and his force of personality.

Duncan Edwards fought the good fight but the artificial kidney designed to keep him alive zapped him of vital strength when he needed it most. He slipped away fifteen days after the crash, aged just 21, mourned throughout the game, and all set to be venerated in death. My world collapsed. He was a link to my youth and a physical manifestation of my football dreams. We all wanted to be Duncan Edwards. A colossus had gone and the game would never be the same again.

Debilitated and traumatised, Manchester United endured a time of confusion and transition, as Jimmy Murphy, taking control of the players while Matt Busby recovered in hospital, sought to put together a team for the FA Cup tie at Old Trafford against Sheffield Wednesday. Preparations were so challenging, with key decisions over team selection taking place right up to the last minute, that the official programme for the match left the United starting line-up blank. An attendance of 59,848 witnessed United's 3-0 victory on a night of high emotion that made news all over the world.

It was in March 1958 that I received a telephone call from Tom Holley, the former Sunderland and Leeds United centre-half, who was now, aged 44, a journalist for the *Yorkshire Evening Post* and an unofficial player agent. A one-time Leeds United teammate of Dennis Grainger, my cousin, Holley had become one of the best-connected men in the game, so a call from him could only be momentous.

'Colin, do you fancy signing for Manchester United?'

It turned out that Holley was helping United recruit players during this problematical period and he felt that I, ostensibly still an England international, could offer experience, knowledge and speed. A move to Old Trafford would have been a step forward from the relegation battle that was afflicting us at Sunderland. And I did not much enjoy playing for Alan Brown. But I rejected Holley's advances for various reasons, most notably that I felt I should not benefit directly from the tragedy that deprived me of two good friends. Had I moved to Old Trafford, I might have played in the 1958 FA Cup final for United against Bolton Wanderers at Wembley. I might have flourished under Matt Busby and alongside Bobby Charlton. I might have lasted long enough to have played alongside George Best. But my job during that dark period was to help Sunderland in the battle to avoid relegation.

When I did visit Old Trafford in the spring of 1958 it was as a Sunderland player: 4 April, a 2-2 draw in front of 47,421 spectators, a result that kept us one place above the relegation zone. The official programme for the match had the headline on the cover, 'United say thank you to Munich', which summed up the extent of the goodwill towards the stricken club.

But all I could think of was how abnormal it felt playing against a United team that lacked the virtuosity and charm of Tommy Taylor and Duncan Edwards. I had got on so well with Edwards during our days together as England internationals that I believe we would have kept in touch long after our playing careers had come to an end. He could have been the England captain at the 1966 World Cup. He would surely have become the greatest English player of all. Maybe he is anyway.

Death made him forever an icon. In his short years, he lived long. And though the cultural theorists and football historians keep him alive and fresh and relevant, it feels wrong that he is no longer here to absorb the applause of his youth.

As for me, I guess I just miss my friend.

Dark age

A big club with big-name players, Sunderland FC was suffering from an identity crisis. The dichotomy between our reputation and our results created a sense of confusion in the dressing room. We should not have been surprised. After all, our regular No. 10 began the season going by the name of Alan Hope and ended it going by the name of Alan O'Neill. We never had a settled team, with too many changes and too many new signings. George Whitelaw, a large Scot, arrived from St Johnstone in late winter 1957 and seemed to have the physical presence we needed up front. But he was from a different century. He looked like a caveman, had little knowledge of how to use a knife and fork, and seemed permanently confused. He would bring his boots wrapped up in brown paper and tied up with string. When he smiled, it was to reveal a set of teeth that had suffered from some frightful dentistry. Whitelaw was a charming enough bloke and he stuck to me like glue, not because of my personality but, rather, because I had a good car.

A 3-1 defeat to Manchester City on 12 April all but ensured relegation for Sunderland. We went into the final match away to Portsmouth needing a 14-0 victory to guarantee safety and send Portsmouth down instead, although results elsewhere could also have preserved our top-flight status. We won 2-0, with both goals by our most recent signing, Don Kichenbrand, a South African who had won the Scottish League Championship with Rangers two years earlier. A great physical specimen, if a touch awkward with his running style, he went by the nickname of 'Rhino'. Sometimes we called him 'Kitchen Sink'.

'Throw everything at the Kitchen Sink', Sunderland supporters would chant. And we did.

And as I lay in the bath afterwards, I still had hope. A defeat for Leicester City away to Birmingham City would have saved us, but Leicester won 1-0. The manager of Leicester was David Halliday, a Sunderland goalscoring legend from the 20s, whose emotions must have been all over the place. We would also have stayed up had Burnley defeated Newcastle United 40-something-nil. It would be the first time in history that Sunderland would compete outside the top division of the Football League. I could not have known, of course, that this match away to Portsmouth would be the last I would ever play in the First Division. I had suffered relegation with Sheffield United but this felt far worse. With a squad containing Stan Anderson, Billy Bingham, Billy Elliott, Don Revie, and Charlie Hurley, we should have done far better. But Alan Brown was never sure whether to play Revie as a deep-lying centre forward or in a traditional, more advanced role. Perhaps the tactical change was one reason why Revie was less authoritative than he had been with Manchester City. One formed the view that he was coming towards the end of his career, even though he had not long turned thirty and was still relatively fit. Perhaps he, too, suffered for the changes at Roker Park.

Brown relied too often on young players who, though talented and full of potential, were not ready for a season of penury near the bottom of the First Division. We were shy and inconsistent in front of goal. We were even worse at the back, conceding 97 goals and revealing a surprising uncertainty. Training was a bore, with more emphasis on fitness than on ball work and tactics. And attendances were diminishing. Perhaps Len Shackleton, a man of great prescience, knew what was coming and got out at the right time. But already his era felt part of a distant past. Sunderland FC was entering its first dark age.

Youth was everywhere

If I needed a reminder that I might already have gone beyond my peak as a player it was when the letters from Walter Winterbottom stopped coming. He had left me out of the England squad for the World Cup qualifying matches in May 1957 against Republic of Ireland at Wembley, Denmark in Copenhagen, and Republic of Ireland in Dublin. During the 1957/58 campaign, England played six matches, but I never heard a thing from Winterbottom. In those days, the only contact you had with a national-team coach was if you had made the squad.

Now I was out of contention, ostensibly forever, Winterbottom had no need to keep in touch with me. Did it upset me? Professionally, yes – especially with the 1958 World Cup in Sweden around the corner. Personally, no – because I understood how the systems and processes worked, and I knew that my ankle problem had taken the edge off my game. Every ache in my body told me that I was older as a football player than I was as a human being. Losing a yard of pace in the First Division did not affect me too much but at international level it was crucial. Apparently I was one of the thirty players from whom the England manager would select his 22-man World Cup squad, but the players were already in Sweden by the time I realised I was one of the eight not to make the cut.

The outside-left for England was Alan A'Court, a blond-haired, diminutive bundle of energy who played for Liverpool, then in the Second Division. While I liked A'Court and rated him as a player and as a gentleman, I felt at the time I had more to offer an England team going into the World Cup. I was more experienced, faster, and had already shown I could play at that level. But Walter Winterbottom ostensibly did not want to take players to Sweden whom he believed were not 100 per cent fit. Had Winterbottom asked me, I would have told him I was fit enough.

Aware that the time was out of joint for me and that my international career was already at a crossroads, I watched the 1958 World Cup on television at home in Bywell Avenue with great interest and greater frustration. The grainy images flashing from our tiny screen, which revealed established players like Garrincha and new players like Pelé, were no substitute for being there in person. Billy

Bingham, my Sunderland colleague, performed well for Northern Ireland as they reached the quarter-finals, going down to France. But Bingham was out of the equation at Roker Park and was already considering a move to Luton Town. And who should win the tournament? Why, Brazil, of course; a younger, quicker Brazil, admittedly, from the one against whom I scored twice in England's 4-2 victory two years earlier.

My past was starting to feel more exciting than my future. I withdrew into myself a little and spent more time thinking than I had ever done when my career was going well. I philosophised, examined and debated the game in my mind. To those of an introspective nature, counterfactuals are a great way to analyse the history of football. Would England have won the World Cup had there been a tournament in 1956? Would I have made the squad? Would England have won the 1958 World Cup had the Munich crash not ravaged the Manchester United team? There were not many squads to match England in 1956. We defeated a Brazil team not yet mature and a West Germany team probably too mature. Amid political turmoil, Hungary had fallen from the heights of 1953. France were great going forward but not so great defensively. Perhaps Sweden, with Nils Liedholm and Gunnar Gren, two supremely intelligent and talented schemers in midfield, and coached expertly by George Raynor, were the team to watch. Even without their best players, they stopped us from performing in Stockholm during our European tour, securing a goalless draw that flattered England. With Liedholm and Gren, they might have proved too sophisticated and tactically adept for England's direct style, especially within the intense environment of a World Cup tournament. By 1958, Brazil had found a system to accommodate Zito, Pelé and Garrincha, and they took the game to a new level, defeating Sweden 5-2 in the final in Stockholm.

Youth was everywhere. I was already beginning to feel old.

I had to remind myself that I was still only 25.

Twinkling tootsies

On 20 February 1958, *The Stage* magazine reported that I had signed a contract with M.C.A. for a £250-per-week, ten-week variety tour during the summer. During the tour, I acquired the latest copy of *Record Mail* and found a photograph of myself on the cover, with an accompanying article:

SONG BOW BY SOCCER STAR

Sunderland's Colin Grainger Scores with First Record

Colin Grainger, star Sunderland footballer who has been seven times capped for England, has made his debut on records as a singer of 'pop' songs. The titles – 'Are You' and 'This I know' HMV-POP-484. Colin, an outside-left who was transferred to Sunderland last year for a fee of £23,000, first became interested in singing after seeing the Al Jolson life-story film. He first sang in public in May 1956 – in a hotel cabaret in Finland while on tour with England.

In September 1956, he made his first stage appearance in the country when he sang at the Sheffield Empire one night with the Hilltoppers vocal group. A spot on Winifred Atwell's TV show followed, and three weeks' variety in Sunderland, Middlesbrough and Sheffield. On two occasions he stood in for singer Ronnie Hilton with the Cyril Stapleton Show Band Show at Newcastle – one night when Ronnie was appearing in a Royal Command Variety Performance, the next when he was unwell. Then he appeared in Eric Robinson's Roundabout TV show.

Colin, who lives at Fulwell, Sunderland, was born at Havercroft, near Wakefield, on June 10 1934. Favourite singers – Ronnie Hilton, Perry Como. Hobbies – golf, athletics, cricket and gramophone records. Ambitions? 'Well,' says Colin. 'I would certainly like to continue both careers – soccer and singing – for as long as I possibly can.'

Record Mail, *Volume 1, number 6: June 1958*

It was while filling in for Ronnie Hilton in Newcastle that somebody introduced me to Des O'Connor, then a young comedian, who had previously played part-time professional football for Northampton Town before becoming a shoe salesman. He was intrigued that I could balance football and singing and I was intrigued at his confidence, which I knew would take him far.

No longer part of the international equation, no longer enjoying my football under Alan Brown, I took solace in my growing reputation as a singer. My dual role was now defining my identity. I was the 'Singing Winger', or 'The voice with a kick in it', or the 'Singing Footballer'. The Madison Confectionary company of London published a set of 48 Disc Jockey collectors' cards. Among the likes of Johnny Mathis, Perry Como, Frankie Vaughan, Frankie Laine, Pat Boone, Debbie Reynolds, Harry Belafonte, Lonnie Donegan, and Elvis Presley was a young man from Havercroft called Colin Grainger.

One popular culture magazine published a feature on actors and singers who had also flourished in sport. Johnny Mathis, a singer par excellence, had been a high-school high-jump champion. Althea Gibson, the brilliant African-American double Wimbledon tennis champion, was due to make a movie with John Wayne and Bill Holden. Dean Martin, a former welterweight boxer, was now 'slaying folk with his velvety vocals'. Toni Dalli, by now a personal friend, was the 'soulful serenader' who was road-walking champion aged seventeen. Primo Carnera, the former heavy-weight boxing champion, was 'a natural for Cinescope', having secured a role in the film, *A Kid for Two Farthings*. The article described me as the 'England outside-left' who has been 'scoring with his voice, as well as his twinkling tootsies'.

There were three official Colin Grainger fan clubs, in Newcastle, Sunderland and Manchester, each run by an enthusiastic part-time secretary. By the summer of 1958, fan mail was reaching the fifty-letters-per-week mark, and Doreen would help me reply to the requests for autographs and basic information about my hair colour, eye colour, and favourite breakfast. Fans asked how they could meet me, some even calling at our house at No. 1 Bywell Avenue. The more forward among the fan-club members would ask for stuff like handkerchiefs and tiepins, but we could never oblige unless the letter came with a postal order for the appropriate amount.

While I was nowhere near the millionaire bracket (no football player was in those days, not even Stanley Matthews), I was doing well enough to buy myself a Riley Pathfinder, the car in which I took my test and passed first time. The car cost £400, a big saving on the retail price of £1,200. To some people, it resembled a funeral car, but with its slick leather seats and speed – it could reach 100 miles per hour – it felt great to drive. Doreen's indulgence was more modest: a boxer dog called Vicky.

Len Young had done a great job fixing me up with regular work. The most lucrative was the week at the Hippodrome in Manchester, where I shared the bill with the Kaye Sisters, one of whom, Carol, was now Young's wife. The Kaye Sisters consisted of three unrelated women: Carol Young, Shan Palmer, and Sheila Jones.

Wearing matching suits and matching blond hairstyles, they hit the big time in 1957 when they appeared with Judy Garland at the Royal Variety Show and earned themselves a spot on *The Ed Sullivan Show* in the United States. Their eyes sparkled, their hair seemed immovable, and their teeth were so clean and white that bacteria could surely not survive anywhere in the same room as these delightful women. I drew confidence just from being in their company, although they were so down to earth that I never felt uncomfortable. The beauty of having Young as my manager was that he put me into all sorts of environments, with various celebrities and every conceivable type of entertainer. One night at the Sheffield Empire, I shared the bill with the Old Mother Riley music-hall act, starring Roy Rolland. Essentially a drag act, Old Mother Riley was a novelty that transcended theatre to become an ongoing film franchise. Life was so agreeable that when it came to pre-season training in July 1958, my heart sank. The thought of Alan Brown filled me with indifference.

An awkward bugger

I made history on 23 August 1958, scoring Sunderland's first goal ever outside the top flight. It was a dubious accomplishment. We lost 3-1 to Lincoln City at Sincil Bank and never got going. On 27 September, a 2-1 defeat away to Bristol Rovers sent Sunderland to the bottom of the Second Division. Everywhere I turned I saw players I barely recognised. Len Ashurst, a teenaged Liverpudlian left-back, had arrived from Prescot Cables and oozed energy and commitment but not necessarily style; not then, at least. An apprentice printer, he made his debut during that difficult autumn in place of Billy Elliott, a former England international outside-left, whom Alan Brown had converted briefly, and unsuccessfully, from a half-back into a left-back. I never really had much to do with Ashurst socially but we never worked well together on the pitch. Brown made it clear that I should play in a withdrawn role, primarily to support Ashurst. I felt sure that Joe Mercer at Sheffield United or Bill Murray during my early days at Sunderland would have encouraged Ashurst to support me. For the first time in my career, I had defensive responsibilities. Brown also had a similar plan for Stan Anderson, deterring him from the desire to play through midfield and instead ordering him to perform as a one-dimensional stopper; essentially, a defensive midfield player, shorn of all responsibility to be creative. If Anderson did not like it, he could always play for the reserves.

Times they were a-changing.

Brown's desire for youth manifested itself in severe changes. Having turned down a move to Middlesbrough, his hometown club, Don Revie scored for Sunderland in a 4-0 victory away to Rotherham United on 22 November and then, a few days later, signed for Leeds United. The surprise was not that Revie left but, rather, that he had stayed so long playing for Alan Brown. The two men could barely stand each other. Their personalities clashed. Their ideas about football clashed. And it could not have helped that Revie was starting to feel insecure about his future.

George Whitelaw, the caveman, took his unsophisticated style to the sophistication of London's West End by signing for Queens Park Rangers. Jack Hedley, the right-back, left Roker Park after a decade of stable performances to sign for Gateshead in the Third Division North; an unfortunate move, for Gateshead would slip into non-League football by the summer of 1960. Colin Nelson, a teenager from Boldon, replaced Hedley. A new goalkeeper, Peter Wakeham, arrived from Torquay United to replace Willie Fraser, who went to Nottingham Forest. I had to hand it to Alan Brown. While I had little regard for him as a person, I admired how much travelling he did in his spare time trying to secure new players. He went to Torquay in person to sign Wakeham. 'The north-east seemed bleak and far away,' Wakeham said, but Sunderland represented a forward step for a player keen to maximise his potential. He kept a clean sheet on his debut against Grimsby Town on 1 November 1958 – a 1-0 victory – and stayed at Roker Park until 1962.

Sunderland signed Ernie Taylor from Manchester United in December 1958 for £6,000, which brought back memories of when I attended the 1953 FA Cup final at Wembley and saw him perform splendidly for Blackpool against Bolton Wanderers. He also played against Bolton in the 1958 FA Cup final, this time for United, but ended up on the losing side. I welcomed his move to Sunderland. He was a marvellous player, full of speed and intelligent passes, and remarkably strong for a man of just 5ft 4in. He was aged 33 when he moved to Roker Park and already showing the signs of a player coming towards the end of his career. For starters, he was reluctant to train hard. On Fridays, when Alan Brown allowed us the freedom to train whichever way we wanted, Taylor would always put on his spikes to give the impression he was planning some serious sprinting. Not a bit of it. He would walk about, talking to players, hoping nobody would notice that he was not actually doing anything.

Whenever we travelled to a hotel before an away match, Taylor and I would share a room. The experience was rarely pleasant. Although I enjoyed his conversation and found him engaging company, I took an instant dislike to his chain-smoking and his penchant for drinking copious amounts of Newcastle Brown Ale. On the occasions I went to his house, he would have crates of Brown Ale piled up behind his armchair, the source of which I had no idea. 'Fancy a bottle, Colin?' I was never much of a drinker, but even on a good evening, knocking back a couple of bottles, I would never have made a dent in his stash of alcohol. Alcohol would have hindered me. It seemed to help him. Surprisingly, given his range of skills and his ability to bring other players into the game, he only played one match for England – the cataclysmic 6-3 defeat to Hungary at Wembley in 1953. He was the reason for an improvement in results, with Sunderland moving from twentieth position in mid-December and into a more comfortable spot.

No time for rehearsals

It was early evening on Tuesday 24 February 1959 when Kirk Stevens, the Scottish singer, telephoned me from his digs at Salem Hill South, Sunderland. I was just tucking into my evening meal before heading out to see him perform on the same bill as the Barry Sisters, the New York-based jazz duet, at the Sunderland Empire.

'Colin, is there any chance you can cover for me tonight?'

'Uh?'

Stevens was suffering with bronchial problems that caused him to lose his voice and affected his chest, the severity of the illness being so great that a doctor told him to pull out of his entire residency. He had done his Monday show but his cold got worse, so there was no hope he could perform again. I agreed to do the show, mainly because Stevens was such a good friend. There was no time for rehearsals, however. I wolfed down my meal and got to the Empire, performing five numbers towards the end of the first half. There was no way I could deputise for the week. Alan Brown would not have allowed it. The next day I was back in training with Sunderland to prepare for the match at home to Huddersfield Town

My father, Daniel, and my mother, Lily, in the back garden of our home at 10 West Street, Havercroft. They supported me every step of my journey. [AUTHOR'S PERSONAL COLLECTION]

With the Ryhill School football team in 1947. I am first on the right kneeling down. [AUTHOR'S PERSONAL COLLECTION]

I was also a keen cricketer. I am on the front row second from left with our school team. [AUTHOR'S PERSONAL COLLECTION]

With my school mates, Curly Worby and Derek Belcher, in Blackpool, 1950. I had already signed for Wrexham by this stage. [AUTHOR'S PERSONAL COLLECTION]

In the famous Green Beret of the Royal Air Force. I would spend two years in the RAF from 1951 to 1953 for my National Service and was stationed at Odiham in Hampshire. [AUTHOR'S PERSONAL COLLECTION]

At the Racecourse Ground during my Wrexham days. This was a photo I sent back home to Mum, Dad, brothers John, Eric, Horace, and sister Lily in Havercroft. [AUTHOR'S PERSONAL COLLECTION]

Pictured with my pals in Wrexham, my first Football League Club. I joined Wrexham at 17 and only played five league games over three years, but my experiences there and in the RAF helped to shape me as a footballer and a person. [AUTHOR'S PERSONAL COLLECTION]

Jumping as if on springs, eyes firmly on the ball, I head for goal during Sheffield United's 2-0 win over Tottenham Hotspur in September 1955. [COLORSPORT]

With leg muscles that could only have come from hours of extra training, I use my pace to good effect for Sheffield United against Portsmouth, November 1955. [COLORSPORT]

Playing for the Football League Representative XI, 1956. Although our side included luminaries such as Johnny Haynes, Tommy Taylor, Jimmy Armfield and Ronnie Clayton, we lost 5-2 at Windsor Park to a side picked from the Irish League. [AUTHOR'S PERSONAL COLLECTION]

Slotting the ball home on my England debut against Brazil at Wembley, May 1956. Brazil's goalkeeper, Gilmar, looks on. My life would change beyond recognition. [PA]

My confidence soaring and England now dominant, I scored a second goal – England's fourth – in a 4-2 victory. A dream debut. Two years later, Brazil would win the World Cup. [PA]

Lining up with my England teammates in the Olympiastadion, Berlin ahead of our clash with the World Cup-holders, West Germany, in 1956. I would score the second goal in a 3-1 win, my third and last for my country. [AUTHOR'S PERSONAL COLLECTION]

Falling to the floor as I clip the ball beyond the reach of West Germany's goalkeeper Fritz Herkenrath in England's 3-1 victory in Berlin. This was a golden period in my life and the height of my fame as a footballer. [AUTHOR'S PERSONAL COLLECTION]

Having emerged in mid-1956 as an England international and a semi-professional singer, the hard work for 1956/57 with Sheffield United in the Second Division begins away from the public eye. [COLORSPORT]

One of my early singing performances at the Empire Theatre in Sheffield, September 1956. I could have quit my £15-a-week job in football to make £5,000 each year on stage. But I always preferred to be one man of eleven in the football stadium. [MIRRORPIX]

On England duty prior to the match against Northern Ireland, October 1956. Right to left, Tommy Taylor, Duncan Edwards, me, Albert Quixall, Roger Byrne, Dennis Viollet, and Tom Curry (Manchester United trainer). Taylor, Edwards, Byrne and Curry would die in Munich in 1958. [AUTHOR'S PERSONAL COLLECTION]

The England team to face Ireland at Windsor Park. I am on the front row, first on the right. The game would finish 1-1 and it would prove to be my last away game in an England shirt. [AUTHOR'S PERSONAL COLLECTION]

Surrounded by 100,000 spectators, I find myself alone with my thoughts as England play Wales at Wembley Stadium, November 1956. [COLORSPORT]

With Jim Iley, my good friend,
teammate and brother-in-law, in 1957.
[AUTHOR'S PERSONAL COLLECTION]

The smile is for the photographer.
But all I feel is anxiety. The train journey
from Sheffield to Sunderland, for talks
about a move to Roker Park, represents
the end of my career with Sheffield United.
[MIRRORPIX]

Sharing a joke with Mercer and the Sunderland director, Ernest Graham, after travelling up
from Sheffield to discuss a proposed move in February 1957. I act happy, but I feel uncertain.
[MIRRORPIX]

My first game for Sunderland, against Tottenham Hotspur at White Hart Lane in the league, February 1957. We would lose 5-2 but, over the next few weeks, played well enough to avoid relegation. [PA]

The Singing Winger.
While on international duty with England in 1957, I take time out to exercise my voice. [MIRRORPIX]

Training with my England teammates at White Hart Lane, April 1957. [PA]

Training with Ray Barlow at White Lane before our clash with Scotland, April 1957. [PA]

With the legendary Trinidadian pianist, Winifred Atwell, in preparation for a BBC television appearance in 1957. Atwell insured her fingers for £40,000. But it was her smile that captivated me. [AUTHOR'S PERSONAL COLLECTION]

With the Sunderland team ahead of the 1957/58 season. I felt privileged to be in the company of some brilliant players on the front row (left to right): Len Shackleton, Don Revie, Stan Anderson, Jack Hedley, me and Alan O'Neill. [MIRRORPIX]

Performing at the Manchester Hippodrome, June 1958. I was on the same bill as the Kaye sisters, all of whom would become friends. [AUTHOR'S PERSONAL COLLECTION]

Pictured with the Kaye sisters on the same evening in Manchester. [AUTHOR'S PERSONAL COLLECTION]

My wife, Doreen, and my son, Colin junior, listen to my new pop record at our family home, January 1960. [MIRRORPIX]

Pictured on the front row, far right, with my Leeds United teammates during my only full season at the club, 1960/61. Though we would only finish fourteenth in Division Two, good things were about to happen to the club. Under Don Revie (the player-manager here, pictured in the middle of the front row) Leeds would flourish for a decade from the mid-1960s. You might also spot a young Jack Charlton behind him, who would also prove crucial to their renaissance. [AUTHOR'S PERSONAL COLLECTION]

Port Vale, 1962. I am on the back row, second in from the right. My three years at Vale Park coincided with the peak of my singing career. These, however, were injury-plagued years on the pitch. [MIRRORPIX]

I wasn't the only one in my dressing rooms who enjoyed a singalong. Here I am performing in the showers with Alick Jeffrey, a Doncaster Rovers legend whom I encountered late in my career at Belle Vue. [MIRRORPIX]

My daughter, Kim, my grandson, Christian and his daughter, Avabella, at Christian's graduation.
[AUTHOR'S PERSONAL COLLECTION]

on the Saturday. Danny Purches, the Surrey-born singer, covered Stevens for the rest of the week and was a worthy replacement. I envied him.

Against nature

We defeated Huddersfield Town 1-0 but I broke my collarbone and missed five matches, not returning to the starting line-up until the trip to Barnsley on 4 April. John Watters, the Sunderland physio, drove me to hospital, where a doctor put my arm in a sling and told me not to drive a car for a month. My prized Riley Pathfinder looked forlorn parked outside my house. The timing of my injury was terrible, the rehabilitation painful, and I began to wonder if I was cursed. I had been enjoying a relatively good season from a personal point of view, with much attention surrounding the possibility that I might return to the England team. The arrival of Len Ashurst might have added to my responsibilities on the left flank but the arrival of Taylor made everything feel like fun again. He provided the craft for Sunderland that Jimmy Hagan provided for Sheffield United during my time at Bramall Lane.

'Grainger can stake new England claim: Ernie Taylor playing vital part for winger,' Malcolm Usher had written on 5 January 1959. 'Outside-left is still one of soccer's top problem spots – even for the England selectors who already this season have called twice on Tom Finney, of Preston, and one on Alan A'Court, of Liverpool. Finney played against Ireland and Russia, A'Court against Wales. A'Court also played for the Football League against the Irish League, and Burnley's Brian Pilkington against the Scottish League. But before long, surely the England selectors will have to consider again Colin Grainger, who cost Sunderland £17,000 [sic] and has been capped seven times. On Saturday, despite a treacle-toffee pitch at Liverpool, Grainger completely eclipsed A'Court for speed, positional play, wing thrusts and strength in moving the ball. In fact, for me, he was easily the game's best forward. Yet this is not one isolated instance of Grainger returning to his old form. He has been progressively improving since the arrival of Ernie Taylor – the finest partner Grainger has ever had at Roker Park.'

The *Sunday Graphic* on 18 January published an interview with me:

I had no confidence at all last season. You know, it's very important for a winger to have the confidence to hold the ball and beat his man.

Otherwise you are wanting to get rid of the ball almost before you get it,
which is what I was doing until recently. Now I really think I'm getting
back to my [Sheffield] United form. And Ernie Taylor must take a lot of
the credit. As soon as he came to us from Manchester United, I realised
that this kind of service suited me down to the ground. Another cap?
Well, that's been my ambition right from the start of the season and I'm
keeping my fingers crossed.

I saw similarities between Taylor and Len Shackleton, but Taylor was easier to play with and more of a team player; a bit less selfish. There was no doubting that Alan Brown had signed some talented young players – there was a new energy on the pitch at Roker Park – but also that Taylor, then in his early 30s, was both the heartbeat and the brain of the entire operation. Think of the queen bee and you get some idea of how important he was in 1958/59. Without him, Sunderland would almost certainly have slipped into the semi-obscurity of the Third Division.

Sheffield Wednesday won the Second Division to secure promotion to the top flight, reviving the Steel City Derby matches against Sheffield United. Wednesday triumphed without my friend, Albert Quixall, who had signed for Manchester United, but they did have a centre-half touched by magic: Peter Swan, a Yorkshireman destined for England honours – and, as we shall see, for notoriety.

Shackleton and I became acquainted again on an April afternoon in 1959 for his testimonial match at Roker Park: Sunderland versus a Shackleton XI. The Shackleton team read like a Who's Who of the game's mavericks and visionaries: Don Revie, Roy Bentley, Tommy Docherty, Jackie Milburn, Johnny Haynes, and a young centre-forward called Brian Clough, who could strike a ball hard and cleanly and who had huge confidence and a mouth to match. Although I'd heard of Clough, who was making waves with his excellent strike rate at Middlesbrough, I did not know much about him. Some players pronounced his surname 'Clow' rather than 'Cluff'. I soon learnt, however, that even within the milieu of a muted testimonial, he could be an awkward bugger; a *sui generis* individual who was not universally well-liked. How could we have known that Shackleton would influence Clough as a young manager in the 60s and that, in the 70s, Clough and Revie would fall out very publicly?

I found it interesting and surprising to discover that my cousin, Edwin Holliday, the Middlesbrough outside-left, regarded Clough as an ally and good friend. In terms of personality, they were opposites. Unsurprisingly, given his idiosyncrasies and insecurities, Clough could be cruel – especially regarding any perceived weakness. For example, Edwin Holliday could become nervous before matches and would often go to the toilet before the kick-off, which Clough found amusing. 'Eh, Ed, I hope you've washed your hands this time,' Clough shouted on one occasion as my cousin returned to the dressing room. With Clough, you never knew if he was playing the bully or just engaging in his odd version of dressing-room banter.

I was less surprised to discover that Clough and Alan Brown rated each other highly and glowed in each other's company; indeed, way into the future, once old age had encouraged rumination, Clough would speak fondly of how much Brown influenced him.

Brown's influence on me was of the negative kind, although I did not feel so bad about it in 1958/59, now that I was producing my best form in a Sunderland shirt and being linked with a return to the England team. I flourished not because of him but in spite of him.

But I did not make the national team squad for the summer 1959 matches in the Americas against Brazil, Peru, Mexico and the United States. If Walter Winterbottom had written me a letter, the postman certainly never posted it. My international career was over, consigned to the history books; and, of course, the souvenirs – the shirts, the caps, the press cuttings, the memories – could not compensate for the fact that the eighth cap I sought never did come. I had played so well against Brazil and West Germany in 1956 that my failure to establish myself as an England player felt to me not only against nature but against logic.

Winterbottom felt differently. He considered all his options for the position of outside-left, which meant a first England appearance, against Wales in Cardiff on 19 October, 1959, for Edwin Holliday, my cousin, who was flourishing with Middlesbrough in a forward line that included Brian Clough and Alan Peacock. I was proud of him and felt not the slightest bit of jealousy. But his England career ended just five weeks later, against Northern Ireland at Wembley, after just three caps.

Even more surprising to me was that Jim Iley, the Tottenham Hotspur left-half, never featured at full international level. Neither he nor his wife, Lily, my sister, enjoyed life in London and I wondered if the uncertainty affected his form. He secured a move to Nottingham Forest in time for 1959/60 and I could hear it in his voice that his new club excited him and that he welcomed the chance to play for Billy Walker, the Aston Villa legend and England star of the 20s. My brother-in-law knew Tottenham under Bill Nicholson were on the verge of something great but he also knew Lily was unhappy and wanted a permanent home near to Yorkshire. Nottingham was close enough.

Revie has put the word in for you

Alan Brown's desire to fashion a Sunderland team in his own image continued to have an unsettling effect at Sunderland in 1959/60. Don Kichenbrand, the talented centre-forward, played his last match for the team in August and returned to South Africa to sign for Johannesburg Ramblers. His replacement was Ian Lawther, a tough Northern Irishman, who seemed able to head the ball harder than he could kick it and had just the type of enthusiasm designed to endear him to Brown.

And yet, there was a chasm between perception and reality. There were not as many changes as Brown might have wanted. Most of the established players played most of the matches: Colin Nelson at right-back made 35 League appearances that season; Len Ashurst at left-back (32); Stan Anderson at wing-half (41); Charlie Hurley at centre-half (38); Ernie Taylor at inside-forward (38); Jim McNab at wing-half (36); Ian Lawther up front (38); Ambrose Fogarty at inside-forward (37). I played 41 out of the 42 matches, missing only the trip to Brighton & Hove Albion on 2 January 1960.

Having lost 6-1 away to Ipswich Town, managed by Alf Ramsey, in September, Sunderland were as high as seventh position after a 1-1 draw at home to Liverpool on 31 October but had slipped to twentieth position after a 1-0 defeat on 2 April to Bristol City, who were second-to-bottom and fighting for their lives. Another relegation battle for Sunderland? Not quite. We secured five points from three matches over Easter to edge away from trouble, finishing sixteenth – one place below our position of the previous season. We were going backwards.

We lost 3-0 away to Liverpool on the final day of the season, 30 April, but the scoreline would have been worse had Charlie Hurley not played so well. Indeed, the *Daily Express* reported: 'Liverpool folk know a footballer when they see one, but I never thought I should see the day when the Kop gave out more polite applause than whacking great roars. It was evident that they enjoyed centre-half back play as Charlie Hurley, of Sunderland, plays it. This man who strokes the ball as if he loves rather than hates it, who never needs to hurry.'

This was a different Liverpool from the one against whom we had drawn earlier in the season. Alan A'Court was, as usual, playing at outside-left, but there was a new outside-right, an eighteen-year-old Liverpudlian called Ian Callaghan, who had replaced Billy Liddell, and who reminded me so much of myself at the same age. But the biggest change at Anfield came in the dugout in the shape of their manager, a crop-haired Scotsman by the name of Bill Shankly, whom I vaguely remembered when he played alongside Tom Finney for Preston North End just after World War Two. We were now entering the era of the celebrity manager. Shankly was electrifying Anfield just four months into his reign. Alf Ramsey seemed to be having a profound effect at Ipswich. And then there was Joe Mercer, who had left Sheffield United in 1958 to take over at Aston Villa. In 1959/60, he led the team to the Second Division championship, a point ahead of Cardiff City.

I looked on from a distance with great envy. Would Mercer try to sign me for Villa? I hoped so. If my time with Sunderland taught me one thing it was that I was a confidence player, who flourished if the environment was right (the right manager or the right players around me) but might become tentative and cautious if the environment was wrong (Alan Brown). Villa Park would have represented for me a return to the top flight and Joe Mercer would have represented a spiritual connection to my halcyon days at Bramall Lane. Doreen seemed happy enough. She liked Sunderland the city and its people – 'Just like Yorkshire folk,' she would say – but there was never the sense that we, as a family of three, had settled at No. 1 Bywell Avenue. Going from a hotel at Seaburn to a club house give us the impression of a nomadic existence. The future looked bleak.

Worse still, I had fallen out with the Sunderland directors. The problems started when I approached Stanley Ritson, the new chairman, to ask the club for a loan so I could invest in a newsagent's shop in South Shields. Their answer was unequivocal: *no*. I was not short of money. I was earning the standard twenty quid a week at Roker Park and I had built up funds from my not-inconsiderable earnings as a singer. But I realised that to secure my long-term future, I needed to develop business interests outside of the game, which, in turn, required serious investment. The Sunderland board had helped other players with loans. Why not me? I was becoming disillusioned. I was neither enjoying my football nor the atmosphere at

Roker Park. The club's policy of only offering one-year contracts promoted a feeling of uncertainty. When I discovered that Brown had offered new contracts to virtually every first-team player except for me, I knew my Sunderland career was over. I handed in a transfer request, which Brown rejected. He said he was planning to offer me a new contract. 'My written transfer request has been turned down, so I see little point in writing out another one,' I told Doug Weatherall of the *Daily Herald*. 'I think I stand a better chance of getting on the list if I'm able to state my case to the directors. Surely they'll be reasonable when they realise how miserable I am at Roker. It's the club which gives me the miseries.'

And then, on 3 July 1960, the *Sunday People* published an exposé of the problems at Sunderland. 'ROKER SHOWDOWN LOOMS', went the headline. 'Stars demand "Thrash-it-out" interview with directors . . .' Four players – Stan Anderson, Ernie Taylor, Alan O'Neill, and Reg Pearce – said they were "fed-up with conditions at trouble-torn Roker and would demand an interview with the directors this week to thrash matters out before the season starts". Anderson claimed that everyone was upset, Taylor said his job was 'uncertain', O'Neill said 'a move is best', and Pearce talked about the sour atmosphere at Roker Park. The report went on: 'This bombshell, hard on the heels of international left winger Colin Grainger's threatened walk-out, is tossed into the laps of the directors only five days before the club's annual general meeting.' Anderson claimed that too much 'grumbling' on and off the field was making it difficult for the players to 'give their best the way things are'. He wanted to know why Alan Brown was ignoring his letters. Even Charlie Hurley joined the mutiny, although he was more diplomatic than most: 'We are not out to stir trouble – there's been plenty of that at Roker – but to try to make things right again.'

When Brown replied to one of my letters, it was to arrange a meeting, just as soon he returned from holiday. He said he wanted me to stay at the club, which did not chime with his failure to offer me a contract for 1960/61. I also knew from his activity in the transfer market that he was sticking to his policy of reducing the team's average age. Although he did not give me assurances that I could leave Sunderland, I made arrangements in early July to move my furniture from the club house at Bywell Avenue back to my parents' house at West Street, Havercroft. Sunderland refused to let me train at Roker Park. Newspapers called me a 'rebel footballer' after I made it public that I would not play any part of Sunderland's fixtures in 1960/61. I was not the game's only rebel. Brian Clough was refusing to re-sign for Middlesbrough until he had assurances about the future of the club. All over the country, players were realising that directors had been too powerful for too long and that it was time to redress the balance.

Elsewhere, the Professional Footballers' Association was well into the laborious process that would lead to the end of the maximum wage. I had long made my thoughts clear to the PFA: the maximum wage was an affront to our profession and to hard-working players. For better and for worse, modernity was just around the corner.

Emboldened, and now resigned to leaving Roker Park, I had a second meeting with Brown, during which I insisted I was never playing for Sunderland again and that *he* was the reason for my decision. Calmly and dispassionately, he thanked me for my efforts and told me I could leave if the price was right. I looked at him, the man now known as a latter-day Greta Garbo: aloof, unsociable, awkward, cold, unnatural. And I wondered how different my life at Sunderland would have been had Bill Murray remained in charge and Brown stayed at Burnley.

'Which clubs are interested?' I asked. Aston Villa, Stoke City and Huddersfield Town were keen, but it was Leeds United that made the best offer: £15,000, a club record and probably more than the directors could afford. Tom Holley, the footballer-turned-journalist, told me that Don Revie, at that time Leeds's most distinguished player, was doing his best to ensure that I moved to Elland Road.

'Y'know, Colin, Revie has put the word in for you at Leeds,' Holley said. 'He's influencing it for you. He wants you there with him.' I was flattered. I liked the idea of a reunion with Revie. It did not much concern me that Leeds had finished second-to-bottom in the First Division in 1959/60 and were therefore relegated to the Second Division. I also contacted my cousin, Dennis Grainger, who had played for Leeds from 1945-47, scoring six goals in 37 Football League appearances from the left wing. Life at Elland Road had been traumatic for him, with many players – including Tom Holley – still there, lingering, from the 30s, and relegation a certainty from the midway point of the 1946/47 campaign. 'The club had no direction in those days,' my cousin told me. 'None whatsoever. And the team was old and tired. But being just after the war, it was a difficult time for everybody.'

The *Yorkshire Evening News* on Wednesday 27 July 1960 reported that I would be meeting Jack Taylor, the Leeds United manager, that day to agree personal terms. 'If this player signs,' Taylor told the newspaper, 'it won't be the last one.' It was just the kind of optimism I liked to hear. A charming man, if a throwback to a bygone era, Taylor told me that Leeds United were a 'sleeping giant', with talented young professionals emerging from a well-organised and well-funded youth-development operation. I left Sunderland with such mixed feelings that I did not know whether to celebrate my good fortune or to lament another wasted opportunity. I loved the club. I loved the players. I loved the Sunderland people. I loved the town. But one man cast a large shadow over everything I cherished: Alan Winston Brown. And eliminating him from my day-to-day existence was essential to my career and to my health.

Leeds awarded me an illegal £300 signing-on fee. Cyril Williamson, the secretary, stuffed the notes into a brown envelope and threw it at me. In the manner of a wicketkeeper, I caught it first time. 'Howzat!' I said.

How I loved those brown envelopes.

CHAPTER IV

Fade to White

1960-61: Leeds United, Jack Taylor, Jack Charlton, Don Revie

The presence of somebody much older

THE FIRST MAN TO MEET ME AT ELLAND ROAD IN AUGUST 1960 WAS Jack Taylor, the Leeds United manager, whose manner and personality was more Bill Murray than Alan Brown. Warmer in person than he looked in photographs, Taylor seemed to lack ego and had no obvious agenda above and beyond wanting to take the club back into the top flight. And maybe that was part of his problem.

The second man to meet me was Don Revie, who seemed as pleased to see me as I was to see him. Memories of happy afternoons at the Seaburn Hotel, Sunderland, in 1957, when Revie and I discussed the nuances of the game at length over coffee, entered my thoughts like a firework display and sent adrenaline coursing through my veins. And yet I noticed a difference about him. Here, in his post-Sunderland incarnation, he seemed more authoritative, more confident, happier, and not at all concerned that his playing career was drawing to a close. He was already planning his future. The Leeds United experience was clearly to his liking and he seemed to revel in his role as a respected elder statesman, even though he was only 33 and still, officially, the club captain.

'You'll like it here, Colin,' he said. I nodded, somewhat enthused, until I recalled that he said the same thing to me when I arrived for the first time at Sunderland three years earlier.

As I cast my eyes around Elland Road, absorbing the sun and considering the possibilities of my new situation, I realised that Leeds the club, for all its attributes and traditions, did not quite match the size and status of Leeds the city. There were few signs at the start of the 60s that the team would end the decade among the best in Europe or that Revie would become one of the global game's luminaries. To reclaim our lost horizon, we needed new players and a fresh outlook to both reflect and embrace the onset of changing social attitudes. It was 1960 but, here, it might well have been 1950.

Taylor signed a centre-forward, Peter Fitzgerald, an Irishman, from Sparta Rotterdam. Flame-haired and full of enthusiasm, he had a big reputation and his arrival suggested Leeds were serious about winning promotion at the first opportunity. He had represented Sparta in the quarter-finals of the European Cup against Glasgow Rangers just a few months earlier, so a drop into the Second Division might have felt like a backward step. But Taylor persuaded him that Leeds had great potential and would return to the First Division in better shape than they had left it.

This was indeed a season of revolution, but it had nothing to do with either my arrival or that of Fitzgerald. It was the acquisitions of Les Cocker and Syd Owen to Taylor's backroom staff that changed the entire face of life at Elland Road and would have far-reaching consequences. Cocker, once a centre-forward with Stockport County and Accrington Stanley, learnt about physiology and fitness during his time with the Reconnaissance Regiment in France, about coaching under Walter Winterbottom on the Football Association courses, and about kinesiology and biomechanics when nobody was looking. He was aggressive, abrasive and strict – everything Jack Taylor was not. Owen, who played in the 1954 World Cup for England, was more of an intellectual; a philosopher, a thinker and a tactician who had been looking ahead to the 60s when most players and coaches were still living in the 50s. He was obsessed with coaching and he took pride in telling us that he never missed any of the FA summer courses.

Almost all of the Leeds squad, a mixture of experienced professionals and fresh-faced prodigies, seemed impressed with the physical discipline of Cocker and the mental discipline of Owen. Occasionally, however, Owen would take us on a long, boring run, a process we would nickname 'run rabbit, run'. Those training sessions seemed needlessly hard and humdrum. Cocker could be just as aggressive.

Change was necessary, however, so it would have been churlish to complain. A club not long relegated cannot accept the status quo. Even the over-fed, cigar-smoking conservatives in the boardroom, the guys who had never done a day's exercise in their lives, realised that revolution was necessary.

But one man did not even attempt to conceal his disenchantment with the new arrangement: Jack Charlton, brother of Manchester United's Bobby. Talented, strong and self-assured, if cynical and argumentative, Jack Charlton was not a player to be pushed around. He challenged authority and could sulk if he did not get his own way. But when he realised his performances were benefiting from the interventions of Taylor's new backroom staff, he knew he would have to back down eventually. Although still a few seasons away from becoming one of the world's best defenders, the chain-smoking Charlton made great strides in 1960/61. I liked him immensely. I liked his irreverent manner, his militant attitude. I liked his mining background. I liked his inherent kindness, a side of his character he revealed one day in 1965 while shopping in Leeds city centre. Doreen was pushing Colin junior and our new baby girl, Kim, in a pram when Charlton emerged from out of the shadows with a huge smile and half a crown for each of my two children. 'He's a nice man, that Mr Charlton,' Doreen said when she got home. Perhaps it was because of his size – he was a big man, 6ft 3in in bare feet, angular and yet somehow solid – that I regarded him as a true leader of men. He was aged just 25 in August 1960, two years younger than I, but he had the presence of somebody much older. While I always felt that the likes of Billy Bingham and Don Revie had *some* of the attributes to be good managers, and were always likely to succeed, I had no doubts that Charlton had *most* of the attributes. When he took the Republic of Ireland to the 1990 World Cup in Italy, turning himself into a media personality and something of a populist iconoclast, I nodded my approval and delighted in his success. I had seen the harbingers thirty years earlier.

The fruits of my singing career

Although Doreen and I had comfortable and familiar surroundings living with my parents in Havercroft, we learnt our lessons from our days in Sunderland and this time decided to buy our first house. We found something appropriate at No. 48 Low Lane, Durkar, near Wakefield, a village so small that it made Havercroft feel urban. Durkar is Norse for 'dirt marsh', but the village is anything but. It has the breathtaking Sandal Castle, nearly a thousand years old, and some beautiful scenery and walks. The air was so fresh it could knock you out. Most importantly, our house there was just ten miles from Leeds and eight miles from Havercroft: close enough to the places that governed my life but far enough away to shut out the world if necessary. Domestically, my life was perfect.

Colin junior was now aged four and old enough to go with Doreen to the occasional Leeds United match. I planned to take the family to Elland Road, a twenty-minute drive away, in my Pathfinder – the fruits of my singing career.

Doreen and I struck up a friendship with Peter McConnell and his wife. Having moved to Elland Road as a schoolboy at Stockport Grammar, McConnell became a wing-half who, at that point, had not established himself in the first team. But on the occasions we both travelled to away matches, we would often share hotel rooms, and talk about the future. His ambition after finishing with football was to own his own pub, which he did: the Hare & Hounds in Rothwell. McConnell thought the world of Don Revie and had a great enthusiasm for life at Elland Road; far more enthusiasm than most of the players, who thought the club disjointed and badly organised.

Terry Caldwell, the right-back, was among those who did not enjoy playing for Leeds. He was never less than fully professional but he never felt comfortable at the club and I formed the view that he was planning his next move from the moment Jack Taylor signed him up. Having grown up in Wakefield, Caldwell gravitated towards me and our similar backgrounds helped us develop a good friendship. Many years later, long after both of us had retired, we had a drink after a funeral. 'How did we survive the Leeds experience, Colin?' he said. We laughed, not so much because of his honesty but because of how quickly the club flourished after 1962. By then, Caldwell was playing for Carlisle United and cherishing his wonderful life in Cumbria. I also became friendly with Jimmy Frew, a Scot, then aged 68, who advised me to take my Football Association coaching badges. Frew had been a left-back with Leeds United as far back as 1920, the year the club formed from the ashes of Leeds City. He later distinguished himself with Bradford City. I did the preliminary badge under him and passed with barely any effort. 'Colin, I think you should get yourself to Lilleshall for the full badge,' he said. And I wanted to, but I had too many singing commitments. Frew lamented my decision and I would come to regret not taking coaching seriously.

A journey of discovery

My Leeds United debut was on the opening day of the 1960/61 season, away to Liverpool, the team, coincidentally, against whom I had played my final competitive match for Sunderland. There was no doubt they were the coming force and that we were fortunate to come away with only a 2-0 defeat. But I felt optimistic. The Leeds team was full of players I rated highly. Jack Charlton in defence was a tower of strength, a one-man fortress, even if his desire to break forward would often leave us short when teams attempted to hit us on the break. Freddie Goodwin, the wing-half-turned-centre-half, signed for £10,000 from Manchester United the previous season, had a steadying influence with his strength and bravery. He had avoided the Munich Air Disaster by being left out of the squad for the trip to Belgrade and I think he felt a bit of guilt over it all. Fierce in the tackle, estimably committed, Goodwin had his admirers. But Don Revie felt his lack of composure and lack of pace weakened Leeds as a defensive unit. We conceded far too many goals for my liking. When Goodwin convinced Jack Taylor to adopt man-to-man marking, neither Revie nor Charlton was impressed and the consequences proved dire.

Our goalkeeper was Ted Burgin, with whom I had played at Sheffield United, and who, even now in his 30s, was still the amateur comedian, always playing practical jokes, always ready with the killer quip. He provided a welcome contrast to the seriousness of the dressing-room atmosphere as created by Jack Taylor, Les Cocker and Syd Owen. I thought Burgin was at the end of his career, but he left Elland Road in 1961 and played more than two hundred League matches for Rochdale before retiring in 1966. He performed well against Liverpool on that opening day and, when it seemed as though Roger Hunt and Dave Hickson would destroy Leeds, did much to ensure that we avoided a greater defeat.

One player stood out for me, not so much for his performance on the day – none of us played well; Liverpool never let us – but for his youth, confidence and enthusiasm. His name was Billy Bremner, then an outside-right aged just seventeen, a red-haired Scot who was mentally tough, full of honest endeavour, hungry, small, but with the heart of a lion. Cocker and Owen decided that the best way to bring out the best in Bremner was to work him hard, partly to build up his

125

body but also to test his attitude and character. Perhaps more significantly, Don Revie decided to act as Bremner's unofficial mentor and the relationship between the two flourished, even though they were separated by a fifteen-year gap and were at opposite ends of their playing careers. Missing his home town of Stirling and his girlfriend, Victoria, Bremner was pining for a move back to Scotland, preferably to play for Celtic, whom he had rejected when aged just fifteen. He might have left Elland Road in 1960/61 had Revie not paid him so much attention. I had a great relationship with Bremner. We would occasionally go for a coffee after training and talk away the afternoon. He would tell me of his hopes and fears, and I formed the impression he would not be at Leeds for long. After a few coffees, he would pull out a small flask and have a single gulp of whisky – anything to calm his natural anxiety.

I had seen Bremner in pre-season training, putting in tackles against men twice his size, playing first-time passes with precision, and running around the track with boundless energy, but that did not tell me much. Only in a match environment can you really assess the strengths and weaknesses of a player. And I knew on that warm Saturday afternoon at Anfield on 20 August 1960, even though he found himself overshadowed by Liverpool's defenders, that Bremner would one day become world-class.

I admired a scouting system that could attract such young players as Bremner and turn them into first-teamers. It was like a conveyor belt of talent. Even younger than Bremner was a sixteen-year-old centre-back called Norman Hunter, another fresh-faced boy existing in a man's body. One of Hunter's roles as an apprentice was to clean my boots. 'Are these nice enough, Colin? . . . Are your studs tight enough? . . . Is that enough dubbin for you?' By the mid-60s, this charming young kid, having turned himself into a strong and brave man, had become one half of a great Leeds defensive partnership with Jack Charlton. But I regret it that I never managed to play alongside him in the first team. His debut, in 1962, came after I had left Elland Road. I delighted in his progress, especially when he made the England World Cup squad in 1966, at the age of 22.

Another player to arouse my curiosity was Gerry Francis, whose place in Leeds United's history owes almost everything to his being the club's first-ever black player. He was a startlingly quick right winger from Johannesburg, South Africa, where he had worked repairing shoes before joining Leeds as an amateur in 1956/57. Unable to play in the National League in South Africa because of apartheid, he paid his own fare to come to England and, once here, enjoyed an education that no university could have provided. He was surprised, for example, to see white women perform domestic chores in their homes. Hitherto, in South Africa, he had only seen black women execute such tasks. Even as late as 1960, there were spectators in English football who had never before seen a black person, let alone met one, so his presence in the team had novelty value and attracted a lot of interest. Inexplicably, he did suffer racist abuse during away matches – the odd ignorant comment from the terraces – but never at Leeds; or, at least, never to my knowledge. I liked him. I admired his courage. I respected his easy manner, his charisma, and his confidence. He was amiable, and his permanent smile, which could light up the poorly-lit home dressing room at Elland Road, suggested to me he felt privileged to have made the grade at Leeds United. Every day to him was a journey of discovery and he had the facial expression – that look of awe, the healthy curiosity in his eyes – to prove it.

Looking back, my early days at Leeds provide me with fond memories. My best friend at the club was Tom Hallett, a reserve-team centre-half, who came to Elland Road through the same Welsh scouting system that later unearthed Gary Sprake and Terry Yorath. Hallett never did play in the Football League for Leeds but he was a good player and great company, as I discovered during many afternoon excursions playing bowls on the local green.

Once both of us moved on, we lost touch, but I was delighted to receive a telephone call from him in 2015 – our first contact in more than half a century. We spoke about our Leeds days as if they had happened a year earlier rather than fifty-odd years earlier. I told him how his friendship helped to make my days at Leeds more bearable than they might otherwise have been. We shared stories and jokes, and, alas, exchanged details about which of the players we had encountered during our careers were no longer alive. 'There aren't many of us left, Colin,' he said, wistfully.

Could never find a winning formula

There was something about Leeds United I could not place. The club at all levels, from the boardroom down to the youth team, was not a close-knit operation and, in its own way, rather schizophrenic, with problems manifesting themselves most starkly in the dressing room. For all his attributes, Jack Taylor had not instilled much discipline, which meant some players just pleased themselves. Eric Smith, the Leeds right-half, who signed from Celtic and was a solid player, revealed in later years his impressions about life at Elland Road: 'The club was fifth rate and the players were undisciplined. It wasn't their fault. Jack Taylor had let the thing go. I thought beforehand I was coming to a top club. I found out otherwise in the first three or four days. We would go on long training runs and at the end, some players, quite senior players, would walk in with ice lollies in their hands.'

I thought back to the advice my cousin, Dennis Grainger, had given me about the club lacking direction when he was a player at Elland Road from 1945-47. Had nothing changed in thirteen years?

Rumours were rife that the club was skint and badly run, which would, in time, encourage an overreliance on supremely talented but young players such as Billy Bremner, Norman Hunter, Paul Reaney, Gary Sprake and Terry Cooper, all of whom signed on as professionals during my time at Elland Road. This need to be expedient, putting faith in younger players, would pay dividends in spectacular fashion, with great success over many years, but one wonders how different the future might have been had the club been flush with cash in that pivotal 1960/61 season. Paying ten grand for Goodwin was probably not money well spent, and I did wonder if they overpaid by signing me for fifteen grand. These were colossal sums of money at the time, especially for a club struggling to deal with relegation from the top flight, enduring internal division at boardroom level, and suffering the inevitable decline in home attendances.

Conversely, there was an aura about Elland Road, even before the redevelopment of the ground. You could see the potential. The training kit was smart and well maintained, the ground staff attentive and professional, and the club treated the players well. But I could never put my finger on what was wrong. It was like a big club that did not know how to *think* big; a club dogged by identity crisis and self-loathing, lacking pride, perpetuating a defeatist attitude. The atmosphere never felt right and had a lot in common with the deep insecurities that dogged Sunderland in early 1957. The difference was that Sunderland was a fantastic club during my time there (Alan Brown's unattractive comportments notwithstanding), whereas Leeds needed to reinvent itself. I fitted in well at Elland Road, enjoyed playing under Jack Taylor, but here there was always the feeling of permanent transition, with the potential for great changes, rash decisions, and transformations lurking around every corner. In such an environment, it can be difficult to settle down.

I had no constraints on the pitch. Taylor wanted me to play as far forward as possible, with an emphasis on beating the right-back, or making late runs to the far post, and with no defensive responsibilities whatsoever. In that respect, it was a return to my days under Joe Mercer at Sheffield United. Our left-back, Grenville Hair, who had been with Leeds since 1948, did not need much protection because he was super-fit and intelligent. He was there to help me rather than me to help him and he told me so. What we could not have known, of course, was what all that training and all those matches were doing to his heart. In March 1968, when he was manager of Bradford City, he dropped dead on the training pitch. A cardiac arrest. He was aged just 36. I was deeply saddened when I discovered the news, for Hair was a lovely guy and a good friend, and I recalled wonderful afternoons when he and I would stroll around Leeds city centre, sharing jokes and wondering what would become of Leeds United. And one of the two men to take over from Hair at Bradford City? Tom Hallett, my pal from Elland Road, who had turned himself into a fine centre-half at the club and stayed there until 1971.

My new freedom at Leeds to break forward as often as I wanted was the good news. The bad news was that my pace was not what it was. My damaged ankle now needed heavy strapping before each match, which, in turn, decreased my movement, taking away that extra yard of speed on which my game had relied so much. Devoid of confidence, I would hesitate when I should have been direct; I would play a short ball when I should have beaten the opposing right-back; and I found myself subconsciously protecting the injured joint. And, of course, there was no avoiding that axiom that if you protect one part of your body, you can be sure another part will feel vulnerable. It only added to my troubles that the Elland Road pitch was of poor quality. I never came remotely close to the form that won me England caps in 1956 and 1957 and nowhere near my form at Sunderland in 1958/59. I hoped the players around me would help me compensate for my diminishing pace, but Jack Taylor could never find a winning formula. He changed the team each match, affecting our rhythm, breeding inconsistency, creating confusion. Some of the players, particularly the older ones, felt that a committee selected the line-up, just like pre-war times, and that Taylor was merely the establishment's figurehead. I could see the reasoning. The team changes seemed random, misconceived, and executed without any consideration or strategy. We were less a coherent team and more a collection of individuals.

I scored my first goal for Leeds United in my fourth match, a 4-4 draw away to Bristol Rovers on 29 August. Five days later, I scored in a 4-2 victory away to Southampton and produced my best performance yet in a Leeds shirt. It felt just like old times. 'Man of the match was Colin Grainger, bought at considerable expense to take Leeds straight back to Division One,' Bert Barham wrote. 'He gave a short, sharp lesson in annihilation with one flashing goal and two pinpoint crosses which brought two more.'

We played out another 4-4 draw at home to Middlesbrough on 17 September in front of 17,799 spectators, a match significant because we used an all-white kit rather than our traditional blue/gold shirts, white shorts, and blue/gold socks. I do not recall the colours or the reasons for the temporary change as being significant, but it was not the first time the team had played in all white. But I do recall the match: a rollercoaster ride that summed up Leeds United in 1960/61. Brian Clough, that brilliant but haughty centre-forward, scored two of the Middlesbrough goals, while John McCole, the Leeds centre-forward, wonderfully adroit in the penalty area, scored his fifth goal of the season. Nicknamed 'Four-goal McCole' on account of his goalscoring prowess, he was a fine player who had performed with distinction for Bradford City in 1958/59, having come to England from Falkirk. Unsurprisingly given his Glasgow upbringing, he was tough, fervent, intense, and sharp of mind. But he was also a drinker. You could smell the alcohol on his breath before matches – he was a one-man brewery – and he always had a brandy flask or a bottle of something ready to pull out of his jacket pocket. He gave the impression of spending every afternoon at the pub, drinking hard and swapping jokes with anybody who happened to be there. In 1982, I heard that he had died in poverty in County Donegal of cancer, at the age of 46.

Empty spaces on the terraces

A new competition entered the fixture lists early that season: the League Cup, a knock-out competition created by Alan Hardaker, the Football League secretary, as part of his plan to revolutionise the game. The League Cup was the cherry on the cake of his so-called 'Pattern for Football' manifesto, something he created in

1957. The Pattern – which would see the number of teams in the league pyramid expanded from 92 to 100 – never did get off the ground but the clubs voted for the League Cup, which, eventually, became an important part of football culture and something of a money-spinner. But in 1960, the competition seemed like a Hardaker vanity project and felt no different from those floodlit friendly matches that were all the rage in the 50s. We began in the second round with a goalless draw at home to Blackpool, then in the First Division, before winning the replay 3-1 at Bloomfield Park. I felt no sense of loss at missing out on the third-round tie away to Chesterfield, which we won 4-0 in front of just 2,021 spectators. No wonder critics referred to the League Cup as 'Hardaker's Folly'. Leeds United lost money on the tie.

In the fourth round on 5 December, a cold Monday night, we lost 5-4 against Southampton in a match that finished at nearly quarter past ten because of two floodlight failures. The result owed everything to Jack Charlton's desire to be everywhere on the pitch at the same time. Eager to be a centre-forward, and never comfortable playing alongside Freddie Goodwin at the back, he kept breaking forward as often as possible, a strategy that contributed as much to the five goals we conceded as the four goals we scored. We went four goals down with Derek Reeves, a small but powerful striker, scoring all of them before we turned the tie around through goals by Noel Peyton, McCole, Charlton and Bobby Cameron. With a replay looking certain, Reeves scored his, and Southampton's, fifth goal with the last kick of the match to send The Dell into paroxysms of joyful madness. Both teams ended up with ten men because of injury. Afterwards, Jack Taylor displayed rare emotion, shaking his head and turning dark red with anger, although, wisely, perhaps, he did not offer Charlton any criticism; not in public, at least. The journey north to Leeds, through the winter night, was long, boring, and melancholic. Nobody shouted out to me, *Come on, Colin, give us a song.*

We were hovering around thirteenth position in the Second Division by then and could never work out why we were struggling to keep clean sheets. The problem was two-fold: a lack of tactical discipline and a lack of cohesion. We were a collection of players rather than a team in the traditional sense. Home attendances were diminishing further, with the average slipping below the 14,000 mark by the turn of the year. Just 9,421 attended our match at Elland Road against Portsmouth on 10 December, a rare goalless draw, and even from our vantage point on the pitch we could see the empty spaces on the terraces.

Revie had forfeited the captaincy because, being of a superstitious disposition, he felt that he, personally, was the cause of our indifferent results. But there was only a slight improvement when Goodwin took over from him. Revie's passing remained of the highest standard and there was no doubting his intelligence, but he could no longer move well. Never the fastest player, he now seemed to function in slow motion, as if running inside a large fish tank, and our haphazard style of play exaggerated the extent of his decline. Fortunately, he was well aware of his limitations and he told me over coffee that he had long been considering his next step in the game: a move into management, as soon as the right offer came along. He would go abroad if necessary. He turned down a chance to coach Adamstown in Australia on a five-year deal, while I doubt he considered seriously offers to manage Chester and Tranmere Rovers. There seemed no appetite among the Leeds directors to keep hold of Revie. He represented a past from which the club was trying to escape.

We did enjoy a brief revival, rising to ninth in the table after going unbeaten in the Second Division during December and January, playing some good football in the process. However, there was always the sense that if Jack Taylor wanted to keep his job, he would have to fight for it – and both his posture and countenance suggested he had probably had enough of life at Elland Road. All that was saving him, arguably, was the likelihood that the club could not afford the £2,500 to pay off his contract. A 2-0 defeat to Sheffield Wednesday at Hillsborough in the FA Cup third round on 7 January 1961 proved significant because it denied Leeds United the opportunity to raise much-needed funds from a good run in the competition. The board of directors, under constant pressure from the shareholders, were horrified. Word reached the players that Cyril Williamson, the club secretary, might replace Taylor as manager. A secretary-manager? Was that not a return to football's anachronistic past? Was the mere suggestion of such a regressive appointment proof that a committee really did select the team?

A cohesive monoculture

It was during a training session the day before the FA Cup tie at Sheffield Wednesday that I noticed an unfamiliar face; a black player, balletic, with great speed and power, but who seemed unsure of himself, a bit out of his depth, uncomfortable, and bemused at the ferocity of the tackling – particularly from Billy Bremner.

'Who's that?' I asked Syd Owen.

'Oh, that's Albert Johanneson. We've brought him over from South Africa on trial.'

Whenever Johanneson had the ball, Bremner would go in hard and send him flying; and on each occasion, as Johanneson lay on the floor, Bremner would offer a hand to lift him up. By the end of the session, Johanneson's kit was caked in mud and his legs bruised, but it was Bremner, that delightful character with ice in his veins and warmth in his heart, who walked with him back to the dressing room. The start of an unlikely friendship. I realised that Bremner was testing the twenty-year-old trialist; as if to say, *If you want to make it at Leeds, you have to get past me first.* So keen was he to impress Jack Taylor, Johanneson never considered the possibility that a Leeds United training session could be a bear pit in which only the strong survived. And survive he did – eventually.

When I asked Johanneson how he was finding his new life in Leeds, he spoke about the type of problems that never entered my head: simple stuff like the weather ('It's so cold, Colin, I cannot seem to get warm') or the communal bath ('I never knew at first if white players would share with a coloured man') or his living quarters ('Terraced houses wherever you turn') or playing in boots ('I grew up playing in bare feet'). And then there was the racism that dogged him that day at Hillsborough when, with Johanneson in the stand as a non-playing member of the Leeds party, Wednesday supporters abused him for the colour of his skin. Knowing Sheffield people as I did, from my days playing at Bramall Lane, the bigots were a small minority. Sheffield folk were, and remain, principled, moral and honourable types, but Johanneson would not have known that. He came to England thinking he had moved away from South Africa's racist excesses and found that that problem was ubiquitous and global. How could I, a white Yorkshireman who grew up in a cohesive monoculture, have understood the tribulations that dogged him?

According to the 1961 Census, the black population in Leeds was 2,186 out of an overall population of 510,676 – about one in every 234 people. Most had come to England after the British Nationality Act 1948, which made them British subjects and therefore entitled to live and work in the United Kingdom. In Leeds, many of the black population worked in the textile industry and most attended church. Almost none of the population were rich. Only one – Gerry Francis – was a professional football player, with Johanneson determined to make it two. Inevitably, given their comparable backgrounds, the two men were drawn to each other, but they were different in character and personality. Whereas Francis was outgoing and bubbly, Johanneson was shy and diffident. And, in the early days of his trial, emotional. After one training session, Grenville Hair, always sensitive to the feelings of others, saw Johanneson alone and in tears, clearly struggling with the transition between his old life and his new. 'Everything will work out fine, Al,' Hair said, putting an arm around Johanneson's shoulder.

The prevailing view at Leeds was that Johanneson would have to toughen up to have a chance of making the grade, which, arguably, made Bremner's fierce tackles on the training pitch genuine acts of love. Even in 1961, Bremner was behaving like a genuine leader of men. Leeds United had found their captain of the future. He helped to educate and enhance Johanneson and to vindicate Taylor's desire to test foreign markets. Of course, it was easy to see the appeal of signing South African players, as they were cheap, risk-free, and required no complicated documentation. But black players in England were rare in 1961. Johanneson therefore had many battles on his hands and the road ahead would be fraught with obstacles. His first battle was to perform well for the reserve team in the Central League. He would not sign a professional contract under Jack Taylor. He spent much of his first few weeks at Leeds wishing he was back in Johannesburg, and a lesser man would have cracked completely.

He matured, physically and emotionally, learnt how play in boots, and finally bought appropriate clothing to combat the cold weather. I welcomed his progress. But as winter turned to spring, I did wonder if he would become one of the many eager trialists who came, foundered, and disappeared without trace.

The world had changed

Although a member of the Professional Footballers' Association, I never had much to do with the campaign to end the maximum wage. But my position was always clear: I would have joined my colleagues on strike in 1960 had it been necessary to end this draconian rule. The Football League, led by its president, Joe Richards, the Yorkshireman who had recommended me for the England team in 1956, feared industrial action so backed down.

The fight to end the maximum wage was, for many years, a cause without a rebel. The PFA wanted Harry Hough, the Barnsley goalkeeper, against whom I scored a hat-trick for Sheffield United in 1956, to lead the players. But Hough was too conventional and had too many interests outside the game. The PFA turned instead to Jimmy Hill, the Fulham forward famous for his big chin and insatiable ambition, who was now considering his options at the end of his playing career.

Largely because of lobbying by Hill, the maximum wage ended on 14 January 1961. Players were now free to negotiate salaries based on the balance between what they thought they were worth and what clubs were willing to pay.

Johnny Haynes, the Fulham forward and my former England international teammate, became the first £100-per-week player. For most of us, however, wages barely increased. My £15 per week remained £15 per week until the end of 1960/61. Some clubs, such as Liverpool and Manchester United, still tried to enforce an unofficial maximum wage, but trying to curb the growing power of the professional football player was like trying to stop water trickling down a hill. The world had changed, the game had changed, and club directors now had to realise that their days of autonomy were drawing to a close. This was the start of player power. And although there were still many injustices, such as the retain-and-transfer system, to be overcome, we had now reached a pivotal point. For me, football divides easily into two parts: what happened before the end of the maximum wage and what happened afterwards.

The Leeds United directors, already encumbered by the club's poor balance sheet and even poorer attendances, welcomed the news as they would a trip to the colonoscopist. Sam Bolton, the chairman, was ashen-faced, as though the blood had drained from his face.

The look of agony

Leeds United's form in February 1961 was that of a team fighting against relegation and was a reflection of Jack Taylor's failure to create a settled team. My performances were commensurate with those of the team, although I did score in the 3-1 defeat away to Plymouth Argyle on 4 March. Surprisingly from my point of view, Jack Taylor offered me a contract for 1961/62 – at £20 per week, an increase on £15 per week. There was no ceiling to how much I could try to negotiate but there was a ceiling to how much Leeds wanted to pay or could afford to pay. The offer seemed appropriate, I signed it, and looked forward to what I thought would be a decent spell at Elland Road.

I missed the fixture on 11 March at home to Norwich City, a 1-0 victory that proved to be Taylor's last match in charge. He resigned two days afterwards and, to all intents and purposes, left the game for good. Cyril Williamson, the man who took pleasure in throwing brown envelopes at players, took over on a temporary basis. Had Taylor not resigned, he would have been sacked. He walked away with £2,500 as compensation for the sixteen months still left on his contract.

In a strange editorial decision that probably reflected Leeds's indifferent results and weak financial situation, the *Yorkshire Evening Post* gave Taylor's resignation only limited coverage. It was as if the club had begun a descent towards irrelevance. In our attempts, as players, to find out what was going on, neither the local newspapers nor the directors were of much help. Indeed, there was more coverage about the forthcoming FA Cup semi-final between Sheffield United (my former club) and Leicester City (Revie's former club), which was scheduled to take place at Elland Road. Syd Owen knew nothing about who would replace Taylor – he did not even want to talk about it – but he trained us harder than ever before as we primed ourselves for the match away to Portsmouth on 18 March. My preparation included a place on the right wing for the reserve team against Huddersfield Town at Elland Road on 14 March. The Central League was never my idea of fun, but one must remain professional, even when the manager is really the secretary and nobody seems to have a clue what is going on and every hour of the day feels transformational.

Behind the scenes, the situation was changing quickly. Having lost his place in the first team at the end of January, Revie told me in February of his intention to apply for the vacant managerial position at Bournemouth & Boscombe Athletic. Don Welsh, the former England inside-forward, who had overseen Liverpool's relegation to the Second Division in 1954, had resigned from Bournemouth, creating an opportunity that aroused Revie's interest. I assumed he would be successful, probably on a player-manager basis, and thought nothing more of it. I would miss him, of course, but I knew our paths would cross again. What I did not know was that his desire to leave Elland Road suddenly made him attractive to the Leeds directors. Having previously considered him an ageing player who might be better moving on, they now saw him in a new light: as a potential player-manager. Still convinced he was on his way to Bournemouth, Revie began to consider which players he would take with him. He said to Jimmy Ashall and Peter McConnell words to the effect of, 'I've been offered the player-manager's job at Bournemouth and I want you both to come with me.' But McConnell's wife was from Leeds and it was doubtful a move would appeal to her. They had a young daughter, Debbie, which made them reluctant to take risks. (McConnell told me that when Debbie was born, Billy Bremner went round to the family house with a teddy bear for the baby. The bear, he said, was nearly as large as Bremner).

Revie might still have gone to Bournemouth had it not been for the intervention of Ronald Crowther, the *Yorkshire Evening Post* editor, who was an influential figure locally and one of Leeds United's most famous supporters. Having already agreed to write Revie's letter of application to Bournemouth, Crowther said to him, 'Why don't you apply to Leeds, too?' In the meantime, Revie had asked Harry Reynolds, the Leeds director, for a reference to send to Bournemouth. While drafting the reference, Reynolds realised that Revie had all the attributes necessary to become Leeds's player-manager. The director was only too aware that Leeds had struggled to find a manager in 1959 and that Jack Taylor only got the job because four other people had turned it down. And that was when they were in the First Division. Now sitting midway in the Second Division, Leeds might spend the rest of the season trying to find the right manager, with no guarantee of success. Better, surely, to promote a man who knew the Elland Road set-up inside out.

While Reynolds was trying to convince his fellow directors about Revie's suitability, the directors at Bournemouth recoiled when they realised they would have to pay a £6,000 transfer fee to take Revie. The stars aligned – Revie became the Leeds United player-manager on 16 March 1961.

We heard the news first from Reynolds, who came into the dressing room before a training session and said: 'Before you go out on the pitch, I've got something important to tell you. I'd like to introduce you to Jack Taylor's replacement. Lads, our new manager is . . .' And in walked Don Revie, looking smart, well-coiffed, and commanding, with a healthy glow that seemed to illuminate him. We all applauded.

Hello, boss . . .

Revie welcomed the challenges of being unable to splash out in the transfer market and of having to sell players to balance the budget. He was lucky in that a group of supremely talented young players from the reserves and youth team were ready to take wing, but he was also clever in that he took time to watch these players in their natural environments when other people might not have bothered. He would benefit from the scouting system that had been in place since the days of Bill Lambton in 1958/59.

I was pleased for Revie. But I knew my relationship with him would never be the same again. He would do what all managers have to do: surround himself with an invisible veneer to distance himself from the players; to send out an immutable message: *I'm the boss now*. He went up to Manchester United for some advice from Matt Busby and to Liverpool for advice from Bill Shankly. Revie became a keen student and a good student. I joined Derek Mayers, Peter McConnell, Gerry Francis, Grenville Hair, Jack Charlton and Jimmy Ashall in a contrived photograph to welcome Revie as manager. I still have a copy of the image. Our smiles just about conceal our anxiety. Charlton is shaking the new manager's hand. In his lavish grey suit, Revie already looks five years older than he did the day before he took the job. His peppy expression tells the real story: the future begins here.

Newspapers considered the implications of Revie's new position. Eric Stanger wrote in the *Yorkshire Evening Post*: 'Nothing would benefit Leeds United more than a long stable period of sound management. In fact, in their financial position, it is their only hope for the future.' Revie signed a three-year contract but did not secure a pay rise. He remained on £20 per week – his wages as a player. A cheap manager for a cheap club. How quickly he would become a sophisticated manager for a sophisticated club. How quickly 1960/61 would become the most pivotal season in the long saga of Leeds United.

Unaware at that point of the historical implications, I made the starting line-up for Revie's first match as manager. Jack Charlton did, too – as a centre-forward. Recalling how Frank Buckley, as manager of Leeds in the early 50s, had pushed John Charles from centre-half to centre-forward, Revie attempted the same with Charlton. Auguries were encouraging, although Charlton soon realised that he preferred to be facing play as a defender rather than playing with his back to goal. He scored but we lost 3-1. Revie's first home match in charge was against Sheffield United the week after. The official programme recorded:

Our new team manager, Mr Don Revie, who has thrown himself wholeheartedly into his new soccer task, is no stranger to our supporters or to the bulk of soccer fans throughout the country... [He] goes into the managerial side with many carefully formulated theories on how to get the best out of a team and how to groom young players for the future. That he is also a practical man, he has already demonstrated with his strenuous efforts since he took over his new post... He may need time and patience to achieve the results that he hopes for, but there will be no lack of conscientious endeavour on his part.

Indeed not, but we still lost 2-1 to Sheffield United in front of just 13,688 spectators. Joe Shaw, my former teammate at Bramall Lane, by now a fine centre-half, scored an own goal to give Leeds a consolation but otherwise he performed well, ensuring that Charlton up front barely got a kick. During the second half, when Charlton revealed his inexperience as a centre-forward, Shaw laughed in his face. Even Charlton saw the joke. And to think that Shaw started off as a wing-half and only became a centre-half after he changed positions to smother Don Revie during a Sheffield United-Manchester City match in the early 50s.

But at least Charlton survived his ordeal up front to tell the tale. I sustained a knee injury that would keep me out of action for the match away to Luton Town on 1 April. Revie put me in the reserves at inside-left on 3 April against Derby County, for whom Ron Webster, a seventeen-year-old later to win the Football League championship twice, had the task of marking me. He did not have to work hard to minimise any threat I might have posed. My knee locked completely – I felt something pop – and I limped along with the look of agony engraved over my features, before I eventually hobbled off the pitch altogether. Afterwards, the fragile joint swelled to the size of a second head. The hospital beckoned.

Meanwhile, having become Revie's first signing, Albert Johanneson had made his first-team debut on the left wing in the match away to Swansea Town on 8 April – a 2-2 draw in which Jack Charlton scored twice. I began to wonder if the shy and diffident South African I had observed for the first time in training in early January was the man to take my place at Elland Road. I had to admit he had flourished in the three months since, showing that he had skill to go with his pace and strength to go with his bravery, whereas I was now a diminished figure, hobbling around on crutches, feeling sorry for myself, and out of contention at just about the worst possible time. When you are injured, you avoid people – particularly the new manager.

I went for an operation, during which the surgeon discovered tissue damage underneath the knee cap. He removed the cartilage and, once I woke up with the headache from hell, he told me that his intervention had saved my career in the short term but that I might only have five years left as a professional player.

My season was over.

I watched from the stand as Leeds played the West Riding Cup final away to Bradford Park Avenue. We won but the real excitement in the city concerned the Leeds rugby league team, who defeated Warrington in a play-off in front of 52,177 to secure the Northern League title. Could Leeds call itself a football city if the rugby league club was far more significant?

Leeds United finished the 1960/61 season fourteenth in the Second Division. Ipswich Town, under Alf Ramsey, finished first, with Sheffield United runners-up. At the highest level, Tottenham Hotspur won the Football League and FA Cup double, with Danny Blanchflower winning the Football Writers' Player of the Year award. Preston North End, having failed to deal with the retirement in 1960 of Tom Finney, finished bottom of the First Division. And as if to emphasise how the 60s were ushering in change, Denis Law, the Scotland international striker, moved from Manchester City to Torino in Italy for a fee of £110,000 – a record for a deal involving a British player.

As for me, a summer of debilitating depression awaited.

And I would never play for the Leeds United first team again.

Emblematic and emotional attachments

I undertook a summer singing tour of variety clubs in Sheffield, Bradford, Rotherham, Skegness and Leeds – anything to take my mind off the pain of my injury and of the insecurity of life at Elland Road. The week in Skegness became an all-expenses-paid holiday when I suggest that Doreen and Colin junior join me. They came most nights to watch my performances. Len Young fixed me up with a one-night performance in Brighton for charity. I travelled down from Sunderland, sang five numbers, and met an eighteen-year-old singer called Adam Faith, who was also on the bill. I admired his youthful exuberance but I had more confidence in his ability than he did. At that time, with his first records, 'Got A Heartsick Feeling' and 'Brother Heartache and Sister Tears', not selling well, he was unsure if he was going to make the big time. If only I had the time I would have told him not to worry. He had the talent and the look. But I had to get back to Sunderland on the overnight train.

The work came thick and fast. One evening in Leeds, I shared the bill with Nat Jackley, a Sunderland-born comedian and actor, whose rubber-neck dance, skeletal build and eccentric speech impediment turned him into a celebrity before I was even born. A man of innate charm and zeal, Jackley had the ability to master all aspects of the entertainment industry. What had not come naturally to him, he could learn with ease. It helped him that he hailed from a show-business family, for his father, George Jackley, flourished as a comedian, most notably in London at the Lyceum Theatre, during the interwar years. Nat Jackley moved effortlessly from seaside theatres in the 20s, 30s and 40s to television in the 50s, putting himself into households throughout the country with his Nat's In The Belfry show on the BBC in 1956 – the year of my England debut.

Jackley and I got on well and we liked the idea of working together on a regular basis. But for that to happen, I needed to give up football, which, given my love of the game, was out of the question. Jim Windsor, a locally famous bookmaker and nightclub owner, asked me for a meeting in his office, situated on the first floor of his club in Leeds.

'Do you fancy spending the summer touring Australia with Nat?' Windsor asked me. 'The money's great, Colin, and it could lead to something permanent over there.'

'It's tempting, Jim, but how long will I be away?'

'Probably until September.'

'Sorry, Jim, but I need to be back before the end of July for pre-season training.'

Australia sounded great, as did an entire summer with Jackley, but I could not put at risk my fragile career with Leeds United, or my fragile left knee. I would have earned more each week in Australia than each month in England playing football, and a few of my friends in the game told me I was mad to put the relative poverty of football above the relative wealth of singing.

Think of the future, Colin.

Think of the money.

Think of the lifestyle.

All I could think of was the 1961/62 football season.

The Elland Road directors published an official handbook in August, entitled, 'Do You Know Your Club?' The question was rhetorical, I presumed, but in my mind I answered it anyway: *No, I did not know my club.* Leeds United was too heterogeneous an institution to characterise.

I was not fit enough to join the squad for the start of pre-season training. Consequently, when the campaign began on 19 August, I found myself, quite properly, in the reserve team – away to Manchester United. On a hot day, I played inside-left, with Terry Cooper playing outside-left, and we looked great in an all-white strip that was now, on Don Revie's insistence, our official kit. If only our performance was great. We lost 5-2, with Alex Dawson, a 1958 FA Cup finalist for Manchester United, scoring a hat-trick.

On the same day at Elland Road, the first team defeated Charlton Athletic 1-0, with Billy Bremner scoring, and with Albert Johanneson occupying the outside-left position and Jack Charlton playing in the defence, where he belonged. The crowd of 12,916 was way below the break-even figure and ensured that the first-team players missed out on bonus money – much to Charlton's irritation. He had not yet tempered his belligerence.

The reserve-team matches came thick and fast as I built up my fitness, but results in the Central League were bad beyond belief: defeats to Blackburn Rovers (2-1), Wolverhampton Wanderers (4-0), Liverpool (7-1), Bury (3-2), Aston Villa (1-0) and Stoke City (2-1). We did defeat Sheffield United during that period, but what stuck out for me, more than our 2-0 victory, was coming up against Tommy Hoyland, with whom I had played in happier times at Bramall Lane in the 50s. We looked at each other as if to say, *how did we end up in this situation?* The empty terraces and the shrill echoes of the players shouting instructions to each other told the story of our plight. Hoyland was on his way to sign for Bradford City.

Leeds United reserves improved and I started to feel that I was over my knee problems. I decided to speak to Revie, to see if I could return to the first team, but he had his own, more pressing reasons for a meeting. He called me into his office in mid-October to deliver some news.

'Colin, I'm sorry to break it to you, but I'm going to have to sell you.'

'Really? Why?'

'The club needs the money. Attendances are down and the directors cannot keep dipping into their own pockets to keep the club afloat. We've got the Johanneson bloke doing well at outside-left. He didn't cost us a penny and he has got great potential. But you are an asset, you're well known, and we can sell you for a decent fee. We've had offers of £6,000.'

I played for the reserves against Newcastle United at home on 18 October and I realised that the next time I returned to Elland Road it would not be as a Leeds United employee. And so, for the second time in my career, a club decided that they would rather have my value in cash than in what I could produce on the pitch. I shook Revie by the hand and I knew, as did he, that we would remain friends until one of us died. 'No hard feelings, Don,' I said, and I meant it. I liked him no less for the tough decision his directors had forced him to make. Eventually, once he made the team and the club in his own image, he became one of the greatest managers in the history of the game. And one of the most complicated.

Two clubs were willing to pay Leeds the six grand to sign me: Preston North End and Port Vale. Preston seemed the better bet, as they were in the Second Division and their manager, Jimmy Milne, had ambitions to take the club back into the First Division after relegation in May 1961. Negotiations did not go well, however. It was standard practice for clubs to hand a new player an illegal £300 *ex-gratia* payment, but Milne was insistent: 'Sorry, Colin, but Preston North End does not do that sort of thing.' I brooded darkly. No up-front payment – and I would have to relocate to Lancashire, all at my own expense.

Not only were Port Vale willing to pay me £300 in cash but moving there meant I could commute each day from my home in Durkar. They also agreed to pay me a weekly wage of £30 – double my Leeds wage in 1960/61. Included in my new contract were the standard win bonuses and a bonus of £1 for each thousand people above the eleven thousand mark. Norman Low, the Port Vale manager, a former Liverpool, Newport County and Norwich City defender, had already signed seven new players and had infectious ambition. He was tall, well-dressed, and was gentlemanly, a man with similar attributes to those of Joe Mercer. In his fast-paced Liverpool accent (not Scottish, even though he was from Aberdeen), Low explained why he was so keen to sign me.

'The guys down the road [Stoke City] are about to sign Stanley Matthews and they're getting all the attention. We need a former England international of our own to build up some excitement. Stoke's attendances will improve. We need ours to improve, too.'

I was flattered, of course, but I was not so arrogant or daft to think I could ever find myself in the same bracket as Matthews, either as a player or as a publicity stunt. He was an icon who had great emblematic and emotional attachments to Stoke-on-Trent. I was not an icon and I had no emblematic and emotional attachments to the area.

Desmond Hackett of the *Daily Express* wrote: 'Don't do it, Stan! Retire with pride – now!' But I knew that Matthews, aged 46, still had more years left in his legs.

For me, the biggest snag of all was that Port Vale were in the *Third* Division and had just lost 4-1 away to Southend United. Not since April 1953, when I was still a wide-eyed teenager with Wrexham, had I played in the Third Division. But three hundred quid in the hand sounded good, thirty quid a week better still, and regular first-team football best of all. I signed for Port Vale on 18 October 1962 and looked forward to my toughest assignment – trying to take all the local attention away from Stanley Matthews.

That evening, I turned on the television to watch the BBC's *Sportsview*, a midweek sports programme introduced by Peter Dimmock. And there, in glorious monochrome, was live coverage of a smiling Stanley Matthews signing for Stoke City. His wage: £50 per week – double what he had been earning at Blackpool. He could have had more money if he wanted it. Albert Henshall, the Stoke City chairman, knew that Matthews' arrival would not only make the club seem larger and more significant but also add spice to the Port Vale-Stoke City rivalry.

CHAPTER V

Valiant Gentlemen
1961-64: Port Vale, Norman Low, the Beatles

Give a pill a name and the magic diminishes

WHEN PORT VALE ACQUIRED LAND AT HAMIL ROAD, BURSLEM, IN 1944, the plan was to build a 'Wembley of the North', an 80,000-capacity arena with the best pitch in the world. During the six years the stadium took to build, the club directors scaled down their ambitions, so that when Vale Park opened in 1950, at a cost of £50,000, the capacity was 40,000 and bore little resemblance to Wembley. The pitch looked great, however; large, flat and lush. But it was all an illusion. When the first rains of autumn 1950 arrived, they exposed drainage problems that caused unnecessary postponements in 1950/51 because of severe waterlogging. Not until 1960 – just a year before my arrival – did the club fix the problem once and for all. The Vale Park pitch became an obsession at Port Vale. On my first day at the club, wearing a decent suit and my best pair of shoes, I attempted to walk towards the centre circle to familiarise myself with my new environment. A brusque voice stopped me in my tracks.

'Eh, off the pitch!'

'Uh?!'

I turned in the direction from which the rebuke had come and found the groundsman glaring at me, as if he had just caught me inside his house helping myself to his wife's jewellery. And so came my first lesson: the Port Vale groundsman was so important that he had the power to bark orders at the club's players, even the new ex-England international outside-left.

I realised that if you can handle the groundsman at Port Vale, you can handle anything – up to and including a debut against Torquay United. My second lesson was that the pitch was a work of art and, in terms of dimensions and quality, was just about the only thing at Vale Park that did resemble Wembley. My third lesson was that Norman Low had put together a group of players that belied the team's position in the middle of the Third Division.

I wondered what Roy Sproson was doing there. Here was a player of First Division standard who seemed to have ended up in the wrong context, like a larger-than-life actor who only performed in low-budget dramas in off-off-Broadway theatres in New York. Having played in every position except for goalkeeper, Sproson had already been with Port Vale for eleven years when I arrived and he still had another decade to go. At the dawn of the 60s, he had distinguished himself at left-back, with a sweet left foot, which meant that he and I would need to create a good understanding. It did not take long against Torquay for me to realise that Sproson had a great football brain. Well aware of my need to be in possession, he would tell me to drop off deep to ensure he could give me the ball as often as possible. He was as important to Port Vale as Jimmy Hagan had been during my Sheffield United days and as Ernie Taylor had been during my Sunderland days.

I nearly played against Sproson as far back as Christmas Day 1950. Aged just seventeen, I was in the Wrexham reserve team for the Cheshire League match against Port Vale reserves, which we won 4-2 in front of 1,028 spectators. The programme listed him in the Port Vale team at No. 6 but he was replaced on the day of the match by Jimmy Todd, a Belfast-born half-back, who represented the Ireland team twice between 1946 and 1947, and served Port Vale until 1953. Sproson was already a Port Vale first-team player in 1950 and would remain so until 1972. Incidentally, the right-half for Port Vale reserves that Christmas Day was Albert Leake, who, as manager, would take me to Macclesfield Town in August 1966.

During my Port Vale debut on 21 October 1961, Sproson was as good as his word, beckoning me to come deep to receive the ball, always keeping an eye on me to see if I was in space, playing for me rather than for him. The ball was attracted to him, as it is to all good players, and I felt liberated. The Torquay United right-back, Colin Bettany, a Leicester lad, had a tough time dealing with my pace. An attendance of 10,383 saw Port Vale record a 4-1 victory, with two goals by Brian Jackson, one by Bert Llewellyn and one by me. One newspaper described my debut as 'triumphant', a compliment that, in the Third Division, reeked of hyperbole. Eventually, a large image of my goal would adorn a wall at the newly constructed Port Vale Social Club, presumably to celebrate the aesthetics of the photography rather than the essence of my skill. I welcomed the attention.

Three days after my Port Vale debut, Stanley Matthews played the first match of his second spell at Stoke City, at home to Huddersfield Town. The attendance of 35,974 eclipsed that of the 8,409 who turned up for Stoke's previous home match, against Preston North End. Norman Low bristled at the news and, fearing a Stoke revival, made an audacious attempt to coax Tom Finney, my former England teammate, out of retirement. Finney was not interested in a move to Port Vale, partly because he would have needed regular injections in the injured groin that forced him to retire in the first place, but mainly because his name, reputation and history were linked so inextricably to Preston North End, it seemed inconceivable that he would play for any other club.

Needing something to counter the excitement that Matthews was inspiring at Stoke City, Port Vale went on a timely FA Cup run that captured the imagination of the town. After defeating Bradford Park Avenue 1-0 away, Crewe Alexandra 3-0 at home in a replay, and Northampton Town 3-1 at home, we secured a fourth-round tie away to ... Sunderland. I would be returning to Roker Park, to one of the English game's finest stadia, but this time as a member of the opposing team. I wondered what, if anything, Alan Brown, the Sunderland manager, thought about a reunion with me. I welcomed the chance to prove to him that he should have made more effort to keep me at Roker Park in 1960. Not since my seventh England appearance, against Scotland at Wembley in 1957, was I so keyed up about a match. My Port Vale teammates asked me for inside information about the Sunderland players, but I told them that our passion would prove far more effective than any knowledge I could disseminate. Besides, I knew Norman Low had done his homework. The Sunderland players were no mystery. Just as I thought Port Vale were a Second Division club playing in the Third Division, so Sunderland were a First Division club playing in the Second Division.

But Low was hobbling about on crutches. In the depths of winter, he contrived to damage his Achilles and ended up in the North Staffordshire Royal Infirmary.

It was from his hospital bed that he made a new signing: Ralph Hunt, a centre-forward, from Swindon Town for £3,500. Hunt turned up for this first home match, against Shrewsbury Town on 16 December, on a motorbike and then proceeded to score a hat-trick in a 4-1 victory. Alas, he was cup-tied – he had played for Swindon Town against Kettering Town – and so could not form part of squad for the trip to Roker Park on 27 January 1962.

At Sunderland, the usual suspects were there waiting for us: Peter Wakeham in goal, Len Ashurst, Stan Anderson, and Charlie Hurley. There were also new names: George Herd, an inside-forward formerly of Clyde in Scotland, and a new centre-forward, Brian Clough, of whom I knew much from his time with Middlesbrough and from the natural bombast that was making him famous.

The odds being against us, I devised a plan to improve our chances of victory. Half an hour or so before the kick-off, I gave each of the Port Vale players a pill.

'Take this,' I said, going from player to player. 'It will give you so much energy, you won't stop running.'

'What's this, Colin?' one player shouted out.

'Just take it,' I replied. 'You'll be glad you did.'

My international experiences with England meant my Port Vale colleagues readily trusted me, and nobody else asked any questions. Nobody considered the implications. Nobody noticed that I never took one.

But the pills worked a treat. We outplayed Sunderland for much of the match – Clough, cutting a neglected figure, barely had a touch – and were unfortunate to only draw 0-0 in front of a massive 48,468 crowd. As a member of the opposition, such as I was, the Roker Roar seemed louder and more intense than it ever did when I played for Sunderland. My own performance, full of fire, speed and skill, had more in common with my halcyon days of 1956. Many of the Sunderland supporters appreciated my efforts and said so as I walked off the pitch after the final whistle. My hitherto damaged ankle did not trouble me at all, nor did my left knee. But my increased adrenaline enabled me to trouble Cecil Irwin, the Sunderland right-back, who might have asked himself, *Why wasn't Colin this good when he was a player at Roker Park?*

After the match, we went for a large post-match meal in a hotel near Newcastle. Used to such treatment, the players knew how to pace themselves, but Sid Alcock, our bus driver, was less experienced in such environments. Thinking that the first course, a bowl of soup, was actually the main meal, he bloated himself with half a dozen bread rolls. When the main course did arrive, he was too full to eat anything else. One of the players ate Alcock's meal.

On the Monday, as we prepared for a light training session, Roy Sproson shouted out to me, 'Eh, Colin, what were those pills you gave us?'

'Aspirin, Roy,' I said. 'Just plain, ordinary aspirin.'

I did not have the heart to tell anyone that I got the aspirins from the medical chest of Lol Hamlett, the trainer, who had captained the club in the early 50s and had become a beloved figure. What I did not know at the time was that Sproson always drank a slug of Scotch before each match, given to him by Hamlett, so in all likelihood he played an important FA Cup tie having broken the rule about not mixing aspirin with alcohol. With no financial cost to me, and no risk to anybody's health, I had given my colleagues a psychological boost – the perception that they had taken amphetamines – in our most important match of the season to date. Placebo can be a wonderful thing, playing tricks with the mind, giving players a strength they did not know they possessed. The drawback, of course, is that I could only pull such a stunt once. There was no point in my offering the players pills for the replay at home on 31 January. Give a pill a name and the magic diminishes. However, I learnt that Hamlett fooled Brian Jackson, our right winger, with the aspirin trick later in the season – this time when Jackson claimed to be feeling unwell.

Norman Low seemed surprised that we drew. 'It is the unexpected that makes the FA Cup competition so attractive,' he wrote in his programme notes for the replay. Unexpected? Not to the Port Vale players. Having brought Sunderland back to Vale Park, our main advantage was the size and quality of the pitch – perfect for Sproson's passing ability and for my pace. And, in torrential rain, we used it to full effect to secure a 3-1 victory in front of 28,206 spectators, many hundreds of whom had been queuing since six o'clock in the morning waiting for the gates to open. Brian Jackson, Harry Poole, and Bert Llewellyn scored the goals. Willie McPheat, an inside-left who joined Sunderland after I left, scored their consolation and, again, Brian Clough barely touched the ball. Defensively, we were superb that night. Ken Hancock, our goalkeeper, damaged his ankle in the first few minutes and was a virtual cripple for the remaining eighty-odd minutes. 'Hail! Vale's Fearless Five,' went the headline in the *Daily Mirror*, paying tribute to the men who protected Hancock and denied the Sunderland forwards. John Nicholson, our Liverpudlian centre-back, was so good that I wondered why

Liverpool had sold him.

As well as I had played in the first match, I improved in the replay, revelling in the extra space, creating chance after chance, playing better *against* Sunderland than I had ever done *for* them. Dispensing with false modesty, I knew I had turned in the type of performance that had attracted me to the England international selectors in 1956. It was all much to Alan Brown's chagrin. Afterwards, as we passed each other in the vestibule area between the two dressing rooms, I tried to catch his eye to say hello. His hair was soaked, his demeanour scornful. My natural instinct was to laugh, but I suppressed it because I wanted to be magnanimous in victory. He looked back at me – a dark stare born of revulsion and awkwardness – and then he looked away quickly, avoiding my olive branch in a manner that neither surprised nor perturbed me. The least he could have done was wish Port Vale good luck in the fifth-round tie away to Fulham on 17 February. Les McDowall would have done. Reg Freeman would have done. Joe Mercer would have done. Bill Murray would have done. Jack Taylor would have done. Don Revie would have done.

I could only admire Alan Brown that, for all his faults, for all his odd idiosyncrasies, he remained true to himself: the charmless bad loser who did not much like players who had been more successful than he had. I was grateful that I at least knew where I stood with him. He was consistent – which is more than I could say for Port Vale during that winter of 1961/62. Amid the euphoria of the FA Cup run, our League fixtures sometimes appeared as obstacles on the road to football's *empyrean*.

We played away to Bradford Park Avenue on 3 February. Charming stadium, nice people, but very Third Division. Norman Low put a veteran, Peter Taylor, in goal to replace Ken Hancock, whose injury early in the Sunderland replay was severe and threatened to keep him out for a month. I had been under the impression that Taylor, a rather morose figure, looking older than his 33 years, had retired after leaving Middlesbrough in 1961. Indeed, in later years, he said he was 'finished' by the time he moved to Port Vale. So it came as a surprise to see him hanging around Vale Park, never really sure if he wanted to play or not, never really fitting in. I do not recall speaking to him even once. He would come to training, barely say a word to anybody, and disappear as quickly as he could. He was on the periphery, aloof, bored and overweight; as uninterested in the club as the club, apparently, was in him. The prevailing view was that he was not particularly bright – thick as pudding, one player said – and certainly not the type you would expect to make a successful career as a coach.

With Jimmy Scoular, the tough-tackling former Portsmouth and Newcastle United wing-half, in superb form for Bradford Park Avenue, they defeated Port Vale 2-1. And so ended Peter Taylor's only match for Vale. Having come to the wrong club at the wrong time, he made it clear to Norman Low that he was nowhere near as good as Ken Hancock; the first example, to my knowledge, of a football player talking himself out of a place in the first-team squad. Taylor moved to Burton Albion as player-manager in May 1962 and then, after a valuable education at Hartlepools United, popped up as an extraordinarily successful assistant to Brian Clough at Derby County and then Nottingham Forest, winning League Championships and European Cups. Thick as pudding? Not in the late 60s and 70s, when he turned himself into one of the game's great talent-spotters. Nothing in football surprised me as much as Peter Taylor's remarkable accomplishments alongside Clough. I never saw any of it coming.

Our FA Cup form in 1961/62 seemed an aberration, evidence of which came when Port Vale lost 2-0 at home to Grimsby Town in the Third Division on 10 February. With Ken Hancock still injured and Peter Taylor not up to the task, Norman Low gave a League debut in goal to John Cooke, a teenager from South Yorkshire. There was no doubting Grimsby's merit – they would secure promotion at the end of the season – and that their right-back, Don Donovan, an Irishman formerly of Everton, marked me with skill and dexterity. But, as a team, we felt heavy-legged and preoccupied, with a sense that Football League fixtures were all so low-key and anticlimactic after the electricity of the FA Cup matches against Sunderland.

Worse still, I could feel a discomfort in the left groin area, a discomfort that turned to pain, a pain that kept me awake at night. My body was giving up on me. I picked up the injury in training when Eric Jones, a new addition to the backroom staff, took the cliché *no pain, no gain* rather too literally. He looked like a violinist but sounded like a sergeant major. He had us all lying on the floor with heavy weights and then shouting at us to get to our feet, still holding the weights. Nobody enjoyed it. Nobody saw the point of it. And then my groin went. I cursed Jones – I wished he would go back to his full-time job with De Graafschap in the Netherlands – and went to see the ever-reliable Lol Hamlett. 'You should go and see your local doctor at home, Colin,' he said. 'You might need some injections to get you through the rest of the season.'

Hamlett and Jones were opposites. Whereas Jones had a foul mouth and, as an overqualified FA coach, took himself too seriously, Hamlett was a true gentleman, who hated swearing and put into Port Vale far more than he took out. Hamlett went to church regularly, whereas Jones saw the training pitch as his place of worship. Whereas Jones had a moderate career on the right wing with Portsmouth before the war and Crewe Alexandra just after it, Hamlett distinguished himself as a stable and loyal right-back with Port Vale. He started with Bolton Wanderers and he was at Burnden Park for the disaster that killed 33 people on 9 March 1946. When he staged his testimonial at Vale Park in 1976, Don Revie agreed to bring eleven players to provide the opposition. We loved Hamlett, and as a term of affection, we nicknamed him Lollipop.

I made an appointment to see Dr Switalski in Wakefield and handed him a letter written by Hamlett. Dr Switalski told me to take down my trousers and lie on the orthopaedic bed he had against a wall. He pulled out a six-inch needle, manoeuvring it into the correct position of the groin area. As he hit the spot and injected a transparent substance, my eyes watered. First pain, then relief. Cortisone can be a wonderful thing. 'That should see you through training, Colin,' he said. 'Come and see me next week.' And so began a new friendship.

Local newspapers kept reminding us, quite rightly, that we had not won in the Third Division since defeating Newport County 3-0 on 26 December. Had we put too much emphasis on the FA Cup at the expense of our bid to secure promotion to the Second Division? It would not have been the first time. Having reached the FA Cup semi-final in 1954 and the fifth round in 1960, Port Vale had built up a reputation for defeating teams from higher divisions. But in between, in 1958, the club found itself in the Fourth Division – just one level above the Port Vale reserve team that played in the Cheshire League. Now, in 1962, the club was again underachieving in the Football League and overachieving in the FA Cup.

Muted atmospheres and empty stadia

Not that the Port Vale supporters cared. On 17 February 1962, more than 5,000 of them travelled down to London on special trains, making for a great atmosphere and evoking memories of 1954. Would the absence of Johnny Haynes from the Fulham team give Port Vale an advantage? *The Times* suggested, somewhat grandiloquently, that a 'Fulham forward line without Haynes is like a play without the central character, or a C. P. Snow novel lacking Lewis Eliot'. Would the return of Ken Hancock, the beneficiary of a cortisone injection, in the Port Vale goal prove crucial? Would my groin injury inhibit me in our most important match of the season to date? After 'being besieged for most of the first half', according to *The Times*, Port Vale 'fought back to good purpose in the second' and looked the likelier of the teams to open the scoring. We thought we had scored when, early in the second half, Brian Jackson struck a low shot from long range and the ball seemed to cross the line as Tony Macedo, the Fulham goalkeeper, fumbled. Macedo then pulled the ball back into play, straight into the path of Bert Llewellyn, who missed an open goal from just a couple of yards out. Macedo admitted afterwards that the ball had, indeed, crossed the line. Ken Dagnall, the Bolton-based referee, who would take charge of matches at the 1966 World Cup, did not consult the linesman nearest to the action and waved away our appeals. Alas, the only footage that remains from the match is the monochrome Pathé film that lasts ninety seconds and is not clear enough to reveal whether or not Jackson's shot crossed the line. But Llewellyn, who was close enough to see, swears we should have had a goal. Worse was to come. With four minutes remaining, David Metchick, playing in an uncustomary outside-left position, went down too easily under a challenge from Selwyn Whalley, our right-back-cum-schoolteacher, inside the eighteen-yard box. Penalty! And for the second time Dagnall endured the wrath of the Port Vale players and supporters.

'It was,' *The Times* reported, 'an unfortunate lapse by the Port Vale defence, which had been playing intelligently under pressure'. Jim Langley scored and Fulham went into the quarter-finals. Had we have drawn, we would have fancied our chances in a replay at Vale Park. My groin problem did affect me to some extent but not nearly as much as the fine performance by the man marking me: George Cohen, who played well defensively and proved equally effective for Fulham overlapping their right-winger, Maurice Cook. I was not surprised when, two years later, Cohen made his England debut and two years after that won the 1966 World Cup. Nor was I surprised to find myself in pain on the journey back from London.

Dr Switalski's cortisone injections could no longer mask the problem. I needed rest. I ruled myself out of Port Vale's match away to Watford on 28 February and did not play for the first team for the rest of the season. I even missed the presentation of a trophy to commemorate Port Vale being the best FA Cup giantkillers for 1961/62, which took place before the match against Bournemouth & Boscombe Athletic. The players received gold cufflinks, or so I heard. I never received mine – despite playing in all seven of Port Vale's matches in the FA Cup. Rest having helped me more than cortisone, I felt able to return to the first-team squad by spring, but Norman Low put me in the reserves and kept me there. I did not complain. Stan Edwards, another player whom Low brought from the Liverpool area, took my place on the left wing, while I familiarised myself with the muted atmospheres and empty stadia of the North Regional League.

A cut-throat shave

Port Vale finished 1961/62 in twelfth position, which, given the talent we had in our squad, represented failure to the point of negligence. We only avoided relegation by nine points. Portsmouth won the Third Division with the brilliant Bobby Campbell at wing-half, Ron Saunders at centre-forward and Tony Barton at outside-right. In the early 80s, Saunders as manager and Barton as coach, and then later as manager, would bring massive success to Aston Villa. Defensively, Port Vale were excellent, and we benefited from having Ken Hancock in goal. We conceded fewer goals (58) than Queens Park Rangers (73), who finished fourth. Our problem was goals; i.e., the lack of them. We only scored 65 in the League – fewer than Torquay United, on 76, who were relegated. How was that even possible when we had forwards such as Arthur Longbottom and Bert Llewellyn? Longbottom scored sixteen in the Third Division, Llewellyn fifteen, while Stan Steele chipped in with eight. My meagre return of one goal in eleven League appearances disappointed me, although I consoled myself in the knowledge that I contributed greatly to the excellent strike rates of Longbottom and Llewellyn. And, of course, my injury problems insulated me from criticism.

For all my frustrations of missing out after February, I felt content at Vale Park. There was a friendly, down-to-earth feel about the club, attributes that Leeds United in 1960/61 seemed to lack. There were no prima donnas, few egos, and an egalitarian attitude that took me back to those tranquil days at Sheffield United when my playing career had more future than past. Being a Scot and a Liverpudlian all rolled into one, Norman Low fostered the kind of approach that put the emphasis on fellowship and familiarity. He hated arrogance. He hated disharmony. On coach trips home after away matches, he would stand next to the driver and entertain us all with his jokes and his impressions, and the thought crossed my mind that he had the skill of timing that could have helped him become a professional comedian.

To perform one impression, he put on a false nose, and I saw players laugh so much they were shaking. I knew of professional comedians who never elicited such a response from an audience. His father, Wilf Low, had flourished with Newcastle United just before the Great War and won the FA Cup in 1910 and a runners-up medal in 1911. A centre-half of some distinction, whom players and spectators nicknamed the Laughing Cavalier, he also played for the Scotland national team from 1911 to 1920. I never got to meet him, as he died in 1933, the year of my birth, but Norman Low spoke affectionately about his father and was proud to have been part of such a good footballing heritage. Port Vale was unique in that there were no cliques, and even Ken Hancock's dogs, which he sometimes brought to training, enhanced the overall conviviality. Low could have put any pair of players into a hotel room before an away match and the camaraderie would have burgeoned.

It was my good fortune that I usually roomed with Longbottom, who never got over the novelty of being a professional player or of being asked for his autograph. He never took supporters for granted and they, usually, could see a bit of them in him. He was a great runner, agreeably whole-hearted, with the type of work ethic that would have endeared him to my dad's colleagues down the pit. Longbottom wanted balls over the top, which made him a nightmare for defenders, but which arguably compromised our tactical approach. Perhaps, with such cerebral players as Roy Sproson and Harry Poole, we should have been more sophisticated and less direct. A trained hairdresser and eminently popular among Port Vale supporters for his all-action style, Longbottom had a wonderful honesty and integrity about him and I had no doubts that he would have been successful at whatever career path he had chosen.

But he hated being a Longbottom. He told me during one away trip that he intended to change his name. 'I don't want my kids to be burdened with such a surname,' he said. And so, one day, through deed poll, Arthur Longbottom became

Arthur Langley – and his children, Mark, Keith and Kirsty, no doubt breathed a collective sigh of relief when they also acquired the Langley surname.

Surprisingly, I never heard any of the players mock Longbottom for his name. Given the proliferation of amateur comedians at Vale Park, one might have expected him to be the butt of the jokes, but everybody spared him, probably because everybody liked him. Even Stan Steele, for whom everything was a joke, decided that the Longbottom name was a no-go area. On the pitch, Steele was vital, marrying great technical ability with his inclination for covering more ground than seemed humanly possible. Norman Low said that Steele did the work of two players, which was no exaggeration.

One could have said the same for Terry Miles, a half-back, who had already been with Port Vale for six years when I arrived. A local lad, he was super-fit on the pitch and eager to please off it, and he expressed pride in having won the Fourth Division championship with Port Vale in 1959. He was the type of midfield player every team needs, and I admired his guts, especially in the depths of winter when pitches became quagmires and less talented midfield players among the opposition blurred the distinction between football and mud wrestling.

If we had a talisman, he was Roy Sproson, whose left foot had a uniquely close relationship with the ball. Being a left winger, I always saw the value of a union between a left-back and an outside-left. On the pitch, where it mattered most, Sproson and I worked well together, and Norman Low, always keen to promote any alliances on the field of play, would not have wanted it any other way.

I do wonder, however, where we would have finished in the table had John Nicholson not been at the heart of our defence. Tall and strong, he had a presence about him, and there seemed no doubt to me that he only left Liverpool because he realised he was never going to displace Ron Yeats for a regular first-team place. Nicholson might not have been good enough for Bill Shankly's first team – not many players were – but he was certainly too good for the Third Division. With his wavy blond hair and his ability to jump high, even from a standing position, he stood out on the pitch, dominant and brave, and was one of two reasons – the other being Ken Hancock – for why we defended so well in 1961/62. Nicholson would remain a part of my story for a few years yet, even if, as we shall see, his own story had only a few more years left to run and would end in tragedy.

At the other end of the efficacy spectrum was Ralph Hunt, a talented forward, who had been playing since 1950 but never really settled anywhere. He had a good spell with Norwich City, averaging a goal every two matches from 1955-58, but he had already played for six different clubs when he turned up at Port Vale in December 1961, six weeks after my arrival. We laughed when he turned up for matches on his motorbike, we respected his talent, but we recoiled when, as was often the case, we smelt the alcohol on his breath. Maybe his proclivity for drink was one reason why Norman Low sold him to Newport County for a couple of grand in the summer of 1962.

And what a summer it was. In May, the entire Port Vale first-team squad went on a tour of Poland to play four matches, during which time we would enjoy an eight-day holiday within the awe-inspiring splendour of the Tatra Mountains. We would also visit Zakopane, Warsaw and Krakow. There were pitfalls along the way, which, paradoxically, was part of the fun. I played in the match against Górnik Zabrze, one of Poland's top teams, and sat out the other three. The match at Bridgoczcy suffered for having a ninety-minute half-time break. We had to wait for the Wyścig Pokoju (the Warsaw-Berlin-Prague Cycle Race of Peace) to run its course, which delayed the start of the second half. We lost 1-0 and Norman Low was furious. He felt the delay was part of a plan to disorientate us. The referee, he told the press in his Liverpool accent, 'was obviously determined that the local team should win'.

The trip to the Tatra River was not without incident. We went out in boats and it was when we were shooting rapids that the rear vessel capsized. Nobody suffered injury, never mind threat to life, but the episode created bad feeling for the rest of the excursion. Low began to wonder if the locals calculated everything just to irritate us.

Poland was, by turns, exciting and boring, enlightening and heterodox, free and restricted. Big Brother was everywhere, usually wearing a uniform and carrying a gun. There was no escaping the sense that we were situated behind the Iron Curtain, existing in a context for which we neither had the skills nor the back-up systems to function properly. This Poland of the second Władysław Gomułka era, for all its designs on modernity, found itself consumed by its own paranoia. The first thing we were told was not to shout in the street. Quietness was essential, particularly at night. Even the appearance of having fun seemed an affront to local sensibilities, so better not to smile. We had no access to television. In the rare time we met locals, they were friendly enough, but they were in the minority compared to the gun-carrying soldiers who occupied every street corner and wore morose expressions, with the lines of joylessness engraved all over their craggy features.

There were many hours of tedium, which meant we had to go to great lengths to keep ourselves amused. One night in Warsaw we went to a club, which aroused the interest of the police, who kept a collective eye on us throughout. The Americans in there kept asking us for drinks. When we got up to leave, the police officers followed us out and into the street. After that, we spent longer in our hotel, dreaming of the flight back home, which exacerbated the boredom. Time moves slowly when you want it to move quickly. We had more spending money than we could spend because there was nothing on which to spend it. In Krakow, Arthur Longbottom had an idea: a cut-throat shave in a nearby barber. So off we went. The two of us. Excited at the thought of filling half an hour with one man and his razor. That is how bad life had become.

The best part of having smooth faces was that we now looked better in real life than we did in our passport photographs.

To fly airplanes

Home at last.

Six weeks off meant time away from football, time with my family, and time to consider my singing schedule. I found myself on the same bill as the Folies Burlesque girls at the Leeds City Variety Hall, with Dennis Shirley, Franklyn & Yorke, Johnny Wager, and Mara Laine also adding to the eclectic mix of entertainment. Again, the compere introduced me as 'The Voice With a Kick In It'. Given my Leeds United connections, the locals gave me a heart-warming standing ovation; the type of enthusiasm that seemed all too rare at Elland Road during my time there.

It made me think about how Don Revie was doing. Not too well, at this point in his managerial career. Leeds only just avoided relegation to the Third Division but the board of directors there gave him all the time he needed, partly because they could not afford another manager, but mainly because they rated him as a visionary and as a tactician, and well able to blood all the talented youngsters. The consequences of the directors' decision would be astonishing – although I could not have known that at the time.

For now, keen to maximise the novelty of my act, I put an advertisement in *Stage* magazine:

International singing footballer
COLIN GRAINGER
Radio: TV: Cabaret: HMV Recording Star
Enq.: Mr. T. Fensome, 48 Low Lane, Durkar, Wakefield, Yorkshire, manager
(No sole agent)

The 'Mr. T. Fensome' was Terry Fensome, the nephew of my wife, Doreen. A charming man with a quick mind, he could not wait to leave school so he could train to become a pilot. I put him in charge of my bookings to give him some extra work before he moved to the United States to fly airplanes on a full-time basis. His involvement with my appointments gave him an idea: why not take the entire Grainger family – me, Doreen, Colin junior – to the U.S.A. and take my singing to a new level? He would manage me there, sending me all over the country to larger venues, alongside more famous acts; to major television shows; to famous clubs . . . anywhere that could manufacture an audience. I liked the fertility of his mind and I admired his passion, but for as long as I was healthy enough to play professional football, my singing would always be an adjuvant pursuit.

Besides, Terry Fensome did not need me. In time, having clocked up millions of miles of flying time, he developed a trusting and successful working relationship with Freddie Laker and subsequently became president of Laker Airways. Doreen's nephew began by flying airplanes and loved the industry so much that he ended up running a major airline.

It was around about this time that I delighted in the progress of Ken Jones, a Havercroft lad, who was emerging as a full-back with Bradford Park Avenue. Jones grew up next door to my parents in West Street – I remembered him as a little boy, kicking a ball about around The Square – and it seemed more than a coincidence that he should make the grade. After playing more than a hundred matches for Park Avenue, he performed with distinction for Southampton until 1971, ending his professional career with Cardiff City in 1972. Later, Cyril Knowles and his brother, Peter, who both grew up near the Monckton Colliery, made names for themselves as fine players in the 70s. Cyril Knowles became a Tottenham Hotspur legend, while Peter became a Wolverhampton Wanderers stalwart. Such a small part of West Yorkshire but so much talent. I felt proud.

Passing the time away

Right, lads. Listen up. Come on! Quick! I want to make one thing clear. This is going to be the toughest pre-season you've ever had. And if you don't like it . . .

Such was the welcome from Eric Jones to pre-season training for 1962/63. Having resigned from his position as manager of De Graafschap in the Netherlands, he took up a full-time job at Port Vale as Norman Low's assistant. While I rarely questioned Low's judgement, this was one occasion when he, no doubt with some help from the board of directors, got it spectacularly wrong. Jones arrived in June with the expression of a man determined to inflict pain on the entire first-team squad. He did not seem to appreciate that preparation for a new campaign is about peaking at the right time and about making sure your best efforts take place in competitive matches, not on the training pitch.

With Jones, it was effing this and effing that, constant abuse, sticking his nose into every corner, and asserting himself in a manner that made many of us believe he was either insecure or naturally choleric. He seemed to relish pushing us beyond realistic and even unhealthy limits. I do not think any member of the squad benefited from this new approach or welcomed it. I felt sure that Low became embarrassed by him. Worse still, Jones would sit next to Low on the bus to away matches, meaning that Lol Hamlett, the club's one-man sedative, had to make do with helping out with the reserve team in the semi-obscurity of the North Regional League.

Norman Low made a number of new signings, most notably John Rowland, an outside-right from Nottingham Forest, who could hit the ball hard and benefitted greatly from the new, lighter balls that had become part of the game in this new era. Another forward, Terry Harkin, arrived from Coleraine in Northern Ireland with a great reputation. Eric Jones' influence manifested itself in the arrival from De Graafschap of Jim Watton, a half-back who would become a left-back. And then there was Mel Machin, a seventeen-year-old midfield player, who signed professional forms, looked extremely talented, and would make a name for himself with Norwich City in the 70s. I heard, however, that Low could never sign the players he really wanted and that the board of directors imposed their will on him.

Free of pain and now moving perfectly, I expected to make the starting line-up for the opening match of the season away to Wrexham. But Low selected Stan Edwards at outside-left, as he did for the next match, at home to Millwall. Just as I accepted Low's decisions the previous spring, so I respected them now. I had no right to a first-team place. Edwards – a nice guy, talented and fast, but more an inside-left than a winger – deserved his chance, while, deep down, I lived in fear that my groin problem would return and rule me out of the entire season. Such thoughts of doom dogged most players, for the average professional was insecure and paranoid and never as assured behind the scenes as he appeared on the pitch. Physical concerns were only part of the problem. Mental fears could do more damage, destroying confidence, creating timidity, forcing a player to pull out of tackles or to avoid sprinting at full throttle. I wondered if clubs might have benefited from employing psychologists. But who did we have instead? Eric Bloody Jones! The joke at the time was that when a bottle hit Jones in the face during the match against Wrexham, thrown ostensibly by a spectator, the culprit was really one of the Port Vale players.

I made the starting line-up for the third match, at home to Reading, during which I scored to help secure a 2-0 victory. And so began what was, for me, by my recent standards, a full season. But it would be a period of frustration and of killing time, partly because my groin problem never quite went away and partly because nature bestowed on Britain the worst winter since 1946/47. The Big Freeze was on its way.

But greater cataclysms were more immediate. In mid-October, the board of directors decided that Eric Jones was doing more harm than good, ripped up his contract and told him to leave. Then, on 30 October, just a few days after Terry Harkin scored twice to give Port Vale a 2-1 victory against Swindon Town, Norman Low resigned. 'I have not always been able to see eye to eye with the board on their buying policy,' he told the press. 'Lately the position has become more acute and I felt obliged to take this step.' Off the record, however, he was becoming furious with Joe Machin, the chairman, and I understand the two men could not be in the same room together without arguing. Had Low not resigned, Machin would almost certainly have sacked him. Port Vale might have been too large a club for the Third Division but it was too small to accommodate Norman Low and Joseph Machin at the same time. Only one man could survive the morass. Low stepped aside with good grace to become a scout with Stoke City, an important position but one that neither reflected his ability nor his personality.

I was shocked at his departure, of course, as I felt we were making progress and had a great chance of securing promotion to the Second Division. I also enjoyed working under Low and I relished those afternoons drinking coffee with his son, who had all of the charm of his father but none of the baggage and cynicism. And so, not for the first time in my career, I suffered for the transitory nature of a manager's position. One day he is there, looking authoritative, making you feel great. The next day he is gone, no longer influential, ushering in a new regime; a regime that might not be to your personal advantage.

Goodbye Norman Low, hello Freddie Steele; yes, the same Freddie Steele who had managed Port Vale from 1951-57 and had led the club to the semi-final of the FA Cup. It seemed an odd choice, for Steele seemed a part of the past, to the days of heavy balls, baggy shorts, and of Vale Park's swimming pool of a pitch. But the chairman wanted a manager he deemed to be safe and uncontroversial, one who could accept interference from the directors. So much for the view that selection committees were a relic of a bygone era. At Vale Park, the directors still had more say in what happened on the pitch than their collective experience and knowledge warranted. The average director probably knew more about football than Len Shackleton had suggested in his book in 1956 but still not enough to sign players, plan tactics, and select starting elevens.

I asked Roy Sproson about what players might expect from working under Freddie Steele. Based on his experiences of the 50s, Sproson painted a picture of a man full of drive, enthusiasm and energy, with an ability to change tactics depending on the occasion or the nature of the opposition. Harry Poole told me that Steele was using 60s methods as far back as 1953, when most people in the English game were still struggling with advancements in Europe and South America. It all sounded good – until I realised that Steele had none of the drive and enthusiasm of which Sproson spoke. After a while, even Sproson had to admit that Steele had lost interest and was, in observance of that age-old axiom, going through the motions. We responded to Steele because we had to and because he still had the ability to make his teams impenetrable at the back. Just as Bill Murray and Alan Brown were complete opposites at Sunderland, so it was with Norman Low and Freddie Steele. I cursed my bad luck and kept my mouth shut.

Before his first match in charge, against Bristol Rovers in the FA Cup, Steele made an odd request of Harry Poole:

'If we're the team kicking off, I want the ball to go to John Nicholson and then to you. Then I want you to kick it in to the crowd. As far as possible, into the crowd. Understood?'

The reasoning was that such an intervention would protect Port Vale from conceding an early goal. My view was that giving the ball away needlessly was the act of an amateur, not a professional. Still, Bert Llewellyn scored twice and we won 2-0, but probably in spite of Steele, not because of him. Our next match, on 9 November, was an experimental Friday night affair against Barnsley. In the 74th minute, I received a booking for dissent. Thirty seconds later, Stan Steele scored to give Port Vale the lead, and then in the 82nd minute, he was sent off for fouling Barnsley's Bob Nicol. After the final whistle confirmed our 1-0 victory, the referee, Jim Pickles, needed a police escort to leave the field of play.

Port Vale defeated Aldershot 2-0 in the FA Cup second round, a match significant for it being Sproson's 500th for the club. We applauded him in the dressing room afterwards and paid homage to his loyalty.

It was during the Big Freeze of 1962/63, when we did not play a League match in January or February, that Steele made two decisions I regarded as inexplicable to the point of lunacy: the first, selling Arthur Longbottom to Millwall; the second, selling Llewellyn to Northampton Town. It was no secret that Steele preferred defending to attacking, and he set his teams up to keep clean sheets and smother creative players. But to dispense with our two leading scorers of the previous season seemed risky at best. What did he want? Forty-two goalless draws a season?

Paradoxically, the Big Freeze abetted me. My groin problem meant I needed more rest between matches, so cancelled training sessions and postponed matches ensured that I remained fresh, putting a smile on the face of Dr Switalski. He feared that I was becoming reliant on the cortisone injections. Given how icy the roads had become, particularly near to Buxton, Port Vale gave me permission to train with Barnsley, and it was at Oakwell that I sprinted up and down the terraces in a bid to build my stamina and my leg muscles. I worked as hard as I would have done had it been pre-season training. I wanted to prove my fitness. Freddie Steele had a different attitude to my injury, however. He thought the pain was all in my head and he sent me to a different doctor, who told me that there was nothing wrong with my groin. The advice: if you feel pain, just run it off. Fortunately, Vale Park had a big pitch, perpetually soft and damp, which preserved me from serious damage. On a hard pitch, I might have been putting my entire career in jeopardy. But I resented it greatly that Steele questioned my integrity. I could live with somebody questioning my ability as a player but not my honesty as a human being.

By this time, I was making news not so much for my football but for my singing. *The Stage* magazine featured on 27 December 1962 my recent performance at the Nuffield Centre, London:

Fair-haired, Yorkshire-born Colin Grainger has in the past found such fame on the football field as to be picked several times as an England international. Whilst with Sunderland F.C., he won nine [sic] caps for his country. As a singer he also achieved considerable success. He's done a Moss Empires tour, played many of the top clubs in the North of England and made four records. And taking time off from his current football club – Port Vale – he came to London recently to appear on the bill at the Nuffield Centre and prove that he has a voice which could – if he got the right breaks – make him a show business star. Confidently and with good showmanship he sang his way through one time hits 'I know' and 'Dreaming', a Jolson oldie 'Mammy' and a pretty ballad 'The Key', and demonstrated that his already mentioned voice is strong, powerful and used well. Two other vocalists on the bill also showed distinctive promise – Billy Moss and Denise Kaye. The former – a handsome, rugged sort of fellow with a casual style inspired by Michael Holliday and Perry Como – left the audience wanting more as he effortlessly and tastefully sang his way through such well-known numbers as 'Just in Time', 'The Party's Over' and 'Stay as Sweet as You Are'. The latter – looking very pretty in a smart black dress – showed an inventive mind as in her sophisticated, appealing song-settling she put inventive interpretations to such "evergreens" as 'Billy Bailey' and 'The Birth of the Blues'. From Hungary-born George Kovati there was a most accomplished display of magic in which he continually had the audience baffled with tricks involving such objects as scarves, cards, string and an egg. Compering the show in a friendly, easy-going manner was Bob Kelly. In fact, this was a remarkable performance – it was his stage debut and he showed great promise. His material was good, his personality pleasing and in his own spot he gagged and played violin.

The warmth of the theatre compensated for the cold of the football stadium. During January and February, Port Vale managed just one match: an FA Cup tie on 27 February, in which we defeated Gillingham 4-2 at Priestfield – a match that had hitherto suffered myriad postponements. We lost count of how many times we travelled to Gillingham only to return once we saw the frozen pitch. It was a relief to play. I scored one of the goals: a penalty.

March meant the end of the Big Freeze and the start of the great thaw. The matches came thick and fast, with two in particular sticking out. We played Sheffield United, my former club, in the FA Cup fourth round in torrential rain at home on 13 March, my goal proving a consolation in a 2-1 defeat. Then, three days later, we played Swindon Town away – one of our most important League matches of the season to date. With Northampton Town likeliest to win the Third Division title, it would be between Swindon, Port Vale, Coventry City, Bournemouth & Boscombe, Peterborough United and Notts County for the second promotion place. We were mid-table but had so many games in hand that we fancied our chances of making up ground. We were leading Swindon 3-2 when, in the final minute, we won a corner on the right. John Rowland walked slowly to the corner flag to take the kick, while our two centre-backs, John Nicholson and Harry Poole, occupied their customary positions around the opponent's penalty spot. But instead of crossing the ball, Rowland stood over it and then back-heeled it into touch for a throw-in to Swindon. The referee was having none of it. He ordered a retake, only for Rowland to repeat his trick.

'What are you playing at, Roly?' Roy Sproson shouted.

'Passing the time away, Rowland shouted back in an accent that did not conceal his Peak District roots.

It was difficult to question his logic. The 3-2 victory gave Port Vale a great psychological boost heading towards spring. Two days later, we lost 3-1 away to Peterborough United only to win the return match 3-2 five days after that.

The match away to Barnsley on 29 March, a 2-1 defeat, represented my sixth match of the month – and perhaps one match too many. My groin went again, which caused me to miss most of the season's denouement. I only played in three of our final fifteen matches and watched from the sidelines as we finished in third position, four points behind Swindon Town, the runners-up, and eight behind the champions, Northampton Town. Only Swindon and Bournemouth conceded fewer goals than Port Vale, giving credence to the view that Freddie Steele had created a citadel. Conversely, sixteen teams scored more goals than Port Vale, bringing into question the manager's decision to sell Longbottom and Llewellyn.

Even in the Third Division, there was talent all over the place. Swindon benefited from a youthful Mike Summerbee, who would win the League Championship with Manchester City in 1968. Curiously, Swindon had been in the Third Division for 43 years, which made their promotion to the Second Division historic. Northampton's most durable players were their two full=backs: Mike Everitt on the left and Theo Foley on the right. But the team scored 109 goals – 37 more than Port Vale.

But there would be no championship medal there for Llewellyn. His Northampton career barely took off – he only played one League match for them in eighteen months – and he was soon off to Walsall. For Northampton, this was another step on their march towards the First Division, which they would reach, memorably, in 1965.

Elsewhere, opponents from my past were forging new futures for themselves. Alf Ramsey, the former Tottenham Hotspur right-back, became England manager in the same week that Freddie Steele became Port Vale manager. Brian Clough, the Sunderland striker, suffered the knee injury on Boxing Day 1962 that all but finished his playing career. Stanley Matthews flourished with Stoke City, winning both a Second Division championship medal and, for the second time in his glorious career, the Football Writers' Player of the Year award. Matthews could look forward to a return to the First Division and to the adulation of the Stoke supporters. All I had ahead of me was a summer of rehabilitation and a full singing schedule.

Please, Please Me

I had two musical agents in 1963: Slim Farrell, working from Sheffield, and Sonny Gross, working from Manchester. It was Gross who fixed me up in June with a week in Liverpool and a week in and around Manchester. Routine stuff – or so I thought.

The Liverpool Cabaret Club was great. The compere each night was Jimmy Tarbuck, a 23-year-old local comedian, who was on the cusp of national fame. He would always introduce me as the 'Singing Winger', probably because that was what Gross told him to do, although, to be fair, Tarbuck knew his football and was a keen supporter of Liverpool FC. Tarbuck and I became friends and remained so, even after he became a celebrity by presenting *Sunday Night at the London Palladium* from 1965 and had his own television show, *It's Tarbuck '65*! It was during that week that I chanced upon a semi-professional comedian called Tom O'Connor, who taught music in Liverpool but was trying to break into entertainment. He was well known in the north for turning up to gigs as a paying punter in the hope that one of the acts would not turn up, which would give him the chance to offer his services.

Len Young, my first manager, had fixed me up with a night at the Liverpool Empire, sharing the bill with Mike & Bernie Winters, a comedy double act, and the Kaye Sisters, that trio of talented women whom I had known since 1957. I joined the 'sisters' for a pre-gig photo shoot, during which they each wore one of my England caps. They wore make-up, too, but evidently not as much as I was wearing. Fortunately, when *The Stage* published the photograph, the old-style letterpress production techniques concealed the effects of my eyeliner and foundation. The Kaye Sisters had become such good friends that whenever they worked near Yorkshire, they always arranged to see Doreen and me at our house, whether that be in Sunderland or Durkar. They adored Colin junior and Doreen's dogs, and they charmed Doreen and me with tales of their tours around Britain and the world. In Liverpool, they charmed the locals with fine harmonies and well-constructed melodies.

I always liked Liverpudlians. That quick wit, sassy charm and lack of deference to the Establishment seemed apt for these changing, post-Macmillan times. And where should I find the perfect manifestation of this Scouse charm? Why, in Manchester, of course!

Sonny Gross had fixed me up with two gigs in one night on 13 June 1963, sharing the bill with a boy band. 'There are four of them and they're from Liverpool,' Gross told me. 'They call themselves the Beatles or something like that.'

I had heard the name before but knew nothing about them. When I saw 'the Beatles' on the posters advertising the gig, I thought there was a spelling mistake. Should it not have been 'the Beetles', like the insect? Gross told me that the Beatles – a beat group, hence the weird spelling of their name – were starting to have chart success, having reached the top twenty with 'Love Me Do', the number-two spot with 'Please, Please Me', and the number-one spot with

'From Me To You'. They made girls scream in a manner reminiscent of early-era Elvis Presley concerts.

The Beatles had accepted the gig many months before, long before their chart success, which meant they could neither pull out nor could they renegotiate their £50 fee. Fifty quid between them – a piffling sum for a group on the cusp of greatness. I formed the view that Brian Epstein, their manager, would have pulled out if he could. I did not have the heart to tell him, or, indeed, his four boys, that I was also earning £50 . . . all for myself.

The first show was at the Palace Theatre Club, Stockport and when I arrived at the dressing room, I introduced myself to four extremely charming men: John Lennon, Paul McCartney, George Harrison and Ringo Starr. At that point, I knew nothing of their music, but they had a confidence and self-assurance that took me by surprise. Even top-level football players had some insecurities, but not these guys. Collectively, they were a force of nature; individually, they had a uniqueness that set them apart from any other acts with whom I worked. Although it meant nothing to me at the time, in later years, when the Beatles took popular music and cultural iconography to heights never considered possible, I had to laugh when I remembered how I made four times for singing in one night what either John Lennon and Paul McCartney made.

I admired their professionalism. I admired their drive for musical perfection. They were not in the slightest bit nervous or even concerned that they might let their audience down. They were good and they knew it. By way of preparation, they behaved as if they were on a cheap package holiday. Lennon and Harrison cracked jokes non-stop, with Lennon particularly quick-witted and mentally sharp. McCartney asked me about my own career and seemed keen to please. And Starr spent most of his time on the floor, playing around with the Dinky cars he brought with him.

It was then that I realised the extent of their following in the north-west of England. Not only was the arena packed but there were hundreds of people – i.e., girls – outside trying to get in. The plan was for the Beatles to open and me to close in Stockport and then do the reverse at the Southern Sporting Club in Manchester, which was about ten miles away.

When the Beatles opened, there was an aura about them. They sang their own material and performed with passion and skill, with wonderful three-part harmonies and high energy. After only a couple of songs, I realised that here was the future of English music. These four Liverpudlians were going places.

After I closed the night at Stockport, I got myself to the Southern Sporting Club as quickly as I could. The Beatles were already there, this time intoxicated on adrenaline after the success of their opening performance. I congratulated them on their songs and their success, and I meant it.

At the end, they each shook my hand and presented me with one of their autographed photographs. Nine months later, I heard about their successful slot in the United States on the world-famous *Ed Sullivan Show*. They had gone from the Southern Sporting Club, Manchester, to being global superstars in the time it takes to play a football season.

I still have the autographed postcard, although I reduced its value significantly by having it laminated. An error of judgement, for sure, but nothing can take away from me the knowledge that I must be the only man in history to share a dressing room with Stanley Matthews and the Beatles.

While the Beatles marched towards cultural immortality, I stayed in Manchester to do a week at the Embassy Club, owned by Bernard Manning, a singer-turned-comedian who made a virtue of his rudeness on stage but was more polite off it. He had not yet mastered the art of television and was still perfecting his act, but you could see how all those years performing at working-men's clubs had toughened him up. He was never better than when an audience heckled him.

If Manning was on the up in 1963, Randolph Turpin was on the way down. A former professional boxer who, in 1951, defeated Sugar Ray Robinson to become world middleweight champion, Turpin had fallen on hard times and was now trying to revive his career as a wrestler. His name was enough to warrant decent-sized audiences but, on the night I shared the bill with him in Bury, he cut a tragic figure. He did not have much of a clue about entertainment and, while I regarded him as a lovely man, I was sad to form the view that he resembled a down-and-out. I felt sorry for him, for he was no longer the sophisticated boxer of his heyday in the 40s and early 50s. I was desperate for him to do well – I was in the audience willing him on – but his act had none of the entertainment value that his audiences expected. It turned out that I was more at home singing in the boxing ring, constructed especially for the evening, than Turpin was fighting in it. Three years later, on 17 May 1966, having declared himself bankrupt, he acquired a gun and committed suicide. He was aged just 37.

Cartwheels of joy

A few days into pre-season training for 1963/64, Billy Bingham arrived as Port Vale's latest signing. Since we last met at Sunderland, he had sparkled with Northern Ireland at the 1958 World Cup, had averaged roughly a goal every four matches from the right flank for Luton Town, and performed superbly with the brilliant Everton team that won the First Division in 1962/63. Two years older than I, Bingham knew that Port Vale would represent his last club as a player and he was already talking about a managerial career. The intervening period had been kind and I noticed an aura around him, an effortless confidence, just as I had noticed the same characteristics in Don Revie when I arrived at Leeds United in 1960. Inside Bingham the player was a manager fighting to get out. Freddie Steele signed him for £15,000, which seemed a lot for a 32-year-old. Conversely, he was too good a player for the Third Division, so his quality was sure to rub off on inferior players.

'What's it like here, Colin?' Bingham asked me in his alluring Belfast accent.

'Great club, great people,' I replied. 'But I'm not sure about the manager.'

'Why?'

'He doesn't seem too interested.'

'And what about you, Colin?'

'I've got this groin injury, Billy, and it won't go away. The manager thinks it's all in my head.'

Albert Cheesebrough joined Port Vale for £20,000 from Leicester City, having first flourished under Alan Brown – yes, *the* Alan Brown; my former manager at Sunderland – with Burnley. But Cheesebrough was unlucky. He left Burnley a year before the team won the League Championship. He then played for Leicester City in an FA Cup final defeat at Wembley to Tottenham Hotspur in 1961. And then he missed the 1963 FA Cup final altogether, falling out of contention at the worst possible time. If he expected better fortune at Vale Park, he was to be disappointed. His suffered a knee injury early on and missed large chunks of the campaign. I only played with him once: on the opening day, away to Shrewsbury Town; a match we lost 1-0 – and a match in which I struggled with my groin. I did not play again for the first team until March 1964.

With John Rowland (by now my roommate for away trips), and then Ron Smith, a new signing from Crewe Alexandra, taking my place on the left wing, I spent the next six months playing for the reserves and nursing my injury. For the first time, I wondered if nature was telling me that my days as a professional player were drawing to a close. Dr Switalski in Wakefield was advising me against too many cortisone injections, while Freddie Steele was of little help because he thought the pain was all in my head. Doreen was sympathetic, but she had more pressing concerns: another baby, due in late February 1964.

Elsewhere, the world embraced a new era – the era of the Beatles, of John F. Kennedy, and of the Swinging Sixties – and it was in this context that Manchester United gave a debut on 14 September 1963 to a 17-year-old Northern Irishman called George Best. Over the ensuing weeks, I read about him; about his natural confidence, his balletic style of play, his agreeable effrontery, and his success among women. He was not yet *El Beatle* – his days of celebrity were still two years in the future – but he was certainly a sign of the future; a future that, in football terms, could no longer belong to me.

In my absence from the first team, Port Vale did what Port Vale had been doing for a decade: overachieving in the FA Cup and underachieving in the Football League. It helped that we signed Jackie Mudie, the Scotland international centre-forward, from Stoke City. I was at Wembley when he won the FA Cup with Blackpool in 1953. Having played in the 1958 World Cup for Scotland, he then won the Second Division title alongside Stanley Matthews with Stoke in 1963. With Mudie in excellent form, Port Vale defeated Birmingham City of the First Division in the third round, which meant a fourth-round tie against Liverpool at Anfield.

Port Vale performed superbly to secure a goalless draw, after which rumours emerged that Paul McCartney of the Beatles had been at the match in disguise. I was surprised. I had been under the impression that he was the Everton supporter and John Lennon the Liverpool supporter. 'Defences triumph in Thriller at Anfield', went the headline to the match report in the *Liverpool Football Echo*, with John Nicholson, playing against his former club, earning particular praise from the reporter. Afterwards, the Port Vale players performed cartwheels of joy and absorbed the noise of a standing ovation from the Liverpool fans at the Kop end.

Two days later, Port Vale went into the replay confident of victory, even though Mudie failed a late fitness test and Billy Bingham was out injured. Just before the kick-off, Roy Sproson said the atmosphere at Vale Park was the best he had ever witnessed. Of course, he had been with the club since they built the stadium, so his opinion carried weight. Roger Hunt opened the scoring for Liverpool in the 35th minute but Port Vale more than held their own, equalising superbly through Albert Cheesebrough in the 79th minute to force extra time. I felt confident we would do enough defensively to secure a second replay, but, with just sixty seconds of extra time remaining, Peter Thompson scored with a long-range drive after John Nicholson blocked a shot by Gordon Milne. When the referee, Harry Hackney, blew his whistle to confirm Port Vale's defeat, thousands of Liverpool supporters swarmed on to the pitch. Eventually, amid the tumult, the police emerged to rescue a laughing but somewhat relieved Thompson. Although heartbroken, the Port Vale players felt a sense of achievement in running Liverpool so close. The delight among the visiting supporters told us everything we needed to know about how well Port Vale performed. We scared Liverpool – and Bill Shankly knew it. Three months later, after defeating Arsenal 5-0 at Anfield, Liverpool won the First Division championship.

By then, I had become a father for the second time when Doreen gave birth to a girl on 27 February 1964. We called her Kim and her presence more than compensated for the constant frustration of playing North Regional League football for Port Vale reserves. Colin junior, aged seven, now found a rival for our attentions. Our family of four seemed complete and perfect.

I returned to the first team for the trip to Peterborough United on 23 March – a 1-1 draw – and then played at home to Millwall five days later – a 1-0 victory, with Billy Bingham scoring – but I functioned in the knowledge that the groin injury had become my nemesis; punishment, perhaps, for working too hard in training for too many years.

I would never play for the Port Vale first team again.

A cheat and a grass

With Danny Blanchflower set to retire from playing, Liverpool set to win the League Championship, and Leeds United marching towards the Second Division title, these were times of great transition in the game. But nothing prepared me for the story that broke in the *The People* on Sunday 12 April 1964. 'TOP SOCCER STARS BRIBED', went the headline, and the story revealed that David Layne, Tony Kay (by now of Everton) and Peter Swan had all backed their team, Sheffield

Wednesday, to lose to Ipswich Town in December 1962. Each got back £150 on a £50 stake.

The *People* also revealed the ringleader: Jimmy Gauld, the former Swindon Town, Plymouth Argyle, St Johnstone and Mansfield Town inside-right, who had been involved in fixing various matches. He dragged a number of players into the scandal, including Esmond Million, a goalkeeper, who had played with Edwin Holliday, my cousin, for Middlesbrough. Also implicated was Jack Fountain, a wing-half, with whom I had played for Sheffield United. He helped to fix a match involving his new club, York City. In all, 33 players were prosecuted, with ten – Layne, Kay, Swan and Fountain among them – jailed and banned for life from the game. It was hard to feel sorry for players who had rigged the game.

Although rumours had been rife that some of Middlesbrough's matches had been fixed during the late 50s (Brian Clough had raised suspicions at the time), I had no idea that such match-fixing syndicates had been so organised. Nobody approached me to assist with manipulating matches. I had played against Gauld but had never spoken to him. To my mind, he was in a different league as a con man. He made £3,275 from betting on bent matches and £7,420 from the *People* for his confessions. A cheat and a grass – what a wretched combination.

A verbal contract

Considering how much money Freddie Steele had spent before and during 1963/64, and given the quality and depth of our squad, it was a failure for Port Vale to finish in thirteenth position in the Third Division. We had the best defensive record and the best defenders, but a chronic lack of firepower up front. Only two teams – Crewe Alexandra and Notts County – scored fewer goals, and they both suffered relegation. Even though our average home League attendance had risen from 8,130 in 1962/63 to 10,056, the board of directors put Steele under pressure to make massive changes. The club could no longer spend such sums of money to finish midway in the Third Division. Port Vale's financial position had become grave.

Steele had already decided to release the goalkeeper, John Cooke, who signed for Macclesfield Town in the Cheshire League. Terry Harkin and Barry Hancock went to Crewe Alexandra and Jim Watton to Doncaster Rovers. And then, in mid-

April, the manager called me in for a meeting.

'There is no new contract for you, Colin.'

'I know.'

The only surprise to me was that he had not told me earlier. While I could never warm to Steele, I had no negative feelings towards him. From Port Vale's point of view, his decision to release me was the right one. I offered him my right hand and thanked him for his time and for the first-team matches he had given me. He should have known better than to question both my injury and my reaction to it, but even if I had been in excellent shape, I doubt Port Vale could have afforded to keep me for 1964/65. The club was about to enter a period of turmoil.

I waited to see what offers would come my way. I had a strange call in early summer from Oscar Hold, the former Everton and Norwich City striker, asking me if a fancied signing for Doncaster Rovers. Strange, because he had already resigned as the club's manager and had accepted the vacant position at Fenerbahçe in Turkey. Over tea and biscuits at my house in Durkar, he said he was still recruiting for Doncaster and had a decent-sized budget for new players. He told me to ignore Port Vale's attempts to wrest a £2,000 transfer fee from whichever club signed me. He and I got down to business.

'How about I match your thirty quid per week at Port Vale and give you a thousand quid as a signing-on fee?'

I did not have time to react.

'And your singing, Colin, we can help you with that. We can give you flexibility and time off.'

I liked Hold and I liked his offer but I sensed he was giving money away too easily – the actions of a man amusing himself with somebody else's bank account. This was Doncaster Rovers of the Fourth Division; Doncaster Rovers whose final home attendance of 1963/64 was a mere 4,262. I knew of established players in the First Division who were only making £30 per week. And yet I could not preclude a feeling that this deal was a good one given my age, my injury problems and my desire to develop further my singing career. It also appealed to me that I could remain living in Durkar. Hold did not have the contract forms with him but we did shake hands on the deal.

'I give you my word, Mr Hold, that I will sign for Doncaster Rovers.'

'I know, Colin.'

But I was still officially a Port Vale player when I gave an interview to *The*

Stage magazine on 11 June 1964 about the dichotomy between my football and my singing:

> *It is said that true artists are always nervous just before they make their entrance – and Colin Grainger, the singing soccer international (of Port Vale F.C.), is no exception. "To me, performing in a music hall or club is as nerve-testing and exciting as any football match – but I try not to betray such weakness. Nerves on the footer field reduce team collaboration and cost points: nerves on stage mar expression and alienate an audience," he analogized. He is a very pleasing vocalist, notable for a small style and ability to sustain long notes. Physical jerks and regular breathing exercises partially account for these pronounced qualities. With northern audiences, 26-year-old [sic] Colin seems to be as popular as an entertainer as he is in soccer circles and thanks to Slim Farrell in the N.-East and Sonny Gross in the N.-West, he gets a fair share of what's going on.*

Messrs Farrell and Gross did, indeed, ensure that I had a fair share of the action. I spent the summer touring clubs and theatres in the north of England. When it was time for pre-season, I accepted an offer to train with Barnsley, whose manager, Johnny Steele, was a delightful Scot, whom I used to watch when he was a player during and after World War Two. News of my agreement with Doncaster Rovers reached Joe Richards, the Barnsley chairman and at that point still the president of the Football League. I was at Oakwell, Barnsley's stadium, when Richards asked me to see him in his office.

'I've heard you've agreed to sign for Doncaster Rovers, Colin.'

'Yes.'

'But I've heard you've not yet signed a contract.'

'That's true.'

'How about if I offer you the same deal of a grand up front and thirty quid a week if you sign for Barnsley?'

I could not believe what I was hearing. Here was Joe Richards – a man of the establishment; a self-styled paragon of virtue – offering to circumvent both football's moral law and the government's tax laws, and encouraging me to go back on my pact with Doncaster Rovers. While I always had an affection for Barnsley, from the days of my childhood when I watched their matches during World War Two, delighting in Johnny Kelly's pace and skill on the left flank, I regarded myself as a man of my word. There was really no decision to make because I had already made it. My handshake with Oscar Hold was, to my mind, a legally binding agreement; a verbal contract. I formed the view that Richards would have offered me more than a grand but still my answer would have been the same.

'Sorry, Mr Richards, but I am a man of my word and I shall sign for Doncaster Rovers.'

'I admire your integrity, Colin. I wish you well.'

But my move to Doncaster Rovers dragged on. Oscar Hold was going backwards and forwards to Turkey at least twice a month, which meant the club perpetuated a sense of disorder and inefficiency. Eventually, and fortunately, Doncaster announced on 10 July 1964 that Bill Leivers, the Manchester City right-back, would replace Hold as manager. I remembered Leivers from when he marked me in matches in the 50s; excellent player, intelligent, and enthusiastic. He knew of my agreement with Doncaster and he would make it official. He was, he said, 'a man of Oscar Hold's word'.

I thanked Barnsley for letting me train there and I joined Doncaster for what remained of pre-season. But still Port Vale insisted on a £2,000 transfer fee. Leivers refused – rightly. The Port Vale directors knew they had no legal recourse. The club might have been short of money but that was neither my fault nor that of Doncaster.

And so, on 7 August, I signed a contract with Doncaster Rovers for £30 a week and earned a not-inconsiderable signing-on fee of £1,000 to be split into four parts – £250 up front and then £250 after ten matches, £250 once I played my twentieth match, and £250 once I played my thirtieth. The club secretary, Thomas Garnett, made the first payment in cash – bundles of the brand-new, brown £10 notes, which were all the rage at the time. On the same day, Colin Barlow, the Oldham Athletic right winger, previously of Manchester City, also joined the club – in his case as a part-time professional. Bill Leivers and Barlow had played together at City, while Barlow had also played under Les McDowall for Oldham Athletic.

As Leivers, Barlow and I posed for press photographs at Belle Vue, twisting our faces into the customary fake smiles, I took stock of how football had changed since my peak period: I was now a Fourth Division player earning more in 1964 than I had as a First Division player and an England international in 1956.

*

CHAPTER VI

For Whom the Belle (Vue) Tolls

1964-66: Doncaster Rovers, Alick Jeffrey, working-men's clubs

So kind, so funny, so agreeably charming

MY FIRST TASTE OF ACTION WITH DONCASTER ROVERS WAS A PRE-season friendly against Chesterfield on 12 August 1964 at the training ground next to the airport. This was one of those places that always seemed windy. And that was not even the worst of it. The pitch was bumpy (better suited to growing cabbages), the dressing rooms spartan, and our kit seemed to be leftovers from the 50s.

'What's it like being in the Fourth Division?' somebody shouted. 'You know, with your England background and all that.'

He was Alick Jeffrey, the Doncaster Rovers inside-forward, whose value to the club transcended the game. His status as local hero – he was born in Doncaster – owed as much to his personal backstory as to his goalscoring abilities, and he aroused a respect among supporters that was not often to be seen in the lower divisions.

He offered me his right hand. I reciprocated and replied: 'The Fourth Division is fine by me, Alick. I'm just happy to still be playing for a living. Football is the best life – whatever the level.'

Jeffrey nodded his approval. The start of a friendship.

But it was not the first time we had met. Our paths had crossed in October 1956 when Jeffrey, as part of the England Under-23 squad, came to train at Bramall Lane during my days with Sheffield United. I was among those who watched from the touchline at the pavilion side as the England lads played a match among themselves. Jeffrey, then aged only seventeen, and already a Doncaster Rovers legend, stood out alongside seasoned players such as Don Howe of West Bromwich Albion and Alan A'Court, who were both four years older. Strong but quick, with prodigious intelligence, Jeffrey reminded me a bit of Duncan Edwards, and I knew I was not the only one to hold such an opinion.

The Under-23 team then played a match against France at Ashton Gate, Bristol, during which Jeffrey broke his right leg so badly that people were said to have heard the sound of the crack from outside the stadium. We did not know it then, but he had only just agreed to sign for Manchester United. Now, so horrific was the injury, his career seemed in tatters. He retired from the professional game and claimed insurance of £4,000 plus compensation from the Professional Footballers' Association of £500. If he wanted to return as a full-time professional, he would need to repay the insurance money. I remember seeing photographs of him in 1958, walking to the Labour Exchange to claim his £4-per-week dole money. He also did some singing around the local clubs to earn extra money, playing the guitar that he had learnt to play with all the time he had on his hands. But I could see it in his eyes that he was not finished with the game.

Another man saw the same thing: George Raynor, then managing Skegness Town just a few weeks after leading Sweden to the World Cup final. Raynor asked Jeffrey to consider coming out of retirement to play for Skegness. Jeffrey agreed, played in a pre-season trial match, and broke his left leg during a collision with the goalkeeper. Fortunately, this time the damage was not severe, but Jeffrey was forced by the terms of his insurance money to play outside the jurisdiction of the Football Association. He moved to Australia, playing for Sydney Prague in 1961 – he and his family lived near Bondi Beach – and Auburn in 1962, during which time Doncaster Rovers, then managed by Oscar Hold, kept in touch with him. By 1963, the Football Association had absolved Jeffrey of any need to return the insurance money, so he boarded a ship and sailed back to England, signing for the club in December 1963.

So well did Jeffrey begin his second spell at Belle Vue that, by the start of

1964/65, Bill Leivers, the Doncaster Rovers player-manager, was suggesting an England call-up, telling newspapers that Jeffrey was as good as Denis Law. In terms of pure talent, Leivers was correct to make the comparison. But I found that Jeffrey held back in training and never put in the work necessary to fulfil the potential everybody knew he had. When the squad went on those four-mile runs each morning, he was always at the back. His best trick was when we used to run into the park next to the Doncaster race track. Jeffrey would find a tree, hide behind it, and then rejoin the squad on our way back to the dressing rooms. Leivers either did not have a clue what Jeffrey was doing or knew only too well but accepted it as a necessary part of life at Belle Vue. Jeffrey was a law unto himself but got away with his excesses because he produced the goods where it mattered: on the pitch.

When it was time to travel to Belle Vue for home matches, the player assigned to pick Jeffrey up was Alfie Hale, a talented Irish centre-forward. But what should have been a routine job became complicated when Hale found that Jeffrey would still be in bed just 75 minutes before kick-off time. 'Get your backside out of bed, Alick,' Hale would shout from outside the front door, to much surprise and amusement among the neighbours. I wondered if Jeffrey had lost his motivation; as if his injuries had deprived him of his ambition. He decided he was going to rely purely on skill, which, in the Fourth Division, was enough to make him a genuine star. Had he worked harder on the training pitch and drunk less alcohol in the evenings, he might have secured a move to a First Division club. But he was such a lovely man – so kind, so funny, so agreeably charming – that, from a selfish point of view, I would have regretted it if he had moved elsewhere.

Yesterday was too far in the past

I had no sense of arrogance over how my present compared with my past. To play football professionally was, and remains, a privilege and only the fool looks at the lower leagues as some sort of bottomless pit. I would treat Doncaster Rovers as I had treated England – a team for whom I would give as much effort as I could. Never would I ask myself, *what am I doing here?* This, the Fourth Division, was where I belonged. And if I was to belong at a higher level, I would have to help Doncaster Rovers gain promotion to the Third Division.

Bill Leivers decided early on that he would put up an invisible barrier between himself and the rest of the squad. On the pitch, on the rare occasions he played, he decided he would be one of us; off it, he made it clear who was boss, and we never really got anywhere near him. You had to tread carefully and watch what you said in his company. The best thing you could say about Leivers was that he was honest and did not appear to have an agenda. But I never got to know him personally. He was not a man to whom you could get close.

Keen to stamp his authority on life at Belle Vue, Leivers did not so much have a clear-out in the summer as stage a revolution. Just ten players survived from the 1963/64 season, Alick Jeffrey among them, and the lack of cohesion was obvious during the opening match of 1964/65, away to Bradford Park Avenue on 22 August. I was one of six players to make a debut for Doncaster Rovers and we lost 5-2, with Kevin Hector, a young striker, superb for Bradford. Jeffrey and Alex Tait, a former Newcastle United striker and England youth-team player, scored our goals. Worse still, we lost 2-1 at home to Southport in our next match.

I formed the view quickly that the Fourth Division was not significantly weaker than the Third Division. If I was going to be successful, I knew I would have to deal with some tough tackling from right-backs who liked the idea of bruising a former England left winger. In this context, my international background was counting against me.

Within the inner sanctum of the Doncaster Rovers dressing room, my international background was counting for me. I did not need to introduce myself to my teammates because, through television coverage and press reports, they had already heard of me. I was noticing, however, that players seemed younger. With fifteen years of professional football behind me, I was now a veteran – even if I felt youthful and adopted a hairstyle commensurate with the era. And if ever I did feel my age, I only had to stand within the vicinity of our goalkeeper, Ken Oxford, who was four years older than I, had made his First Division debut with Manchester City in the 1947/48 season, but had the demeanour, behaviour and fashion sense of somebody from the late-Victorian era. We called him the Old Man as a term of endearment but also as a statement of fact. He could have been a grandfather to any of us. Oxford and I had something in common. We had both played under Norman Low: Oxford for Norwich City, me for Port Vale, and we spoke often about a man for whom we had a lot of respect. Having flourished with Norwich and Derby County, Oxford earned a reputation for being a fine goalkeeper and he was able to use his natural intelligence and bravery to cover for the reflexes that were no longer quite there. But he would only play the best part of half a season for Doncaster.

Oxford had missed the first three matches of 1964/65 – Fred Potter, previously of Aston Villa, began our campaign in goal – but after he won a place in the starting line-up, results improved. From his first match back in the side until the defeat away to York City on 9 October we lost just one game in twelve outings in all competitions. During that run we secured a 5-3 victory away at Southport, with Alick Jeffrey scoring twice, and a 6-3 victory at home to Darlington, with Jeffrey scoring four. I scored my first goal for the club in a 4-2 victory over Halifax Town.

But often this was not a level I recognised. The game could be fast, a bit disorganised, and the ball would spend more time in the air than it would do in the First Division. I saw less of the ball than I would have liked, partly because Jim Watton, our left-back, preferred to kick the ball long rather than give me the short passes that would give me the chance to turn and beat the opposing right-back. I do not blame Watton. Bill Leivers did not see the benefit of short passes on muddy pitches. Consequently, I spent much of my time chasing lost causes – much as I had had when I played for Sunderland on the same flank as Len Ashurst. Watton's recent career had mirrored mine. His Port Vale career began hopefully, just as mine had, descended towards anticlimax, just like mine had, and he found his way out by signing for Doncaster Rovers in the summer of 1964, just as I had.

For all the lack of sophistication about life in the Fourth Division, I found a great team spirit. We might have had the smallest squad throughout the English professional game, but we had the type of atmosphere that can make going into training each day such a pleasure.

Keith Ripley, our half-back, had forged a stable career with Leeds United, Norwich City, Mansfield Town and Peterborough United before doing his best work with Doncaster from 1962. He was a Wakefield lad so it was no surprise that he and I should gravitate towards each other. We often drove to training together, taking it in turns to do the driving. Before long, the two of us formed half of what we called the Gang of Four: the quartet of Doncaster Rovers players who spent long afternoons after training drinking coffee in the local café and sharing jokes.

Alick Jeffrey was the third member. The fourth member was either Phil Robinson, our right winger, or John Wylie, our right half. Robinson had been with the club since 1961 yet still felt young, fresh and a player for the future. As if to prove the generation gap, he was nine years younger than I and I admired his enthusiasm. Wylie, Newcastle-born, formerly of Preston North End and Stockport County, joined Doncaster in the same week as I signed and proved to be a tough, reliable player. He was one of those men who regarded life itself as some sort of drug. Each new day was an adventure for him and he never grew tired of smiling, as if the child within him had never really gone away.

John Henderson, our inside-right, was a Scot who never quite made it at Doncaster Rovers and he barely lasted half of the 1964/65 season. He was a decent enough player but I always thought he was better at golf. He and I would often spend an afternoon on the course and he would beat me every time. Albert Broadbent, Dudley-born and vastly experienced after spells with Notts County, Sheffield Wednesday and Rotherham United, turned himself into a fine attacking player after I took his place on the left wing. Graham Ricketts was a midfield player who had decent spells with Bristol Rovers and Stockport County before he joined Doncaster a couple of weeks before I arrived. Our right-back was David Raine, with whom I spent a few months at Port Vale in 1962 before he signed for Doncaster. A nice, quiet man, he had a great work ethic and treated each training session as though it was a match. But his days at Belle Vue were numbered. After playing half of 1964/65, Raine fell foul of Bill Leivers' desire to build a team capable of winning the Fourth Division championship.

Our main centre-forward was Alfie Hale, a Republic of Ireland international, who had played under Joe Mercer at Aston Villa. His quality was obvious, particularly in the penalty area, where he would come alive and seem to have more time than most other players. I loved him. He was quiet, unassuming, but professional and serious. He had all the cerebral skills that make a good coach, and he would flourish for thirty years, from 1969-99, with various clubs in Ireland. What I did not see in 1964 were the entrepreneurial skills that would enable him to set up a succession of sports shops and pubs, making him a millionaire.

And then there was Jack Nibloe, a player whom I met once just before he left Doncaster Rovers to sign for Stockport County and whom I would never see again. After he played away to Newport County on 28 November 1964, he met his death when his car skidded off the road in icy conditions near Stocksbridge. There was stunned silence among the Doncaster players at training two days later. A month later, my former teammate at Port Vale, Ralph Hunt, died when, as a Chesterfield player, the car in which he was travelling crashed. He was returning, along with his teammates, Peter Stringfellow (the driver), Ron Powell and Doug Wragg, from watching a match involving Peterborough United.

I remember this as being a frustrating time. Billy Bingham, my old friend at Sunderland and Port Vale, broke his leg while playing for Vale away to Brentford in early September. His career was over after that, although consolation for him came in the shape of a managerial career, firstly with Southport – the club for which my cousins Jack and Dennis Grainger played.

My groin problems returned at the same time but never got so bad as to put me out of the equation for long periods of time. I would miss a match here, a match there, and I struggled to get any sort of momentum. I opted against cortisone injections and, instead, rested when the pain became too acute.

We produced a particularly weak display away to Aldershot on 19 December 1964, losing 3-0 in front of less than 3,000 people, during which I limped off when I felt something pop in my groin. Afterwards, outside Waterloo Station in London, the Doncaster players all got on what we thought was our team bus. We did not recognise the coach driver but thought nothing of it. Only when the Newcastle United players arrived did we realise that we were actually occupying their bus. They had been playing away to Southampton and were just about to head back to the north-east. And who should be among the Newcastle players? Jim Iley, my brother-in-law, now their captain, who knew not to laugh because he realised I was in so much pain. 'You'll be fine, Colin,' he said. But I was not so sure.

I missed two matches and returned to the starting line-up at the beginning of 1965. I was playing reasonably well without making headlines but I was rarely getting into the positions that would help me score goals. Everything seemed to go through the middle, to Alick Jeffrey or to Alfie Hale. And whenever I had a lot of the ball, there would always be an over-keen full-back, no doubt aware of my England international background, ready to hit me with a fierce tackle. I took it all in my stride and regarded it as part of the game. But on 6 March 1965, at home to Brighton & Hove Albion, I lost my temper and my head. The culprit was Wally Gould, the Brighton right winger, who seemed to have something of a grudge against me; a grudge that went beyond merely trying to stop me from playing. From the moment the match kicked off, he would kick me off the ball, swear at me, grab my shirt, hit me hard with late tackles – everything designed to put me off my game and irritate me. Finally, when he tripped me up after I had crossed the ball from the left, I went for him, punching him in the nose and, initially, feeling no sense of remorse. Gould tried to hit me back but we were separated before the fracas became a full-scale fight. The referee, who had hitherto done little to protect me, sent us both off. There were still a few minutes left before half-time. I did not see the rest of match, which we won 2-1 thanks to two goals by Alick Jeffrey. The Sunday newspapers made grim reading. Gould had broken his nose, apparently, although it turned out that I had only caused bad bruising.

I awaited my punishment. A 21-day suspension was likely – the Football Association had no sense of humour about players attacking each other – and I sensed that my season was all but over. But Gould sprung a surprise by asking for a personal hearing, which would not reach the Football Association disciplinary committee until the end of 1964/65. Quite why, I did not know. Was he hoping to avoid censure? His decision meant that I could continue playing but that my inevitable suspension would rule me out of the beginning of 1965/66. Except that I could not continue playing: my groin let me down again and I only played in one out of the final seven matches of the season – away to Chester, which ended in a 3-0 defeat. I was fit enough to play in a Sheffield & Hallam County Cup match against Rotherham United and for the Doncaster & District Football Association XI against a Select XI to raise funds for the family of John Nibloe. Stanley Matthews had hoped to play for the Select XI but he pulled out at the last minute, much to my disappointment. He had only just retired from playing professionally, having spent most of 1964/65 playing for the Stoke City reserve team. I still could not come to terms with the reality that his professional career began more than three years before I was born.

On 20 May, the Football Association suspended me for 21 days, beginning on 16 August, meaning I would miss four League matches and one League Cup match. Wally Gould suffered a fourteen-day suspension and £5 costs. The only good news during this frustrating spring was that Doncaster Rovers put me on the Retained List for 1965/66, guaranteeing me at least another season of professional football. But the suspension and my groin injury, in addition to my regular bookings as a singer, meant that I knew my career as a Football League player was drawing to a close. For how long could I rage against the dying of the light?

I watched the 1965 FA Cup final on television at home: Leeds United against Liverpool. Here, perhaps, was proof of how much the world had changed since I left Elland Road in in 1961. Seven of the Leeds starting line-up at Wembley were at Elland Road when I was there, including Albert Johanneson, who was now flourishing on the left wing. Jack Charlton and Norman Hunter were now two of the best defenders on earth, while Billy Bremner was now the world-class player we all knew he would become. Leeds did not play well on the day and Liverpool won a dull match 2-1. But both clubs would, along with Manchester United, Manchester City and Everton, dominate the rest of the decade.

During the summer, I undertook my usual singing tour around the clubs of the north-east and north-west and I occasionally went to see Alick Jeffrey perform as part of a trio with his father and the comedian/singer, Charlie Williams, who made a virtue of the racist abuse he often elicited. (Williams ended up marrying the best friend of my wife, Doreen.) With Jeffrey playing the guitar, they harmonised beautifully and I promised Jeffrey that he and I would perform together. We did, first on a fundraising night for the Doncaster Rovers Floodlight Fund and then in unofficial arrangements afterwards, usually for no money, and purely for the love of it. I grew to admire Jeffrey. I admired his love of life, his live-for-the-day attitude, and his fortitude in fighting back after two broken legs. I only wished he had pushed himself harder in training and drunk less alcohol, for he still had the ability to play for England. But he was never going to play international football while performing each week in the Fourth Division and doing the least amount of training possible. He knew it and he did not seem to care.

He liked being a hero in Doncaster; a big fish in a small pond.

When I look back at all the conversations I had with Alick Jeffrey, I do not recall him ever talking about his broken legs or his bad luck or the potential he never quite realised or the fame he never really had beyond Doncaster.

He was not that type of character. Today was all that mattered. Yesterday was too far in the past, tomorrow too far in the future.

'Dropped'

Alick Jeffrey played every one of Doncaster Rovers' 46 matches in 1964/65, scoring 36 goals and proving as talismanic to us as Jimmy Hagan had been to Sheffield United during my time at Bramall Lane, Charlie Hurley to Sunderland during my time at Roker Park, and Roy Sproson to Port Vale during my time at Vale Park. But we only finished ninth in the Fourth Division – ten points behind the fourth promotion place and twelve points behind the champions, Brighton & Hove Albion.

Bill Leivers made it clear that he would make changes in time for 1965/66. We had already lost Ken Oxford, the goalkeeper, who moved to Port Vale. Then, one by one in the summer, David Raine, Alex Tait, John Henderson and Alfie Hale all left. Coming in to the club were Andy Wilson, a right winger from Scunthorpe United, Paul Durrant, a forward from Bury, and Laurie Sheffield, a Welsh forward from Newport County.

Although I was suspended until the first week of September, I did play the second half of the pre-season friendly against Skegness Town, a match organised as a legacy of Alick Jeffrey's move from Skegness to Doncaster Rovers. Consequently, I missed the opening match of a season, a 4-0 victory against Lincoln City, with Sheffield scoring twice. I also missed the match at home to Hartlepools United, another 4-0 victory, which made a lot of local press coverage because it was the first time we used our new £15,000 floodlights. There was more history away to Southport on 28 August, for that was when Doncaster Rovers made use of the new substitute rule for the first time, with Keith Ripley coming on in place of Sheffield. (In 1965/66, a manager could only make a substitute in the case of a player being injured.)

I returned from suspension for the League Cup first-round replay at home to Barnsley on 7 September and played against Bradford Park Avenue four days later. So far, so good. But the day before the match away to Hartlepool on 13 September, I read the *Yorkshire Evening Post* and discovered that I had been 'dropped'. Paul Durrant would play on the left wing instead. As I watched Doncaster Rovers lose 2-0, I began to realise that 1965/66 would probably be my last at Belle Vue. Instead of being involved against Aldershot in the next match, I played for the reserves away to South Shields in the North Regional League.

Flights to and from Dublin

It was during this period that Doreen received a strange message. Would I go to the phone box near the Post Office in Durkar to take a call from Alan Hardaker, the autocratic and rather brusque secretary of the Football League? It felt odd and surreptitious waiting inside a phone box for a public telephone to ring, especially with people walking by wondering what I was doing. If you are in a phone box, you are supposed to be talking through a handset, not looking like a loner behaving oddly.

The phone rang.

'Hello, Mr Hardaker. This is a surprise. What can I do for you?'

'Hello, Colin. How do you fancy playing for Drumcondra in a European Cup match against a team from East Berlin?'

'Drum . . ?'

'They're an Irish League club.'

It turned out that Drumcondra were looking to sign an established Football League player to boost their European campaign. The idea was not new. I had been aware of Tom Finney playing for Distillery of Northern Ireland at the age of 41 in Europe against Benfica two years earlier. Apparently, Royden Prole, the Drumcondra manager, was offering me £20 per match, plus all flights to and from Dublin, plus a bonus should the team beat Vorwärts Berlin and qualify for the next round of the competition.

'I am not sure, Mr Hardaker.'

'Well, would you consider it, Colin, and get back to me tomorrow?'

'I don't think so. It would look bad if I flew to Dublin to play in the European Cup when I should be staying here trying to get back into the Doncaster Rovers first team. And I also have my singing commitments, of course, so I am not even sure I have the time to play for Drumcondra. Thanks for the offer but I'm sorry. Give the lads over there my best wishes.'

And so ended my only chance of ever playing in the European Cup. Drumcondra won the first leg 1-0 but lost the second leg 3-0 to bow out on a 3-1 aggregate. In the next round, the East Germans lost 5-1 on aggregate to Manchester United.

A free agent

Bill Leivers recalled me to the Doncaster Rovers first team for four successive matches in October, against Torquay United, Luton Town, Stockport County, and Tranmere Rovers. We lost three of the four and I did not register a single goal. I cannot say that I played particularly well. I did not know it then, but that trip to Tranmere on 15 October 1965 turned out to be my last official match ever in the Football League. I say 'official' because I did start the match at home to Colchester United on 22 October but that was abandoned because of fog after 36 minutes, with Doncaster a goal down. For the match away to Barnsley the week after that, I was the substitute – an unused substitute, as it happened.

As autumn turned to winter, I remained out of contention, either playing for the reserves or not playing at all. I did not even make the first team for the match against Wormatia Worms to officially open the Belle Vue floodlights. I could cope with being dropped for first-team matches. That is part of the game and it happens to every player. But dropped for a friendly? That is almost as bad as being an unused substitute in a testimonial.

It was no surprise, then, when I read in the press on 20 December 1965 that my contract would not be renewed and that I was free to find another club. There was no acrimony. I did not even talk to Bill Leivers about it. He and I both knew the immutable truths: that I had far more past than future; that I was aged 33, heavily involved in touring the clubs with my singing act, prone to a groin injury, and that Doncaster Rovers Football Club was chronically short of money. Had I been offered a contract for 1966/67, I am not even certain I would have signed it.

For me, the World Cup year of 1966 began with a reserve-team match at home to Hull City. On 18 January, the *Yorkshire Evening Post* described the reserve-team match away to Hartlepools United a 'Showpiece for the Sales', with 'Colin Grainger, Andy Wilson and Paul Durrant all available for transfer.' The report went on to state that several Football League managers planned to attend with a view to seeing if we might have something to offer. But, as if to sum up my vexations during that winter, the match was postponed because of a waterlogged pitch.

Leivers continued to make new signings, with John Nicholson, my former colleague at Port Vale, the most notable. A dominant centre-back, probably too good for the Fourth Division, he would provide great stability as Doncaster Rovers launched a serious attempt at winning the Fourth Division title. Bobby Gilfillan came from Southend United, Tony Coleman came from Bangor City, and Alan Finney came from Sheffield Wednesday. The first-team squad barely resembled the one that began the 1964/65 campaign. Such were the changes, there were times in early 1966 when I saw players on the training pitch and had no idea who they were.

It was with surprise, then, that I discovered on 10 February that Leivers had resigned. I read it in the newspapers. 'Personal reasons' was the official line – a meaningless statement that covers a multitude of possibilities – but I knew there was more to it than that. Word around the squad was that he was becoming annoyed at how little money there was. What did he expect? This was the Fourth Division. I was not pleased to see him go, but nor was I sad. For a man who made so many changes, he seemed unable to stamp his authority on life at Belle Vue. He was aloof and disconnected, never giving the impression that he was enjoying himself or that he was in love with life.

The directors put Frank Marshall, the trainer, and Jackie Bestall, the chief scout, in charge as joint caretaker managers until a suitable replacement could be found. I understood that neither man received a pay rise, which told the players everything about how tight money was at the time. Bestall only earned £10 per week, a pittance even though it was 1966 and this was the Fourth Division. The two men did a great job, however, taking the club from sixth position at the time of Leivers' departure to the top by the beginning of May. I liked both men. Marshall had played with Jack Grainger, my oldest brother, during the 50s, while Bestall – a tiny man, but eminently charming and omnipresent – had played for England once, in 1935, having made his name as an inside-forward with Grimsby Town. The joint-caretaker-manager arrangement seemed odd – not that it affected me: I never played under them – but nobody could argue with the results. And when Luton Town lost to Newport County on 25 May, Doncaster Rovers had secured the Fourth Division title for the first time ever. Sharp of eye and a yard ahead of most defenders, Laurie Sheffield had scored 28 League goals, with Alick Jeffrey scoring 22. As a striking partnership, they were devastating and had no business playing at such a low level. They were probably the standard of the Second Division.

I was happy for my teammates, of course, and never once did I resent it that my five League matches that season proved insufficient for a medal. My contribution had been minimal and I had known for more than six months I was leaving the club. It rankled slightly that I never heard about the club's official 'Championship Dinner & Dance' celebration at the Danum Hotel on 8 June. After all, my contract still had 22 days to run, so I was still officially part of the squad. Spiritually, however, I had left the club and was now a free agent. My final match in Doncaster Rovers colours was for the reserve team against Gateshead at Redheugh Park on 7 May in the North Regional League. With barely anybody there to watch, all we could hear were the ghostly echoes of players barking incoherent instructions at each other. Redheugh Park, of course, had been Gateshead's ground during their days in the Football League, but now it was falling into disrepair, with water leaking into the dressing room and weeds growing through the terraces – metaphors, perhaps, for the state of my career at Doncaster Rovers.

I was not the only player to leave the club at the end of 1965/66. Keith Ripley, my friend, also found himself on the 'not retained' list. For him, it was the end of a playing career that had begun at Leeds United twelve years earlier. He and I kept in touch, playing golf together until well into old age. By then, our knees were artificial but our anecdotes, which we shared with enthusiasm, were authentic.

I spent the summer of 1966 touring nightclubs, singing my heart out, and sometimes making £100 in a weekend. I turned down tickets for the World Cup matches at Ayresome Park and Roker Park. I watched on television in glorious monochrome as England, with Jack Charlton at the heart of the defence, defeated West Germany 4-2 to win the final. I watched Alf Ramsey's understated reaction at the final whistle and remembered how my performance against him in 1954 helped end his playing career. I watched Norman Hunter, sitting with the non-playing England squad players, and I remembered how he used to clean my boots at Leeds. But my most intense thoughts were the ones I had for a man who was not even there: Duncan Edwards. Had he not died at Munich, I feel sure that he would have earned a winners' medal at the 1966 World Cup, perhaps even as captain. On that day, 30 July 1966, he would have been still a few months short of his thirtieth birthday and likely would have been at his peak. As Bobby Moore held aloft the Jules Rimet Trophy, I looked on with mixed emotions: happy, yes, but wistful, too.

I welcomed the symmetry

Now to find a club for 1966/67. I knew it would be a non-League club. My aching groin would never let me forget that my Football League days really were consigned to history. Bridlington Town of the Yorkshire League offered me a decent weekly wage and the flexibility to pursue my singing career full time. Wellington Town of the Cheshire League did likewise, although their location, in Telford, would have added significantly to my travelling. Poole Town of the Southern League offered me the chance to move the family to the south coast, with a weekly wage higher than what I had earned at Doncaster Rovers. I wondered what it said about the nature of the non-League game that so many clubs could compete financially with clubs in the Third and Fourth Divisions.

But my outlook was now changing. For me, convenience was more important than money. I was becoming averse to long motorway journeys. So when Albert Leake, the Macclesfield Town player-manager, called up and offered me £17 per week to play in the Cheshire League, I felt enthused. I welcomed the symmetry, for it was in the Cheshire League that my professional career began with the Wrexham reserve team in August 1949. I could even remember that cold Christmas Eve in 1949 when I played for Wrexham against Macclesfield: me, the boy; everybody else, the men. My shirt and shorts were too big, the mud prohibitive, and the tackles fierce. But the Cheshire League in 1949/50 was as important to me as a university education, so I would never look at this level of football with a feeling of condescension, not even as a 33-year-old former England international.

Leake and I had a couple of features in common. He was an RAF man, like me. He had played for Port Vale, like me. In fact, we just missed each other. He left Vale Park in January 1961, just before I arrived. We swapped stories about playing under Freddie Steele at Port Vale and about the vagaries of life at non-League level.

'You can earn as much playing in non-League as you can playing in the Fourth Division, Colin, but have more time to do other things,' Leake told me. 'It's great. Most Macclesfield players use their football incomes to supplement what they get from their jobs. Most of the lads are Football League-standard but want the security of a career outside the game. This, for them, is the best of both worlds.'

And so it came to pass that in August 1966, my professional life went full circle. From being a footballer who supplemented his income by singing, I became a singer who supplemented his income by playing football.

CHAPTER VII

Postscript and Post-Postscripts

1966-present: Non-League, Corinthians, Harry Hough, Sundays

Residual fame

THERE IS AN AXIOM THAT THE OLDER YOU GET, THE QUICKER THE years pass; but for the football player leaving the Football League, time goes into overdrive, as if in possession of a fast-forward button. But even I had no idea how quickly my time at Macclesfield Town would pass. I blinked and felt as though I had missed it all.

My first act there was to pick up a brown envelope containing £300 in cash. It was nice to know that I could still educe a signing-on fee, even if the days of four-figure sums were long gone. I liked the look of the club. The Moss Rose stadium was quaint, the pitch lush. We trained there twice a week, which, for me, being used to full-time training, felt like an extension of the summer holiday. I barely broke sweat. Eventually, I decided to train by myself on non-training mornings. I still had too much energy. I also had a fear of putting on weight. I did not want to be one of the former Football League players who fell too quickly into physical decline.

Two things I noticed about the Cheshire League: smaller crowds than in 1949/50; and my attitude was different because, unlike in 1949, when I was a mere boy and a bit nervous, now I was a man and not the slightest bit nervous. I also had a reputation and track record. I knew in advance that seasoned non-League players would be out to kick me. Such would be the fate of a former England international winger. I knew, also, that the Cheshire League was full of players who had the ability to play at Football League level. Officially, the move from Doncaster Rovers to Macclesfield Town was a step down, but the reality was more nuanced than that. You did not have to look far to find talent. The main difference I found between the Fourth Division and the Cheshire League was not in terms of ability but, rather, in terms of fitness. Constrained by external commitments, the semi-professional usually did not have the time to acquire the physical conditioning of the full-time professional. But never believe that the non-Leaguer suffered from a lack of skill. It did not take me long to discover that all of the Macclesfield Town players had the attributes necessary to make a career out of the game.

The player to whom I got closest during my time at Moss Rose was Frank Beaumont, mainly because he was a lovely, warm, vivacious man, but partly because we shared a Yorkshire background. He was born at Hoyland Common, near Barnsley, and exuded all the positive characteristics of his heritage. He had done well enough as a forward with Barnsley, scoring 37 goals in 107 appearances, from 1957-61, later turning out for Bury and Stockport County. It was from Stockport that he signed for Macclesfield in the summer of 1966, and we struck up a friendship almost immediately. The one feature of his play that stood out most for me was his work ethic. He pushed himself as hard as any player I had seen since my career begin in 1949, and that includes some of the game's legends. He knew nothing of lost causes and he was as dynamic in the final minute of the match as he had been in the first. By the time I played my first match for Macclesfield, at home to Buxton on 20 August 1966 (a 1-1 draw), he was more of a utility player – at home either in the forward line or at the back – and something of a fulcrum.

Among the other Macclesfield Town players to impress me during those early days at Moss Rose were John Collins, a right-back, who played alongside Beaumont at Stockport County. John Cooke, the goalkeeper, was a professional with whom I played during my Port Vale days. He never established himself at Vale Park but there was no doubting his talent. Although too good, in my view, for the Cheshire League, Cooke would emerge as one of non-League football's great goalkeepers. David Latham on the right wing had begun with Manchester United, where he played for the reserve team in the early 60s. George Sievwright, from Dundee, was a tough right-half who played for Oldham Athletic, Tranmere Rovers, and

Rochdale before he moved to Macclesfield Town in 1965. George Forrester, the left-back, was part of the Accrington Stanley team that played in the club's ill-fated 1961/62 campaign, when the club resigned mid-season from the Football League. There was no doubting that Albert Leake had created a strong squad with great spirit, and I looked forward to what I hoped would be a long, successful time at Moss Rose.

But life never works out as you plan it. Now that my singing had become more important than my football, I soon found that trying to combine two careers was next to impossible. I played four matches for Macclesfield Town – twice against Buxton in August, at home to Frickley Colliery in the Cheshire League Cup on 10 September, and against Witton Albion two days later – before I realised that there were not enough hours on a Saturday to play, travel and sing. I had to pull out of one match, the FA Cup tie against Alfreton Town on 3 September, because of a singing engagement. It was before the match away to Bangor City on 1 October that I wrote a letter to Leake asking him to release me from my contract. Playing football was now putting me out of pocket. He understood my position and agreed to make my departure smooth and amicable. I respect him for that, for under a different manager at a different club, the business could have turned chaotic. I offered to return the £300 signing-on fee and Leake refused to accept it. I was stunned – and, naturally, happy. Macclesfield Town was the first time I felt I had taken out of the club more than I had put in, and I did feel a sense of guilt when I walked away for the final time. Consolation came in the friendship I maintained with Frank Beaumont, which lasted until his death in 2011.

I could not support a family of four on my singing wages alone and there was no point in my looking to play for another club. My playing days were essentially over. I had to face the economic reality: I would have to find a nine-to-five, Monday-to-Friday job with a guaranteed regular income. Leaving football did not affect me psychologically as much as I thought it would but I did feel a slight sense of loss. The crowds, the camaraderie, the physical and mental highs, the fame, the discipline ... the vagaries of the football life would be hard to replace. Conversely, I could feel each of seventeen years of the game in my fragile groin and fragile ankle. And after so many years of travelling around Britain and Europe, I liked the idea of spending Saturday mornings and afternoons with Doreen and my two children, Colin junior and Kim.

I applied for a job as a sales representative with a company called Gross Cash

Registers, whose managing director, Don Nesbitt, appealed to me from the moment I met him. A Scotsman with a heart of gold, he made me feel that I had a lot to offer the world of sales. He had no idea of, or interest in, my career as a football player, a situation that suited me perfectly because I wanted to succeed in business on my own merits, not because of any residual fame from my playing days. He offered me a job and, pleased to accept, I put as much effort into learning the processes and procedures. My job was to sell tills to shops and businesses, and every time I opened a new account it felt like scoring a goal. Eventually, I became the area manager for Yorkshire, and one year, out of more than four hundred sales reps on the Gross Cash Registers books, I posted the best figures. My success felt how I imagined a player-of-the-year award to feel.

He was a martyr

But tragedy was never far away. On 3 September 1966, John Nicholson, my former colleague at Port Vale and Doncaster Rovers, the most endearing of Liverpudlians, with his shock of blond hair and quick wit, died in a car crash. My heart broke for the family – a wife, a son and a daughter – he left behind. I will always look back at Nicholson as being a strong player, fearless and brave, but a young, sensitive man.

Forever young – alas.

And then, in autumn 1968, came the cataclysm I had been dreading: the death of my beloved Dad, Daniel Grainger, from pneumoconiosis, a disease born of too much exposure to coal dust. In the final week of his life, I watched a strong, proud, wonderful man fade away. I took time off work to help look after him. I shaved him. I comforted him. I told him that I could not have wished for a more inspiring, caring father. It seemed so wrong to me that he could not get out of bed. I cherished every minute of what I knew was the final phase of his life. One day, I went home to Durkar to get my pyjamas so that I could stay at West Street, Havercroft and be closer to my dad. When I arrived at Havercroft, I heard the dreaded news from my mam: 'Your Dad has passed away.' Her words devastated and disorientated me, and I could see it in her eyes that she was distraught. The knowledge that my dad was dying did not insulate her from the mental torture when death finally came. Nothing, not even the knowledge that death is imminent, can prepare you for the finality of it all.

Time heals, of course, but I do not think I have got over the death of my father. Even now, fifty years on, I think about him and of how he always gave far more than he took. I think of how much better my life was because of the sacrifices he made. I have no doubt that whatever attributes I have as a father and as a grandfather came from my dad.

He was a martyr. My brothers and I were the beneficiaries of his sacrifices. Sometimes I wish it was the other way around.

A heavy heart

I could not stay away from football for long. But my return to the game owed everything to a coincidence: a neighbour in Durkar who happened to be the secretary of Newmillerdam FC, a club based in a nearby Wakefield mining village. His name was Kerry Ridsdale, an agreeable man, a right winger of no small amount of skill and speed, who had been asking me since 1966 to play for the team. It only took me three years to make a decision. I signed for the club at the beginning of the 1969/70 Leeds Red Triangle League season and vowed to play as often as possible, as if to prove that I loved the game for its own sake and not merely as a means to boost my bank account.

I assumed the role of player-manager, which meant I took the training sessions each Tuesday and Thursday evening. I did not hold back. I wanted the team to be the fittest in the league, even if we would not necessarily be the best. I also kept fit by running around the rural parts of Durkar. The standard at Newmillerdam was more than decent – I brought in players whom I thought could improve the team – and I felt sure that some members of our squad had the ability to play semi-professionally. I stayed for three seasons. There was no doubting that a bit of my pace had disappeared from the years of my peak but I was surprised at how fit I remained. I certainly felt I had the fitness and playing ability to survive at a high non-League level. Some of the players in opposing teams remembered me from my England days and felt that I deserved special attention on the pitch, forcing me to endure some fierce tackling. What else could I do but take it as a compliment? The alternative was to be anonymous.

A 3-1 victory against Horbury in the 1971/72 Wakefield Cup final marked the end of my tenure at Leeds Red Triangle League level, and I left with a heavy heart but in the knowledge that I had played a part in an exciting period for the club. I missed appearing in front of large crowds but no matter what the level, there is something unique about football's team spirit – its male bonding, its social potentialities, its exaggerated masculinity; the laughter, the tears – that makes it such an attractive milieu.

My wonderful, magical world

On a warm August evening in Leeds in 1970, after another well-received performance, I called time on my professional singing career. I had known for six months that this particular denouement was coming. It got to the point when, after some gigs on Sunday nights, I would not return home until the early hours of Monday morning, which left little time for a decent sleep in preparation for a week's work at Gross Cash Registers. I continued to perform after 1970, but usually only for free and only locally, which did not involve any significant travelling.

I knew without even asking her that Doreen was pleased to see the end of my performing days. From our early days together, she secretly welcomed my fame. She certainly welcomed the extra money. But she saw less of me than she would have liked. And even I could not argue with the reality of what makes a marriage work. Doreen and the children must always come first.

Nevertheless, singing was the great surprise of my professional life. I always felt, from the age of fifteen, I would become a professional football player, but crooning to audiences seemed to happen quickly, spontaneously, almost by accident. This sphere provided me with priceless memories, great friends, and, for a time, more money than I earned for football. There was something surreal about that final night in Leeds. I did not feel emotional or even sentimental, but a part of my life did flash before me: the Beatles, Joan and Jackie Collins, the Hilltoppers … such was my wonderful, magical world. And to think I even ended up as part of a music collectors' card collection alongside Elvis Presley.

But the candle would burn down eventually – nothing lasts forever, not even the Beatles and Elvis – and I at least had the judgement and prescience to know that fantasylands are transitory. Your only hope is that you can experience the pleasure for what little time it lasts.

Positive stereotypes

By 1972, my days as a professional football player felt so long in the past that I sometimes read about myself in newspapers and magazines – usually 'Where Are They Now?'-type features – as if I had inhabited a distant, monochrome epoch. But the Leeds United team that won the FA Cup that year, containing Billy Bremner and Jack Charlton, two of my former colleagues, reminded me that I still had some relationship with youth. And I was able to prove it when I returned to the semi-professional sphere as a left winger for Woolley Miners Welfare in the Yorkshire League in time for 1972/73.

The offer came from Harry Hough, the former Barnsley goalkeeper and club legend, against whom I had played and with whom I struck up a friendship. He and I played together in a couple of charity matches in 1972 for a Former Barnsley XI against Wath. (For some reason, I kept turning out for a Former Barnsley team even though I had never actually played for them.)

'Do you miss playing, Colin?' Hough asked me.

'Well, I've just finished playing for Newmillerdam in the Leeds League and enjoyed every second of it.'

'So why not play for Woolley?'

Who was I to turn down Harry Hough? As I recalled saying to Alick Jeffrey at Doncaster Rovers, football is the best life – no matter what the level. I agreed to give Woolley a go, although Hough made it clear that this might be semi-professional standard, and Woolley an FA Trophy-level team, but I would not receive even expenses, let alone a part-time wage. I did not care. I loved to play and I liked the idea of competing in non-League football, for it was there that my career had begun in 1949. Some full-time professionals did look down patronisingly on the non-League game, but I never did because I realised early on that this level was as important a part of the game's structure as the England international team. No matter the standard at which you play, there is somebody somewhere – a man with a heart of gold; a volunteer whose value is priceless – who delights in what you do. Not all of the Woolley players had a mining background but all were local, loyal and conformed to the positive stereotypes about West Yorkshire folk. I felt as though I was perpetually among friends.

Woolley Miners Welfare emerged in 1965, having morphed from a club called

Darton Colliery. Starting out in the Sheffield County Senior League and the Barnsley League, Woolley joined the Yorkshire League and took advantage of the physical, and spiritual, proximity to Barnsley. Harry Hough was not the only player with a Barnsley connection to join Woolley; in later years, John Stainsby, Bob Wood, Frank Beaumont, Malcolm Lang also saw value in giving the club their experience. It was nice to reacquaint myself with Beaumont, for he was, like me, continuing to play the game for the sheer love of it. We were of like mind and I always respected him for the fact that he gave football more than he took out of it. How much better would the world be if everybody had the attitude of being willing to give more than they take?

Woolley began 1972/73 in the Yorkshire League second division, having secured promotion the previous May. Among our opponents at the higher level were such local luminaries as Leeds & Carnegie College, Harrogate Town, Ossett Albion, Scarborough reserves, Guiseley, and Worsbrough Bridge Miners Welfare. Scoring 88 goals but conceding 51, we finished runners-up behind Leeds & Carnegie College to secure promotion to the top flight. In the FA Trophy, we lost 5-1 away to Barton Town in the first qualifying round, which, to my mind, was a sign of the strength in depth of non-League football at that time. I played most matches and more than held my own. We struggled in the top flight in 1973/74, however, finishing bottom of a table that saw Lincoln United win the title, with Emley runners-up and Farsley Celtic third. We did defeat Glossop North End, a former Football League club, in the FA Trophy but then lost to Worksop Town in the second qualifying round.

Unfortunately, the second division seemed to be our true level and we seemed far too comfortable there in 1974/75, never threatening the promotion places or enduring the threat of relegation. We defeated Frickley Colliery after a replay in the FA Trophy before losing to Louth United in the first qualifying round. Frickley, of course, were one of the three teams against whom I played during my brief spell with Macclesfield Town.

But the Football Association demoted Woolley to FA Vase status, even though we had preserved our status in the Yorkshire League second division. When I turned out for Woolley against Rawmarsh Welfare in the FA Vase first round in 1975 I considered that I must have been one of the few men in football history to have played for England and also played in the FA Cup, League Cup, FA Trophy and FA Vase.

Woolley had slipped back into the Yorkshire League third division by the time my spell with the club drew to a close in 1978. I would have been happy to carry on playing but a meeting with a former colleague gave me new options for Saturday afternoons.

Nothing to do with my ego

Not long after Billy Bingham took over as manager of Mansfield Town in 1978, he invited me over for a coffee in his office – just like the good old days when we played together for Sunderland. He had, he said, an offer for me.

'I need to put in place a scouting network and I want to know if you'd be interested in covering the north-east area for me.'

I liked the sound of it and agreed. One of my first matches was Tow Law Town versus Durham in the Northern League to watch a young left winger called Chris Waddle, who had hunched shoulders, an odd running style, but a remarkable facility to control the ball and run with it. He was deceptively good, with excellent crossing ability, and I reported straight back to Bingham that Waddle was a player Mansfield Town absolutely had to sign. The club sent another scout to another match to watch Waddle, presumably in an attempt to either authenticate or invalidate my opinion. The report about him came back: 'Not good.' Waddle moved to Newcastle United in 1980 instead and turned into one of the world's finest wingers, playing for England in the World Cup tournaments of 1986 and 1990. I do not take any pleasure in being vindicated. My primary emotion when I think of Chris Waddle is that Mansfield Town should have signed him on my recommendation. This has nothing to do with my ego and everything to do with running a scouting network properly. The best part of scouting for Bingham was that we revived our friendship. My respect for him, both as a human being and as a football man, never wavered. He was, and remains, one of the key figures in my life and a true inspiration. He had changed, of course. Football management does that to a former player. You could see in the stress of the job engraved into his face. But he remained the lovely, charming, kind man he always was.

Bingham left Mansfield in 1979 to become the manager of Northern Ireland, leading the national team to the second phase of the 1982 World Cup, and I took scouting roles with Barnsley and Leeds United, both under Allan Clarke,

Huddersfield Town under Mick Buxton, and Bury, Oldham Athletic and Sheffield United under Neil Warnock. I loved scouting.

I loved meeting people in the game, many of whom, up to and including Bobby Charlton, remembered me from my England days. Charlton introduced himself to me at a reserve-team match and we shared some happy anecdotes. I reminded him of how we played against each other when he was still in his teens. I would like to think neither of us had changed much during the intervening years.

I went back to Sheffield United to scout and was still scouting for Huddersfield when I turned 80 in 2013.

Stinking of alcohol

Scouting for players on Saturdays did not preclude my involvement on the playing side. From 1978, I played at Sunday league level for a team called Walton in a local Leeds league. I ran virtually the entire playing side of things, although it was never easy because often players would pull out at the last minute, leaving us a man or two short. In every match, at least one player would turn up stinking of alcohol from the previous night's excesses. Once or twice, I would try to pass on some tactical advice to a colleague, then I would smell the beer on his breath, and then I would realise that I might as well be trying to push water up a hill. Sunday league has its own rubrics and its own vernaculars.

Organisation became difficult but, perversely, that was part of the fun. I played most matches on the left wing, where I surely belonged, and put as much effort into it as I had when I played for England, although obviously I was not quite the finely tuned physical specimen that I had been twenty-odd years earlier.

Still, for a man of 45-plus, I felt remarkably fit and healthy.

A genuine force of nature

My mother died in 1979. She survived my dad by more than a decade and I admired her fortitude and the unity she inspired within the family. She fell ill with what a doctor described as a 'tired heart' but she seemed to recover after spending two weeks in hospital. Then, when she returned home to West Street, she fell ill again and faded away. We were all devastated, of course, but she left us with lessons and memories that will never fade.

In some ways, it was more shocking when my brother, Jack, died in January 1983. He was somebody to whom I always looked up. He played a part in my metamorphosis from wide-eyed youth to professional football player. But by early winter 1982, he was starting to lose his appetite for food and for life. His wife would make him sandwiches to take to work but, latterly, he would struggle to eat them. Eventually, after he lost a lot of weight, he went to a doctor who, in turn, sent him straight to hospital. The diagnosis was as bad as it could get: liver cancer.

We were in mourning even before he died. Watching a strong former professional football player fall into physical decline and then pass away brought home the harsh reality of mortality. He was a Rotherham United legend but to me he was always our Jack – a genuine force of nature.

Barely drank alcohol

I enjoyed nearly seven years at Gross Cash Registers and then took a position as a sales rep for Townends of Hull, a locally famous wine merchants. I stayed there from 1973-78 before I joined another wine merchant, Halewood International of Liverpool, the brainchild of an entrepreneur, John Halewood. I stayed there for fourteen years and felt that I had played a big part in the massive success of the company. I never did get the bonus I was promised – agreed with John Halewood over a handshake – but I was proud of the work I did.

Now employing more than a thousand people, with annual revenues of more than £160 million, Halewood International owns such famous labels as Crabbies, Lambrini, Red Square Vodka, Caribbean Twist, and Whitley Neill Gin. I found it funny that a man who barely drank alcohol should spend so much time selling it.

A 'Gallant Lad'

My brother, Eric, died in 2008 at the age of 82. Of all my siblings, he was the one with the sharpest brain. But latterly his eyesight faded and he took solace in the bus trips around Britain we arranged for him. We would describe scenes to him and he would picture them in his mind – a mind forever working overtime. It was a sad day when he passed away.

Another brother, Horace, died in March 2014. The shock was great because I regarded him, at aged 84, as still a young man. He was always fit, vibrant and healthy; the one person you thought might see his hundredth birthday. Once he developed bowel cancer, however, I knew that the prognosis was not good.

The *Yorkshire Post* obituary described him thus:

> *Horace Grainger, who was the most expensive rugby league player of his time when he moved between two Yorkshire teams for a transfer fee of £2,000, has died aged 84. He was a versatile athlete playing both football and rugby, known as a sporting gentlemen who upheld traditional values. He first showed promise as a sprinter when he worked for the railways and ran for Doncaster Plant Works Athletics Club winning many medals and trophies. It was his speed which later made him such an accomplished football and rugby player.*
>
> *The family was immersed in sport, his brother Colin was an England international footballer in the 1950s playing for a number of clubs, including Sheffield Wednesday [sic: it was Sheffield United, of course] and Doncaster Rovers, before retiring and becoming a professional singer.*
>
> *Mr Grainger was born in the village of Ryhill, near Wakefield. He was the middle of five children born to Daniel, who was a coal miner, and Lily Grainger. He was educated locally at the village primary school and then Felkirk Secondary Modern School. When he left he worked in the brickworks at Monckton Colliery, later moving to the railways. In 1949 he was called up for National Service serving with the King's Own Light Infantry where he was battalion boxing champion and football captain. While working for the railways at the age of 22 he was sought by Burnley Football Club, then one of the country's most successful teams, but he never played for the first team and eventually moved to Chesterfield where he spent two seasons, but never settled.*
>
> *He was uncertain what to do next until his cousin Jack encouraged him to join Eastmoor Amateur Rugby League Club, Wakefield, one of the oldest amateur clubs. There he played on the wing and almost immediately he was talent scouted by both Wakefield and Dewsbury, choosing the latter club. It was after a couple of seasons with them that in 1958 Hunslet paid £2,000 for him to transfer to them making him the most expensive rugby league*

player of the time. He later played for Bradford Northern before retiring in 1964. But sport was in his blood and he went on to fill a number of roles in both rugby and football. He wanted to help younger players so trained at Lilleshall to be a coach and joined Grove Dreadnoughts in the Wakefield League. He also qualified as a soccer referee in the Wakefield League until he gave it up in the 1970s. About the same time Burnley asked him to be their East talent scout, a post he thoroughly enjoyed until he gave that up in the 1970s. He was also a director of Bramley RL club in the 1970s and 1980s, until he was poached by Hunslet to be their ground director at the time they were playing at Elland Road, the home of Leeds United. At Bramley he became representative on the Yorkshire County Rugby League committee, a position he was allowed to continue when he moved to Hunslet, and in the mid 1980s he reached the pinnacle of his career when he was elected president for a year. Mr Grainger was married to his wife Mabel for 58 years. They lived in the same street in Ryhill but met seriously in 1951 after a village 'hop'. On their way home youths were throwing fireworks and one fell on her. A 'gallant lad' as she described him, rushed forward to brush it off her clothes then walked her home.

As I read those words, I thought of what Charles Chaplin wrote in 1964: 'And so the world grows young. And youth takes over. And we who have lived a little longer become more estranged as we journey on our way.' But only slightly more estranged.

Until Jim Iley, the former Newcastle United, died on 17 November 2018, I saw him regularly and we glowed in each other's company. We reminded each other that for as long as we had breath in our lungs, we remained young, vivacious, alive, excited, with the child inside each of us perpetually bursting to get out. But even the best of us cannot acquire immortality and I know it will be a long time before I stop grieving for the legend that is Jim Iley. RIP, brother. RIP.

My match

When England played Brazil at Wembley on 6 February 2013, I was the only survivor of the England team that defeated Brazil 4-2 in 1956. The day before the 2013 match, the Football Association at short notice sent a limousine to my house near Huddersfield to take me down to Wembley as an invited guest. The entire event was an assault on the senses, for both the past and the present merged to form a collage that, for a time, disorientated me. Wembley had changed beyond recognition, as had the game I loved. Whereas when I played there was too much charm and too little money, now there was too much money and too little charm.

It was nice to be remembered. It was nice to meet luminaries of the modern game. It was nice to sample the excesses of Football Association hospitality.

It was nice to know that I was part of Wembley's rich history, even if this Wembley was an Ikea version of the one at which I played more than half a century earlier. England won 2-1 with goals by Wayne Rooney and Frank Lampard. But as the limousine took me back home afterwards, I knew that the 1956 match – *my* match – would remain historical and that the 2013 match would never come close to being historical. Charm makes history in a way that money never can.

The audience

Venice 1990. I am in Piazza San Marco, with its overpriced coffee bars and its proliferation of pigeons. Near to the canal there is an Italian guy singing on a stage in broken English. Or is it an English guy singing in broken Italian? Hard to tell. In an involuntary action that takes my wife by surprise, I ask if I can join him. He calls me up and suddenly the adrenaline courses through my veins. I am high on life, as if on drugs, but still in control of my senses.

I take the microphone.

'Wait a minute!' I shout to polite applause. 'Wait a minute! You ain't heard nothin' yet!' And then, to growing cheers, I croon with a confidence that nobody knows I possess. Suddenly I am Al Jolson again, just as I was when I crooned in public for the first time at the Havercroft Working Men's Club in 1947, and just as I was in Finland in 1956 when Nat Lofthouse said, *Come on, Colin, give us a song* to create a catchphrase among the England players.

I have to laugh. The more things change, the more they stay the same.

I feel sure that nobody here in the Piazza knows I played football for the England national team, let alone shared the bill with the Beatles. And I do not care. What matters is that I have an audience, even if, on this occasion, it is somebody else's audience.

The audience makes me feel alive.

The audience makes me feel special.

The audience is everything.

But when I perform in my mind's eye, as I do all the time, whether as a singer or as a football player, there is only ever an audience of two:

My mam and my dad.

And theirs is the applause that matters most of all, for they are the martyrs of my story. They were the ones who toiled so I did not have to. They were the ones who fashioned my future with a simple command:

Son, no way you're ever going down a pit.

About the author

A NATIVE OF LIVERPOOL, HYDER JAWÁD ACQUIRED A DOUBLE FIRST-class BA in history, an MA in European history and an MRes in humanities. In early 2019, he submitted his PhD thesis – *Miscegenation, Urban Apartheids and Diasporic Spaces in Liverpool, 1878-1988* – to Birkbeck College, University of London.

Jawád is a journalist, radio broadcaster and author, winning a prestigious *Press Gazette* national journalism award in 2005. He wrote and edited for the *Liverpool Echo*, the *South China Morning Post*, the *Birmingham Post* (as chief sports writer), *The Times*, and the *Independent*. He has written eleven books, including the best-selling John Aldridge story (Hodder & Stoughton, 1999). Jawád is a keen traveller who has visited 75 countries. He has covered seven World Cup tournaments and four Olympic Games. He is the publisher and editor of *Soccerama*. His first novel, *For The Love of Freddy*, will be published in 2020.

decoubertin.co.uk